ANUTA

Second Edition

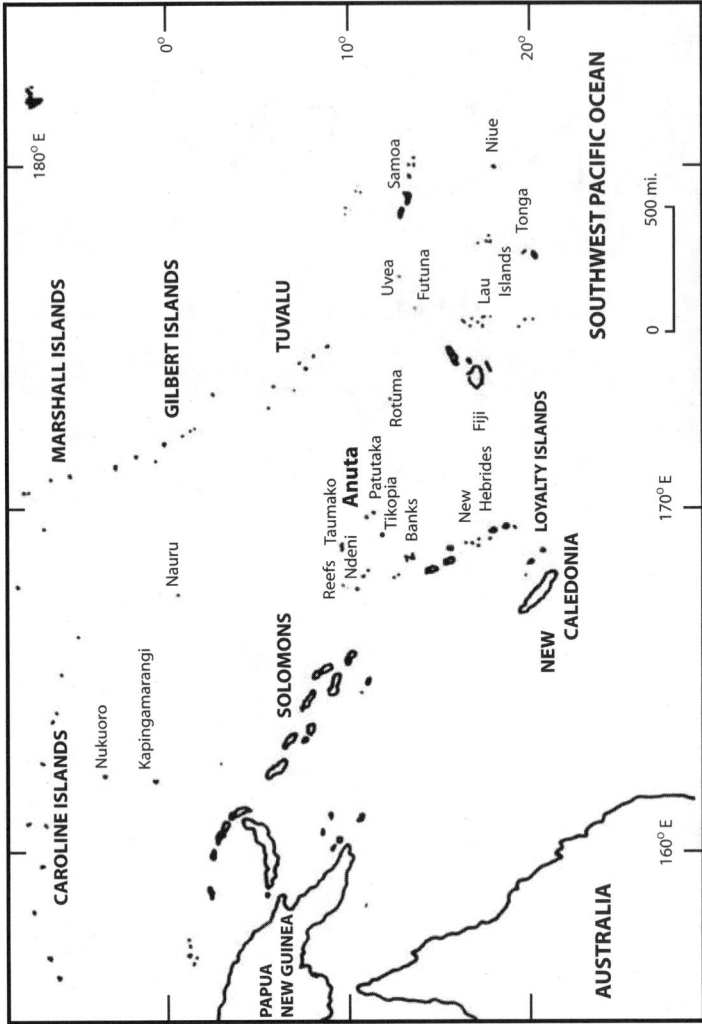

(Adapted from Yen and Gordon 1973:3.)

Map of Central Pacific Ocean, showing relationship of Anuta to other islands and island groups.

ANUTA

Polynesian Lifeways for the 21st Century

Second Edition

RICHARD FEINBERG
Kent State University

WAVELAND
PRESS, INC.
Long Grove, Illinois

For information about this book, contact:
Waveland Press, Inc.
4180 Route 83, Suite 101
Long Grove, Illinois 60047
(847) 634-0081
info@waveland.com
www.waveland.com

Dedicated to

the Memory of My Parents,

Dr. Rose S. Hartmann Feinberg and Dr. Isadore (Tex) Feinberg.
For the unfailing emotional and intellectual support
that made this work possible.

Contents

ACKNOWLEDGEMENTS

Many people have contributed in countless ways to the creation of this book. Most critical are my Anutan hosts who welcomed me to their island, adopted me into their community, and taught me everything I know about their way of life. Special thanks are due to Pu Paone; senior chief Pu Koroatu; the chief's brothers Pu Tokerau and Frank Kataina (Pu Teukumarae); and John Tope (Pu Avatere) for their friendship, hospitality, and assistance over a period that has spanned three decades. Pu Nukumarere and Moses Purianga generously shared their prodigious knowledge of Anutan genealogy and oral tradition, and Pu Nukumanaia was my most important teacher of navigational lore. Sister Lilian Takua Maeva dedicated her life to helping others through devoted service to the Church of Melanesia. She courageously intervened to help calm the civil war that devastated the Solomon Islands in 1999 and 2000, and she died suddenly while organizing cyclone relief for people of the eastern Solomons in 2003. Her contribution to this book is diffuse but nonetheless profound. Other Anutans facilitated my research and saw to my comfort and well-being in ways too numerous to mention; my debt to all of them is beyond measure.

To the late Sir Raymond Firth I owe my choice of Anuta as a research site. His intellectual guidance and support continued unabated from the time that he suggested Anuta as a focus for my investigation until his death in 2002.

My initial study of Anuta was funded by a graduate student training grant under the auspices of the U.S. National Institute of Mental Health, administered by the University of Chicago's Department of Anthropology. Several subsequent periods of field research were sponsored by the Kent State University Research Council, the university's Faculty Improvement Leave program, and Kent State's Anthropology Department.

Most of the material in chapters 2–7 first appeared in a volume entitled *Anuta: Social Structure of a Polynesian Island*, published in 1981 by the Institute for Polynesian Studies at Brigham Young University's Hawai'i campus. I am indebted to the Institute and its director, Dale Robertson, for cooperation and encouragement in the production of this volume.

I must thank Tom Curtin of Waveland Press for taking on this project. Don Rosso has seen me through the copyediting and production process. This book is much the stronger for his patience, care, and thoughtful guidance.

Finally, I owe my family a debt of gratitude that words alone cannot describe. My parents, Dr. Isadore Feinberg (1922–1978) and Dr. Rose S. Hartmann Feinberg (1918–2001) helped shape my sense of curiosity, my interest in understanding human relationships, my attraction to the sea and tropical islands, and my appreciation of the natural environment. Their unwavering support—emotional, material, and intellectual—was indispensable to my success in school and my initial foray into Pacific research. My wife, Nancy Grim, and children, Joe and Kate, accompanied me to the field in 1983–84 and 1993, and they put up with absences of many months in 1988 and 2000 while I pursued my ongoing investigations. Their interest in my research and writing has been a source of constant inspiration.

To all those mentioned here, and to others who have helped enrich my life of anthropological scholarship, I say *tangi pakaaue; toku aropa ki a kotou kairo oti* ('I call out in gratitude; my affection for you all is beyond measure')

Chapter 1

Introduction to Anuta

I stood on the deck of the Solomon Islands government ship *Kwai* and strained my eyes against the early morning mist. Anuta, the island that would be my home for the next year, had just appeared on the horizon. Its outlines gradually came into focus: first the rounded hill that occupies its northern section, then the low-lying coastal flat, and finally the beach and fringing reef.

I knew Anuta would be small, but this was a mere speck—a half-mile in diameter and 75 miles from its nearest populated neighbor. We sailed around the island once, then anchored several hundred yards offshore. An outrigger canoe soon pulled aside the ship. Several men, clad only in bark waist-cloths, swam out from the beach. After a few moments of animated conversation, which I endeavored unsuccessfully to follow, a group of passengers disembarked in the canoe.

Amid the pandemonium, one of the swimmers clambered to the deck and introduced himself to me as Matthew. When he ascertained that I was planning to stay on the island, he proclaimed that he would be my "friend" and insisted that I "follow" him. The man's Anutan name, I later learned, was Pu Paone, and he was among the island's most distinguished leaders. True to his word, he quickly grew to be one of my closest friends and most important teachers of Anutan custom.

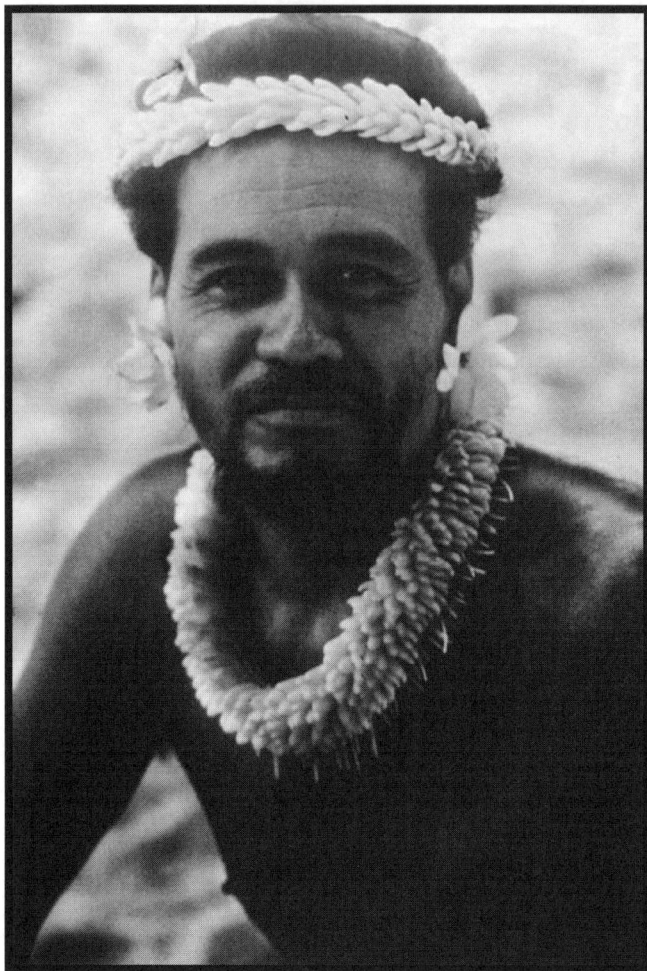

Photo 1.1 Pu Paone, author's close friend and community leader.

Soon others crowded around. One young man seemed particularly agitated. He seated himself on the deck in front of me and started shouting in a language that I could not understand but took to be Anutan. I struggled to make sense of what was going on, but his companions told me to ignore him. They explained that he was *karange* ('cranky') and believed himself to be addressing me in English. *Karange* is a word in Pijin, a kind of pidgin English spoken throughout the Solomon Islands, and it refers to someone who is mentally incompetent.

In the space of a few minutes I had met the most and least admired of my soon-to-be compatriots. Meanwhile, Pu Paone slipped away, and the ship's crew decided that the supposed dignitaries—the colonial district officer, a police sergeant, and I—should go ashore in the launch. Clutching my camera case and a small bag of irreplaceable papers, I descended into the little boat and hoped for the best.

The few published descriptions of Anuta (particularly Firth 1954) mentioned a "very narrow" channel through the reef. I soon discovered that there was *no* "channel" if that is taken to mean a deep-water opening. The so-called passage was simply an area where the surf beat a little less fiercely than elsewhere, and we headed toward that spot. One crew member stood in the stern and propelled us with a long sculling oar; two others stood and paddled in the bow. We reached the breakers, tried to surf behind the crest of a large wave, and almost made it to the beach. When we were perhaps fifteen yards from shore, another wave caught up with us, swept across the transom, and completely filled our boat. I grabbed my bag of papers and managed to keep it out of the water while calling out, "the camera!" A member of our party quickly retrieved the vinyl bag, and the equipment survived with surprisingly little damage despite several seconds of immersion. I had been warned that landing on Anuta could be an adventure, and the event lived up to its billing.

Once safely ashore, a number of small children and some teenage girls began to carry my supplies to what I assumed would be my house. Pu Paone reappeared and led me to the island's water source, a few hundred yards from the village area. Here I found an aqueduct fashioned from hollowed logs, about six inches in diameter and suspended seven or eight feet above the ground. My new friend showered to remove the sea salt, then led me to "the house of the number one chief."

At length, we came to a leaf structure where we crawled through the low doorway on our hands and knees. I saw a 60-year-old man who I later learned was Pu Tepuko—the junior or "number two" chief—sitting cross-legged on the floor. Following my guide's example, I crawled toward him and tried to place my nose on the chief's knee. He quickly thrust his hand beneath my chin and raised my head so that I pressed my nose against his neck instead. The Ariki Tafua—the second-ranking chief of Tikopia, the neighboring island—was also sitting in the house, and I greeted him in similar fashion.

I then experienced my introduction to Anutan cuisine—a banana leaf adorned with a pile of *ma* and several fish. *Ma* is a food made from any number of starchy fruits or vegetables, which are either grated or cut into small chunks and buried in underground pits. Bacterial activity turns the starch to vinegar, and in this fermented state the food may be preserved for many years. At one time, islanders throughout the Pacific relied on *ma* as a hedge against natural disas-

Photo 1.2   Anutan chiefs with entourage. From left to right: Pu Akonima, senior chief; Pu Koroatu, junior chief; Pu Tepuko, Pu Nukumata (then known as Pu Parekope), and Pu Pareaatai. Photographed in 1973 in White River, Guadalcanal.

ter. Today, Anutans are among the few people who still prepare this pungent delicacy, and it has become an emblem of cultural identity for them. It has also made them infamous throughout the Solomons, where not everyone shares the Anutans' culinary passions.

The *ma* tasted vaguely like a sour batch of mashed potatoes. The fish were fresh and still warm from the fire, but they were very small and had been cooked with head, bones, scales, and gut intact. Typically, Anutans clean them as they eat. But since I had to use my fingers and there was no water for washing, my hands soon were covered with scales and bones, rendering them useless.

In the midst of my memorable breakfast, the senior chief joined us. He was younger than his counterpart—35 to 40 years of age—but descended from a higher-ranking line. Like his colleague, he was a large, muscular man with curly, black hair and a dark beard. Unlike the Tikopian chief, the Anutan leaders wore the traditional waist cloth made from the inner bark of a tree known as *te mami*.

Months earlier, I had been warned that two critically important words were *kai* ('eat') and *maakona* ('full' or 'satisfied'). Now I was repeatedly admonished, *"kai."* After objecting several times that I was *maakona*, the piles of food were finally removed. The senior chief offered me a cup of water to drink and a greasy strip of bark cloth for me to try, as best I could, to clean my hands.

When we finished eating, the chiefs passed around some betel nut and offered me a piece. Betel is one of the world's most widely used intoxicants, chewed by tens of millions of South Asians and Pacific Islanders. It is actually a mixture consisting of several ingredients: a nut from the areca palm; slaked lime, a white powder produced by baking coral rock in an earth oven; and the leaf, stem, or flower from a kind of pepper plant known scientifically as *Piper betel*. The mixture turns saliva red and teeth black, causes profuse salivation, and creates a mild stimulant effect akin to a "nicotine high." I accepted in the interest both of scientific curiosity and sociability. The nut was soft and juicy, with a slightly acrid taste; the leaf seemed spicy; and the lime burned my tongue. Otherwise the effect was minor, as my hosts, concerned about my health and comfort, had given me the mildest nut that they could find.

At this point, it began to rain quite hard. I remember the junior chief uttering the first Anutan words ever spoken to me in natural conversation that I was able to decipher: *"Te ua ku too"* ('the rain has begun to fall'). Then, as I was basking in my momentary linguistic conquest, someone rushed in to announce that many of my supplies were still out in the rain. When Pu Paone and I left the beach, the children had apparently stopped hauling my gear to its designated storage place.

Abruptly brought back to reality, I struggled to communicate my wish to go out and check on the supplies. My butchery of the language gave rise to uproarious laughter on the part of both chiefs, but at length I got my point across. I staggered out into the rain and rather than relying on the children, Pu Paone and I applied our own backs. We soon moved everything into a building that I later discovered to be the school.

The senior chief then informed me that I would be living in his house. His words did not mean that we were to sleep in the same structure; rather, I would share a dwelling with his younger brother, Pu Tokerau. Since they were members of the same property-owning group, Pu Toke's house was also the chief's.[1]

Next, Pu Paone wanted me to meet his family. We walked a couple hundred yards to a thatched house resembling the one I had just left, but closer to the center of the village area. There his wife, his mother, two of his daughters, and assorted unidentified persons seemed to be lounging around. He asked me to stay for lunch, and I spent the next few hours practicing Anutan while waiting for the meal to start. Again, I experienced the Anutans propensity to laugh at my linguistic difficulty. At the same time, I was struck by the extent to which Anuta's language has been influenced by that of the neighboring

Tikopia. Frequently, I heard the Tikopian word "*siei*" ('no'), and would respond, "*Siei pe kairo?*" ([Is the correct word] '*siei*' or '*kairo?*') The answer was invariably an embarrassed giggle followed by "*kairo.*"

After lunch, Pu Paone took me to visit another of the island's leaders, a man named Arthur (Pu Nukumairunga). Arthur was the radio operator, medical orderly, and sometime school teacher. He looked to be in his late thirties and was disabled by polio, which had badly withered his right leg. Still, he seemed quite cheerful and enjoyed his prominent position in the community. He spoke excellent Pijin and was one of only two men on the island at the time who spoke more than a few words of English. The house next door to his was vacant, and he offered to let me sleep there.

The idea of having my own place was, in some ways, appealing. Granted, I would not have been in the island's social and political center as I would were I to share quarters with Pu Toke and the chief, but it would have given me a degree of privacy in which to think, work, write, and unwind. When I mentioned this proposal to the chief, however, he responded that there was a "crazy man" at large and he wanted me to be in a location where he and his brothers could look after me and my possessions. He was referring to the fellow I had met aboard the ship, and while I was willing to take my chances, the chief had a reasonable point. From that moment on I became associated with the chief's family, and on my subsequent visits to Anuta I have always shared his dwelling.

After dinner with the chief and his family, I tried to write by the dim glow of a kerosene lantern, but the house quickly filled with people caught up in animated conversation. Crowds of visitors seemed to break out laughing every time I looked up to ascertain whether some comment was being directed at me. It had been an exhausting day and I had not gotten much rest the night before, so I abandoned my attempt to write, opened my camping cot, lit a mosquito coil, and tried to go to sleep around 8:30 P.M. Thus ended day one in my new island home.

Preparation for Fieldwork

In one sense, I had begun preparing for this expedition two and a half years earlier, when I enrolled as a graduate student in the University of Chicago's anthropology department in 1969. In another, I had laid the groundwork many years before. From childhood, I was attracted to outdoor life and to the water—to camping, hiking, fishing, swimming, sailing, and canoeing. I imagined a tropical island surrounded by clear waters and coral reefs to be an ideal environment and I hoped some day to experience life in such surroundings—not as a tourist but a long-term resident.

Also while growing up, I became aware of social strife, both in my home country and elsewhere. Then as now, the media were filled with stories of poverty, crime, ethnic conflict, racial prejudice, gender discrimination, and religious persecution. I saw people caught up in a ruthless competition to make money and accumulate material possessions, often at the expense of others. Throughout school and in the media, I was exposed to all the anger and suspicion that were part and parcel of the Cold War. Guardians of the old social order met the Civil Rights movement's challenge with beatings, lynchings, and bombings. Overseas, the United States became increasingly committed to the military conflict in Vietnam while my friends and neighbors grew progressively more polarized over their attitudes toward the war.

It seemed to me that there must be a better way for people to relate to one another. I also knew that Western social theorists from Plato and Aristotle through the likes of Locke, Mill, Jefferson, and Marx had offered and debated plans to improve society based on their respective understandings of human nature. Yet despite the efforts by some of the world's most thoughtful commentators, we seemed to be in a morass and sinking deeper every day. I wondered if the problem was that we had been working for the past 2500 years with a limited set of shared assumptions about the nature of the world and people's place within it. It occurred to me that we might extricate ourselves from this unproductive mindset by looking outside of the Western tradition. It was that hope which drew me into anthropology. I did not expect to find an earthly paradise, but I thought it likely that there were communities which had avoided some of our most pressing problems. And I hoped that knowledge of such peoples might provide a few suggestions for addressing crises in my own society.

Given my objective, I wanted to study a community as different from my own as possible. I was also interested in working with people who lived close to nature, people who depended on themselves and each other rather than on modern technology and the world market economy to satisfy their major wants and needs. The prospect of conducting research on a remote South Sea island seemed to offer all that I was seeking. Therefore, from the time that I began my graduate studies, I prepared for anthropological fieldwork in the most undisturbed Polynesian community I could find.

In fall of 1970, Raymond (soon to be *Sir* Raymond) Firth was a visiting professor at the University of Chicago. Firth had done extensive research on Tikopia, a remote Polynesian enclave in the eastern

Solomon Islands. His Tikopian fieldwork dates from 1928, and the many ethnographic publications that grew out of his research are now considered anthropological classics. While trying to identify a field site for my own studies, I asked Firth's advice. He was familiar with Anuta, 75 miles northeast of Tikopia and responded, "If you're looking for an isolated island, Anuta is about as isolated as you can get." He suggested that I look into Anuta as a research site, and my inquiries proved fruitful.

Prior to that time, Anuta had never been subjected to systematic investigation. A few early European ships had sighted the island, but their records are not particularly informative. In 1954, Firth published the first scholarly article on Anuta, growing out of comments by Anutans he had met on Tikopia in 1928–29 and 1952 plus a one-day visit to Anuta in 1952. Firth's article is remarkable for its detail, especially considering his limited contact. Not surprisingly, however, he viewed the island through a distinctly Tikopian lens. Then, in 1970, archaeologist Roger Green spent a day on the island, collecting an Anutan word list, which he published in 1971. His main informant, however, was a Tikopian immigrant, and his word list was permeated with Tikopian locutions.

Considering this background, I had little direct indication of what I was to find on Anuta. I knew, however, that it would resemble Tikopia in many important respects; so I spent most of 1971 immersing myself in Firth's ethnographic writings. In addition, Raymond generously donated his time to help me obtain a basic grounding in the Tikopian language. Still, as I left Chicago's minus-15-degree January chill, I had only the most rudimentary idea of what to expect.

The last week before my departure was consumed with errands: arranging for my grant money to be deposited in a bank account that could be wired to a remote colonial territory half a world away; purchasing supplies; packing; saying good-bye to friends; arranging for a ride to the airport; and finding someone to sell my broken-down car after I had left. So I had little time to come to grips with the fact that I would soon depart for over a year in one of the most isolated locations anywhere on Earth.

The first portion of my flight took me to Honolulu and gave me time to collect my thoughts. I eagerly looked forward to my trip but also viewed it with some trepidation. I wondered if I would be able to complete my proposed research. Would I find exciting, new, original material and transform it into a doctoral dissertation that would satisfy my advisers? Would I be able to learn the language? How would I be received? Would I get along with the Anutans? Would this be a rich, rewarding experience, or would I feel isolated, alien-

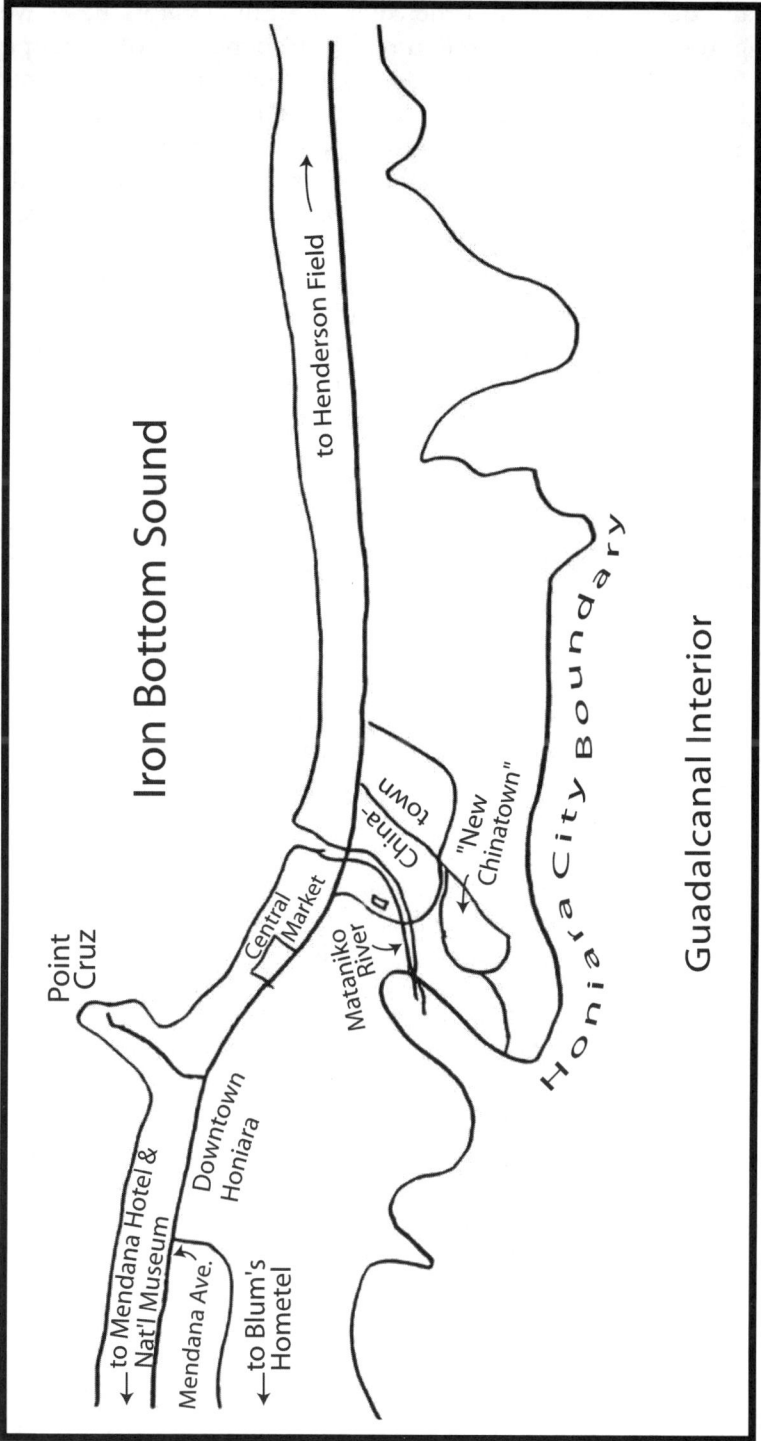

Figure 1.1 Map of Honiara.

ated, and depressed? Would the colonial administrators be as welcoming in person as they were in our correspondence over the past year? Had anyone else organized a conflicting expedition to Anuta while I was getting ready in Chicago? Would I run out of money and be stranded far from home? Would my health hold out, particularly in a place where it could take a month or more to get to a hospital? I was concerned about the separation from my family. I would have little communication with the outside world, with ships visiting no more than once a month. Should there be a crisis it could take months for me to find out and months more to reach someplace where I might be able to help. And so on, ad infinitum. Still, after two years of preparation, I was anxious to begin my research. When the plane touched down in Honolulu, I caught my first glimpse of O'ahu's rugged Ko'olau mountains and felt the humid 75-degree air. In that instant, all my doubts dissolved in a euphoric haze. I had landed on my first Pacific island.

While in Honolulu, I made contacts at the University of Hawai'i and the Bernice P. Bishop Museum. The latter was particularly fortuitous. I learned that ethnobotanist Douglas Yen, and archaeologists Patrick Kirch and Paul Rosendahl, had just spent two months on Anuta. Yen and Kirch were still overseas, but Rosendahl had returned to the museum, and we spent many hours talking about life on Anuta and in the Solomon Islands. He showed me some photographs of the island and allowed me to study the team's preliminary findings, including a detailed map.

The plane from Honolulu stopped briefly in American Samoa, crossed the International Date Line, and landed in Fiji. There I caught a small prop plane northwest to the New Hebrides (now the independent nation of Vanuatu) and on to the Solomons. I arrived in Honiara, the Solomon Islands' capital, on February 2nd.

Honiara is located on the island of Guadalcanal, made famous during World War II as the site of major battles between American and Japanese forces. (Those battles were recently reenacted in the film *The Thin Red Line*.) In 1972, Honiara was a sleepy town of perhaps ten thousand people. The "highway" from the airport to the city was unpaved and dusty. I had expected tropical rain forest but discovered most of the surrounding area to be covered with tall grass, which is frequently burned. Sometimes the burning is accidental, but often it is purposely done to clear land for vegetable gardens.

The main road in town was named Mendana Avenue after the early Spanish explorer, Alvaro de Mendaña, who died while attempting to establish a colony in the Santa Cruz Islands of the eastern Solomons. Standing approximately at right angles to Mendana Avenue, but across the Mataniko River from the administrative and business center, was Honiara's Chinatown, which stretched along a single street for a distance of perhaps four blocks.

Mendana Avenue and two or three side streets had been graced with asphalt. There were few cars and no traffic lights. Most of the buildings were wooden and badly in need of a new coat of paint. The structures were one-story—or at most two—and almost all the shops were clustered either along Mendana Avenue or in Chinatown. Most of the shops were owned by Chinese merchants and had the character of "general stores," selling everything from food and hardware to medicines, clothing, tape recorders, radios, batteries, and kerosene.

Initially, I stayed in a guest house called Blum's Hometel, started by an American who first visited the Solomons during the war, liked the place and the people, and decided to make a life there for himself. The "hometel," a block inland from the main road, was the less expensive of Honiara's two places of accommodation. It has since been purchased by an international chain, expanded, upgraded, and renamed the King Solomon Hotel. The Blums' daughter is now the U.S. consular representative to the Solomon Islands.

During those first few days at Blum's, I met a number of people who helped ease me into life in the western Pacific. One was a Harvard graduate student named Gilbert Hendrin. Gil, his wife Diane, and their young child were taking a break from anthropological research on Ulawa, a small island about 80 miles east of Guadalcanal. I also met Wynn Hughes, a geologist from north Wales, who had tried unsuccessfully just a short time before to land on Anuta. A few months later, while I was on Anuta, Hughes drowned attempting to get ashore at Tinakula volcano in what is now Temotu Province. My most important contact of those first few days, however, was an American couple, Bruce and Cecile Szal, who had come to the Solomons to work as teachers at St. Joseph's mission school in Tenaru, several miles east of town.

I met the Szals at Henderson Field—a remnant of the American invasion of Guadalcanal in the early 1940s, which still serves as Honiara's international airport. A friend of theirs had been on my flight. They picked him up at the airport and offered me a ride into town. Along the way I noted the tropical heat and clear blue sea that beckoned just a few yards from the road, and I asked where there might be a good place to swim. Bruce responded soberingly, "It depends on whether you'd rather be eaten by sharks or crocodiles. It's the ocean for the sharks; the rivers for the crocs." A few days later, while visiting the Mendana Hotel, I noticed a sign that read "Warning! Because of sharks, swimming in these waters is unsafe."[2]

Over the next few days, I became friends with the Szals. We had several meals together, as they continued to advise me on survival in the Solomons. They introduced me to staff members at St. Joseph's School, a Peace Corps couple named Dave and Sue Wellman, and the first Solomon Islander whom I came to count as a personal friend—John Gina from New Georgia Island in the western Solomons. John was well educated and well traveled, having trained at Scotland Yard before working as a police detective in the Solomon Islands. When I met him, he had left the police and was employed as a statistician for the colonial government. He also was a fine guitar player and the leader of a popular Solomon Islands band.

A few days after registering at Blum's, I learned that the lodge was overbooked, and I was asked to find another place to stay. The only other public accommodation, the Mendana Hotel, was prohibitively expensive for someone on a student's income. Bruce and Cecile again came to the rescue, offering me a bed at their place in Tenaru.

Culture shock is the sense of disorientation that travelers, including anthropologists, often feel when they arrive in a place where behaviors, rules, and expectations are radically different from those in their home communities. My first experience of culture shock on this trip came when I arrived in Honiara and discovered that the protectorate's capital looked more like the set for a John Wayne movie than a seat of imperial power. The second came the following day, when I searched for the Immigration Office.

Before I arrived in the Solomons, the Immigration Service had sent me a provisional entry permit and a letter instructing me that I must surrender a return plane ticket as bond immediately upon arrival. But the clerk at Immigration declared that her office could not hold the ticket for me. She could not issue my extended residence permit until I surrendered the ticket, but she had no idea to whom I should surrender it. Eventually, we hit on the idea of giving the ticket to the local bank in return for a letter that could then be deposited with the Immigration Department. The bank manager, Mr. Waddell, was more than happy to oblige. But that was all I would accomplish in one morning. By the time I finished with immigration and the bank it was 11 A.M., and all the stores and offices in town closed for their "lunch hour"—which, I learned, lasted until 2 P.M. Mr. Waddell wisely counseled that I "should not be in a hurry to get anything done around here."

When I inquired about shipping to the Eastern Outer Islands, I discovered that the government had two boats that were supposed to make the trip. However, one was out of service, and the other had been caught in a cyclone. No one in Honiara knew where it was or when it might be back. In the end I was lucky and only had to wait three weeks.

Photo 1.3   Mendana Avenue, downtown Honiara, in 1972

I spent those three weeks purchasing supplies, arranging transport, and getting to know the few Anutans then living in Honiara. The local Anutan community was located in White River, a suburb on the western end of town. The first Anutan I met was Frank Kataina (Pu Teukumarae). He was gracious and helpful, and I was immediately struck by his extraordinary poise, dignity, and command of English. Frank is the senior chief's youngest brother and was then a sergeant in the Royal Solomon Islands Police. Thirty years later, he is still among the most worldly of Anutans. We talked about conditions on Anuta and what I should expect to happen when I got there. He reassured me about Anutan receptiveness to my study and helped me expand my Anutan vocabulary. Frank remains one of my closest Anutan friends.

While in Honiara, I also met Roger Green, a leading figure in Pacific archaeology. He was on his way to the Eastern Outer Islands as part of a large comparative project. We spent time together in the capital and later shared a cabin on the ship out to the eastern Solomons. I benefited from his wealth of knowledge and experience, and he later became a member of my dissertation committee.

Life on Anuta

I landed on Anuta just over a month after my arrival in the Solomons. During the initial flurry of excitement described in the last section, the ship unceremoniously blew its whistle and departed. As I watched the *Kwai* weigh anchor and sail off toward the horizon, I felt a brief but profound sense of isolation. I knew that it would be at least a month before I next had contact with the outside world. In fact, it was a good three months before I saw another ship. In the meantime, I would have to satisfy my needs with the materials I had with me. Should I require something that I had neglected to bring on the trip, I would either have to improvise or change my view of what is necessary. If I got sick or learned of a family crisis, I could not be evacuated until the next ship. This was the reality I had hoped for and worked hard to achieve; now I had to live it.

Feelings of isolation, self-doubt, and disorientation are common for anthropologists when they first arrive in the field. Yet every expedition by every anthropologist is, in some ways, unique. In contrast with many well-known cases (e.g., Evans-Pritchard 1940; Berreman 1962, 1963), I did not have to struggle to build trust or rapport with my community. When Raymond Firth conducted his research on Tikopia, he got along extraordinarily well with his hosts; and when he returned to England, he proceeded to write a series of books that made Tikopia one of the best-known small-scale communities anywhere. The Anutans were aware of the Tikopian experience and understood that my work would resemble Firth's. Furthermore, they were sufficiently proud of what they had created on their little piece of terra firma that they were happy to have me record their accomplishments. They were anxious that I share the secrets of their special way of life with others. Some even expressed the hope that I would make Anuta as well known as Tikopia. In many respects, then, I had stumbled on an anthropologist's dream site. Still there were adjustments to be made as well as myriad frustrations.

Often anthropologists face extreme isolation. On Anuta I was never wanting for human companionship. In fact, I was constantly surrounded by people who were curious about my activities and behaviors. However, I *was* isolated from friends and family, people who shared my language and culture, and those who were concerned about the issues that had been my focus of attention up to the time of my departure from the United States. Many times during my year on Anuta I longed for someone with whom I could discuss the Vietnam War, the presidential election, or even the World Series.

Initially, my single greatest frustration was the inability to communicate. Pu Tokerau and Pu Nukumairunga spoke enough English to carry on a conversation; but no one else knew more than a few words of my language. Fortunately, I had some rudimentary knowledge of Anutan when I arrived, owing to Sir Raymond's efforts and my later work with Anutans and Tikopians in Honiara and on the ship to Anuta. Thus despite my limitations, I had a foundation on which to build.

My best language teachers in the early days were young children. Pu Paone assigned his nine-year-old son, Robert Pakapu (now a married adult known as Pu Taumarei), to be my guide and escort; and everywhere I went I was assured of a large, youthful entourage. Before arriving on Anuta, I had mastered a few key questions, the most important of which was "*Mea ko tea?*" ('What is that?') I spent hours walking through the village and the bush, pointing to everything I saw, asking my self-appointed advisors, "*Mea ko tea?*" and recording their answers. I would then transfer my newly-acquired lexicon to index cards and spend several more hours drilling myself. After committing the new vocabulary to memory, I would try to use each word repeatedly in conversation until it was thoroughly familiar to both my mouth and ear. In this way, I gradually developed a respectable repertoire of nouns. That procedure was of limited value, however, in learning other parts of speech, and abstract concepts were extremely difficult. Were it not for Pu Toke's moderate command of English, I can only guess how long it might have taken me to figure out such words as *paia* ('because').

Within about a month I gained sufficient control of the language that I was able to begin conducting a house-to-house census. Census interviews consisted of repeating a set of stereotyped questions such as: "Are you married?" "Were you married before?" "Is your eldest child a boy or a girl?" "What is his/her name?" "When was he/she born?" "The next child?" and so on. This allowed me to obtain a good deal of basic information with a limited vocabulary. In addition, each interview led to a least a few new words, and my linguistic facility continued to grow.

After a couple of months, I also began to tape speeches, sermons, and ordinary conversations, and I transcribed the tapes with the help of my more patient hosts. This helped me develop my ear for Anutan pronunciation and gave me some sense of how Anutans put words together to produce more complex thoughts. After about six months, when I began to dream in Anutan, I convinced myself that I now spoke the language.

Language learning was facilitated by the fact that Anutan, like other Polynesian languages, is relatively easy for English speakers to pick up. The phonology is similar to Spanish, and the grammar is not particularly complex. But there is a trade-off; while Anutan is fairly easy to speak, it is difficult to speak well. Even now, after thirty years of research and writing about Anutan language and culture, I lack the flowing style and graceful use of metaphor that marks indigenous speech. When Anutans address me and make an effort to be clear, I have little trouble following their thought. But when they speak very rapidly to one another with mouths full of betel or while holding pipes between their teeth and, seemingly, without moving their lips, spoken Anutan can still appear as a stream of undifferentiated sound. In short, while my facility with Anutan is serviceable for most purposes, it is not that of a native speaker.

To learn a new language is not simply a matter of inserting new words in place of familiar ones. A language reflects the way in which members of a community categorize their surroundings and, in the view of many anthropologists, it shapes their perceptions of reality. Thus, the process of learning new words and their meanings may require an uncomfortable shift in the way one thinks about one's social and natural environments. This was pointedly brought home to me in two of my earliest conversations.

During my second day on Anuta, I was surrounded by young children and decided to begin sorting out kin relations. I asked one youngster how he was related to a man standing nearby. The answer was *"toku tamana,"* an expression that is most easily translated as 'my father.' That seemed fine until I asked the same boy about his relationship with another man and received the same answer. I had studied kinship in my graduate classes and understood on some level that many people apply the term for 'father' to a number of men. Still, by the time my young consultant had finished pointing out his sixth 'father,' I was ready to tear my hair in frustration.

I quickly learned that what one takes for granted as common sense and elementary logic in one community may be anything but common-sensical in another. When Pu Paone introduced me to his two sons, he informed me that Robert Pakapu, the elder boy, was my *iraamutu* ('nephew'), while Pakapu's younger brother, Joseph Maatua, was my *tama* ('son'). It seemed obvious to me as an American that full brothers share the same genealogy and, therefore, if two people were brothers, I should be in the same kin relationship to both of them. Thus, I was convinced that I must have misunderstood something about the boys' relationship to one another or to Pu Paone. Only much later, when I discovered that kinship on Anuta is as much a statement about social and political as genealogical relationships, did this conversation begin to make sense.

Fieldwork inevitably places one in the midst of people whose behaviors, values, rules, and expectations seem strange and sometimes threatening. Even such an elementary matter as going to the toilet can be a challenge. Anuta has no plumbing, or even outhouses. When I first mentioned a need to relieve myself, a young man escorted me to the beach. As far as I could see, I would be in full view of anyone within a quarter mile. I felt self-conscious, rushed, and the whole experience was, as we might say, less than satisfying. Eventually, I learned that there are separate sections of beach for men and women. Proper etiquette stipulates that one not venture into the wrong area, and that one not look should he or she be close to the toilet area for the opposite sex. One goes below the high tide line, and the toilet flushes twice a day—probably as good a substitute for modern plumbing as there is on a small, isolated island.

Still, sanitation—or lack thereof—continued to bother me for a long time. The germ theory of disease is so ingrained in most Americans' consciousness that it is hard not to feel threatened by people who have no understanding of infection or how to prevent its spread. Thus, I was less than overjoyed when, on my first visit to the junior chief's house, several of his relatives seemed terribly ill and were coughing profusely, yet they insisted that I join them for a meal. A day or two later, I joined Pu Tokerau as he went to treat a very sick woman with a skin infection that had become systemic. Again, while we were visiting, our hosts insisted that we share a meal.

People eat with their fingers from leaves or mats spread out on the floor. The polite host serves his honored guest by picking up the vegetables in his hands and placing them directly in front of the visitor. He also picks up pieces of fish, using his fingers to rub off the scales before serving his guest. He does this even if he is sick or, in the case of Pu Tokerau, if he has been treating others who are sick. At one point, I suggested to Pu Toke that he ought to wash his hands before serving food. My suggestion did not make much sense to him, but he wished to be ingratiating. Thus, the next time he served me a meal he first took a mouthful of water, which he proceeded to spit onto his hands to wash off all visible dirt.

Anuta is a beautiful island, the perfect image of a romantic South Sea paradise, reminding one of a Hollywood movie set. Its lush, green jungle is ringed by a brilliant, white-sand beach, crystal-clear water, and a stunning coral reef. Coconut palms sway gently overhead while exotic-looking men and women go about their daily business without upper body covering, often wearing traditional bark-cloth garments around their mid-sections. Hollywood, however, usually neglects to show the less appealing sides of paradise.

Anuta has the highest concentration of flies and mosquitoes I have seen anywhere. If one goes to the bush within a week or two after a significant rain, one is quickly and quite literally covered with mosquitoes. To sleep without a mosquito net is nearly impossible. I was told that prior to the introduction of mosquito nets, which came with European contact, people sometimes had to lie on the beach and bury themselves in the sand in order to get any sleep. Health authorities report that Anutan mosquitoes do not carry malaria, but they often make life most uncomfortable.

Flies can be as troublesome as mosquitoes. They do not bite through unopened skin and, therefore, do not inflict immediate itching and pain. However, they swarm around any uncovered food, sometimes giving it a velvety black sheen. Often meals must be consumed by teams, the hosts fanning the flies to keep them off the food while their guests eat. After the guests have satisfied their hunger, they exchange places and take possession of the fans while the hosts dine in some semblance of peace. In the absence of indoor plumbing, flies get into piles of feces and spread gastrointestinal diseases. They also gravitate to any open cut or sore, ensuring infection. Even when the sore has begun to heal and formed a scab, that is no guarantee of safety. Flies congregate on the scab and pick away until the wound has been re-opened.

A third ubiquitous insect pest is the cockroach. Tropical cockroaches can be two or three inches long, and they fly. They also eat paper, including notebooks. Their egg cases, which they lay on such cloth surfaces as clothing and mosquito nets, are covered with a chemical that dissolves the material and leaves large holes. They congregate in dark recesses of supply boxes and crates, so whenever I removed a can of food to give away as a present or to prepare for a meal, a dozen roaches would stream out of the space that the can had occupied. I kept a guitar in the rafters of my house; and whenever I took it down to play, several dozen roaches would run out of the sound hole. These large insects also leave substantial chunks of excrement, which foul everything they contact. After a few weeks, my guitar had accumulated enough cockroach feces that I could use the instrument as a rattle. A good mosquito net usually keeps cockroaches and other insects away while one sleeps, but if an intruder should get inside, it can be difficult to remove. Many times I was awakened from a peaceful slumber by one of these prehistoric faunal relics. Armed with a flashlight and a can of insecticide, I would scour my mosquito net and bedding in pursuit of the interloper. Most often after a futile search I would give up, put out the light, and attempt once more to go to sleep. Naturally, as soon as I began to drift off, the cockroach would return to scurry across my body, tickling—and sometimes biting—me along the way.

One of Anuta's appeals is its proximity to a boundless expanse of warm, clear ocean. The water covering the fringing reef, however, is usually too shallow to permit swimming. Whenever I wanted to swim, I would have to walk across the jagged reef to the surf line, brace myself to keep from being knocked down by the surging breakers, and, as soon as there was a lull in the wave action, run forward until the water was deep enough to allow me to swim. In the process, I would inevitably get cut or scratched on the reef. If the cuts were not immediately treated and bandaged to protect them from flies, they would become infected. Infected sores could then become tropical ulcers, a serious and potentially life-threatening medical problem.

As an anthropologist who had been taught the virtues of participant observation, I was determined to join in fishing expeditions, many of which occurred on the fringing reef. Often such forays take place at night, when it can be surprisingly cold. Shivering, I would walk along the jagged reef bent over at the waist and look down into the water with my diving mask. The current on the reef flat is always powerful; combined with the surge from the surf, it would inevitably push me against the coral, causing further cuts and scrapes. Still worse were sea urchin spines, which can penetrate the flesh, break off, and lead to serious infection. Wearing sandals protected the soles of my feet, but they were awkward and made walking in the current still more difficult. They were constantly at risk of washing off and drifting out to sea, and they did nothing to protect the sides or tops of my feet.

Unlike the Anutans, I had not built up a lifetime of calluses on the soles of my feet, so walking on the reef was always more difficult for me than for them. Because of that, they mistakenly assumed that I would be inept in other water-related activities; and they tended to be over-protective. People discouraged me from going to sea or participating in fishing expeditions unless conditions were perfect. The first time I went swimming in the ocean with Pu Toke, he grabbed me every time a wave came by. This was intended to steady me and keep me from being knocked down on the reef. In practice, it made it impossible for me to maneuver and deal effectively with the turbulent sea. Over time, Anutans came to recognize that I was very much at home in the water, but it took a long time before they trusted me to take care of myself.

Many anthropologists (e.g., Chagnon 1997) have remarked on the lack of privacy in the field and the difficult adjustment that it requires. My experience on Anuta was no different. I almost always had people around, watching me, scrutinizing my behavior, and asking about my actions and intentions. Whether I was eating, sleeping, exercising, or dressing a wound, I constantly had curious onlookers. When I worked in the makeshift study that I had established in a leaf house, I could almost always look up and see a dozen pair of five-year-old eyes peering at me through the thatch. When I walked through the village, everyone I passed would ask, "Where are you going?" or "What are you going in order to do?" This was inevitably followed by, "Let's go eat!" I could walk a hundred yards from my house to the canoe storage area near the main passage wearing a swimsuit and holding a spool of fishing line and meet a dozen people along the way. Each one would ask, "Are you going to the ocean?" Or I could be walking to the men's toilet area, a roll of toilet paper in hand, meet the same dozen people, and every one would ask, "What are you going in order to do?"

Intellectually, I understood that this was the normal Anutan greeting and that people usually expected no more information than Americans typically do when they ask, "How are you?" Still, I found it difficult to keep from responding testily that it was none of their business and they should leave me alone. Over the years, I have become accustomed to Anuta's style of greeting, and it no longer bothers me so much as it did in the early days. Nonetheless, at times I still can find it irritating.

Anutans continually asked me for supplies and favors. My early annoyance was intensified because their language has no word for "please," so requests are typically phrased as demands; e.g., *"Au mai poi rau paka maaku!"* ('Give me some tobacco!'). Despite the fact that I was living on Anuta, that my neighbors were looking after my well-being, and that my research depended on their good will and cooperation, I often found it difficult to suppress the feeling that I was being exploited—that I was tolerated simply for the goods I might produce. Eventually, I realized that membership in the Anutan community requires incorporation into their kinship system and that sharing is the essence of Anutan kinship. People expected to share whatever they had with me and assumed that the relationship was reciprocal. The requests were then a measure not of my exploitation as an outsider but, to the contrary, of my acceptance as a member of the community. Again, however, it took time for my emotional reactions to catch up with my understanding.

Even such matters as laughter—what people find funny, when and how they laugh, what it means, and one's appropriate response—can present a challenge. This was powerfully brought home to me during my third day on Anuta. I was trying to light my kerosene pressure lantern, which needed to be heated with denatured alcohol for it

Photo 1.4 Anutan woman walking on path beneath coconut palms near beach.

to ignite properly. At first the lantern was inadequately sealed, and the flame kept going out. Each time it died, the dozen or so people in the house would howl in laughter, adding to my gradually building level of self-conscious irritation. Finally, I fixed the leak and the lantern glowed with a bright white light, similar to an incandescent bulb. Then, to save alcohol, I removed the wick and tried to blow out the fire. Instead, I caused the flaming alcohol to drip onto my lap.

As I sat on the floor, flames shooting from my legs, I expected others to rush to my aid. Instead, they virtually rolled on the floor in still more uproarious laughter. Fortunately, I did not yet speak enough Anutan to express my feelings. The closest American analogy, it seemed to me, was the classic laughter at someone who slips on a banana peel. But whereas Americans might find such an episode comedic, we also recognize it as bad form to laugh at another's misfortune or discomfort. Here I was not dealing simply with discomfort but the possibility of serious injury, yet my hosts showed not the slightest restraint in their levity.

Initially I thought that they were laughing at my ineptitude as a foreigner who had not mastered the most basic skills. Later I discovered that Anutans routinely laugh at each other's—and even their own—mishaps. One who trips over a root or stubs his toe on a stone along the path, who bangs his head on a low-hanging branch, or who gets knocked down by a large breaker and is scraped on the reef becomes the target of collective laughter. But rather than reflecting a malicious pleasure at another's suffering (see Nachman 1986), I eventually learned that Anutans view such laughter as altruistic. They regard happiness as a prime value, and Anutans associate it with smiling and laughter, both of which they call by the same word, *kata*. According to the local theory, any injury or minor misfortune is likely to make one unhappy. Thus, the appropriate response for anyone in the vicinity is hearty laughter. Since laughter is contagious, when the victim hears others laughing, he or she begins to laugh as well, and the pain is converted to pleasure.

Even with that knowledge, it took a long time for me to condition myself to react with the equanimity Anutans expect in response to such laughter, and I never completely adjusted. But at length my reactions came to be more in line with local proprieties.

In addition to emotional adjustment to new cultural surroundings, anthropological fieldwork can involve physical danger. On my most recent visit to Anuta, the Solomon Islands were going through a period of civil war; and while outsiders were not being systematically targeted, there was some risk of getting caught in the crossfire. Moreover, looting was a pervasive problem from which no one was safe.

During my first visit in 1972, I spent a good deal of time swimming in the ocean beyond the fringing reef. This included some rough days when the current was particularly strong and I had to struggle to regain the passage. Had I been unable to overcome the current, the nearest islands to the north and east were well over 500 miles distant.

Once, I accompanied a group of Anutans on a four-day canoe voyage to Patutaka, an uninhabited island about thirty miles to the southeast (Feinberg 1988a: chapter 7). Upon our return to Anuta, as we were carrying the canoe up the beach, the entire bow broke off. I asked Pu Tokerau what we would have done had the vessel broken a few hours earlier when we were miles from shore. He responded with a chuckle, "We would probably have died at sea."

Perhaps the greatest danger was the fact that on Anuta I was weeks—and sometimes months—from a hospital and would be wholly on my own should I contract a life-threatening illness. Fortunately, I was fairly healthy on all of my Anutan visits. However, in 1984 my wife contracted cerebral malaria while we were conducting research on the similarly isolated Nukumanu Atoll in Papua New Guinea. Her temperature rose to 105 degrees, and she became delirious. We were fortunate that Nukumanu had a medical aid post, and the orderly was able to give her an injection of quinine—one of the few medications on hand. Within an hour her fever dropped to 101 degrees; without treatment, her condition would almost certainly have been fatal (cf. Rodman and Rodman 1990).

Despite the many trials and uncertainties, most anthropologists persevere in their field plans, and their experience usually proves positive. That was certainly the case with me and the Anutans. I have now been associated with the Anutan community for thirty years. I feel privileged to count a number of Anutans among my closest friends. Although I cannot claim to have a native's knowledge of the island, its language, and its culture, I have come to know the people and their way of life well enough to write a half dozen books and scores of articles about them. In addition to my 1972–73 research, I visited Anuta in 1983 and 2000, and I have worked with Anutans in other parts of the Solomon Islands in 1983–84, 1988, 1993, and 2000. Since my early research on kinship and social organization, I have written on subjects ranging from indigenous seafaring and navigational techniques to oral traditions to political and economic development. This book is based primarily on my early work. It is intended to provide an introduction to Anutan social life, how it is organized, and the cultural premises that guide it.

Conceptual and Organizational Plan

In this work, I focus on the fundamental constructs that permeate Anutan social structure. I ask how Anutans divide themselves into groups to accomplish the essential tasks of everyday life, and I explore the nature of those tasks. Insofar as the book recognizes common human challenges—the need to provide food and shelter, to procreate, and to ensure that people follow the rules of their communities—and asks how the Anutans meet those challenges, it reads like the British social anthropology of Bronislaw Malinowski or Raymond Firth.[3] However, I try to reach beyond organizational questions and ask cultural ones—what are the units into which Anutans divide their physical and social universes, and how are those units defined and conceptualized? What are the meanings, symbols, values, and understandings that Anutans share, which enable them to come together as a more-or-less unified community? I try to avoid prior assumptions about Anutan categories and the symbols through which they are represented, and I allow the terms of my discussion, insofar as possible, to flow from the Anutans' own statements. Thus, rather than assume that Anutans recognize a category of people who are connected through ties of birth and marriage, I ask *whether* they have a category that is defined in terms of genealogical connections. In this respect, my

approach is most closely aligned with the American cultural anthropology of Clifford Geertz, David Schneider, and their followers.[4] I will
demonstrate that Anutans define what one might call kinship and family groups in terms of compassion and economic support rather than
the essentially genealogical criteria on which Americans tend to rely.
Anutans are by no means unique in this respect, but they are unusual
in the degree to which they think of kin relations in terms of emotional
and socioeconomic rather than genealogical connections.

Chapter 2 introduces Anuta's history, physical environment, and
subsistence practices. Chapter 3 explores how Anutans think about
and organize kinship relations. This involves the question of whom
Anutans recognize as kin and the criteria according to which they distinguish kin from nonkin—a discussion which highlights the concept
of *aropa*, a core value that involves positive feelings for another person
as expressed through economic support and mutual assistance. An
interplay between *aropa* and genealogical connection impresses itself
on the internal structure of Anuta's kinship universe, distinguishing
different kinds of relatives from one another. Later chapters show that
same interface running throughout Anutan culture, shaping the community's family structure, descent groups, political and economic systems, and religion.

Chapter 4 details a grouping to which Anutans refer as the *patongia* or *pare*. This is roughly what we might call a 'household.' It is
Anuta's elementary unit of property ownership, production, and consumption, and it is the smallest unit entitled to make independent economic and social decisions. Individuals act on behalf of the domestic
unit, and that unit is held responsible for its members' behavior. Ideally,
such groups approximate patrilateral extended families, but Anutans
define them in relation to the way that people interact rather than on the
basis of genealogical criteria.

Domestic units come together to form larger groupings either
through voluntary alliance or common descent. Chapter 5 focuses on
marital exchange, the way in which each marriage and birth alters the
island's kindred structure, and the way in which marriage and kindred organization bring together those households whose connections are most in need of reinforcement. Chapter 6 focuses on the
island's four *kainanga*—groups of domestic units whose leaders are
said to be descended from a founding ancestor who lived approximately ten generations ago. That chapter and the following one also
involve a systematic discussion of Anuta's political organization.

Chapter 7 presents the overall community, or *kanopenua*. After
examining the basis on which the community defines itself, it
explores the island's religious foundations—both Christian and pre-

Christian. Lastly, chapter 8 explores some of the changes that have occurred on Anuta in the three decades since my first study, the struggles and challenges that have faced the community, and how Anutans have attempted to work through their problems in light of the principles of kinship and *aropa*. Before examining the intricacies of Anutan social organization, however, we must take a closer look at the island and its people.

A Note on Translation

My focus on meaning and my desire to present Anutan concepts as accurately as possible raises the problem of how to translate indigenous terms for English-speaking readers. Too much local vocabulary can make a work unreadable for the non-specialist, but excessive reliance on English glosses may convey a false apprehension of Anutan cultural constructs. As a compromise, I use terms from the local language more extensively than do most ethnographers who write for a general audience, and I rely more heavily on English translations here than in publications for professional colleagues. To minimize confusion, I include a glossary of key Anutan terms at the back of the book, and I try to convey the special sense in which English terms are sometimes employed by careful use of quotation marks. An English word appearing in single quotes is a gloss for an Anutan term and may have a meaning quite distinct from that in normal English usage. Double quotes usually signify a direct quotation. Occasionally, double quotes convey the sense of "so-called," suggesting that a word is being used in a manner that is fairly common, yet somewhat misleading. In discussing kin terms, for example, the word "consanguineal" sometimes appears in quotes. In anthropological parlance, consanguineal means related by blood, in contrast with affinal, which means related by marriage. I use "consanguineal" (in double quotes) to indicate that although Anutans think of certain persons as non-affinal relatives (in their terms, *kano a paito* but not *kano a paito i te paai o te papine*—see chapters 3 and 5), it is erroneous to assume that Anutans consider them to be related by blood in the way that Americans think of consanguineal kin. Absence of quotation marks indicates that a term is being used in its ordinary American English sense. Through these conventions, I hope to retain a sense of the complex multiple significations attached to many of the terms appearing in this volume.

Chapter 2

The Setting

Anuta, or Cherry Island, is a small volcanic outcropping in the Solomon Islands' Temotu Province. It is the country's easternmost populated island, located at approximately 169°50' east and 11°40' south.[1] The nearest island of any appreciable size is an uninhabitable rock that the Anutans call Patutaka, lying thirty nautical miles to the southeast; the nearest populated island, Tikopia, is about seventy-five miles to the southwest.[2]

Next to Tikopia the nearest bits of terra firma are the Melanesian islands of Vanikoro, Utupua, and Ndenö; the Reef Islands with their mixed Melanesian and Polynesian populations; and the Polynesian Duffs (Taumako), all over two hundred miles away. Further to the south and a bit west are the Banks Islands of northern Vanuatu (formerly the joint British-French "condominium" of the New Hebrides). To the east, the nearest island is Rotuma, five hundred miles away; beyond that are the Polynesian communities of 'Uvea and Futuna and the Tongan and Samoan archipelagoes. Between six and seven hundred miles to the northeast is Tuvalu (Ellice Islands), and about the same distance to the southeast is Fiji.

Anutan oral traditions record over 300 years of regular contact with Tikopia and the Polynesian islands to the east. Prior to the twentieth century, however, they report only the most sporadic communication with the Melanesian islands to the west. This view of interisland contact is supported by Anuta's Polynesian language and culture as well as its people's physical appearance. Genetic studies carried out by Gajdusek and his associates (Blake, et al. 1983) on the *Alpha Helix* expedition of 1972 confirm the Anutans' distinctiveness from all other Solomon Islands populations, even those of Tikopia and other Polynesian outliers.

Historical Background

Pre-Contact History

Most anthropologists are skeptical of using oral tradition as a tool for historical reconstruction. However, written records on Anutan history are virtually nonexistent, while archaeological and historical linguistic analyses leave many unanswered questions.[3] Moreover, the relatively short time span that the Anutans' oral traditions cover, their internal consistency, and their correlation with sociocultural and linguistic evidence all lend credence to the Anutans' version of their island's past, at least in its broad outlines.[4]

Anutans, like many Polynesians, have stories claiming that their island was pulled up from the ocean floor sometime during the mythical past by the demigod Motikitiki.[5] The first inhabitants' origin is unknown, and Anutans evince little information about them until the time of Pu Ariki, an important Tikopian chief.

At some point during Pu Ariki's reign he voyaged to Anuta and spoke with the two indigenous chiefs. He told them of the storms, droughts, tidal waves, and famines he had come to know back home but which Anuta had not experienced. When he heard that such events were unknown on Anuta, Pu Ariki cringed with shame and vowed his hosts would soon make their acquaintance. He returned to his homeland, invoked his deities' assistance, and a short time later Anuta was struck by a horrific storm. Crops were destroyed, and a ferocious surf prevented acquisition of food from the sea. After the storm, the sun came out and shone unmercifully; the water dried up, and the people perished.[6] These events allegedly took place about fifteen generations ago.

A short time later, two canoes descended to Anuta. One is said to have been Tongan, and its crew was led by Pu Kaurave, the man who would become the first chief of Anuta's current population. The second was from Uvea (probably East 'Uvea or Wallis Island) and was led by Pu Taupare, the founding ancestor of Anuta's present chiefly line.[7]

Pu Kaurave and Pu Taupare married each other's sisters and lived peacefully together for some time. Eventually, however, they

Photo 2.1 Pu Tokerau holding Kaurave war club. Islanders say this club was brought to Anuta by Pu Kaurave, the first immigrant from Tonga, approximately fifteen generations ago. The club is understood to possess supernatural powers and is under the personal control of Anuta's senior chief.

came into conflict. Pu Kaurave left Anuta in search of overseas adventure, eventually landing in the Santa Cruz Islands. One version of the story states that he sailed to Taumako; another identifies the site as Vanikoro. In either case, he met his end when his hosts bathed him in "the chilling water." Kaurave's son, Ruokimata, accompanied him on the trip. Upon his father's death, Ruokimata returned to Anuta and succeeded to the chieftainship, but he had no offspring of his own. Thus, when he died, Pu Taupare's son, Toroaki, assumed the chieftainship. It has remained in the Uvean line from that time onward.

During this early period, more canoes arrived from Tonga and Samoa. Their crew members settled on Anuta, adding to the population's genetic and cultural makeup. Then, three generations after Toroaki, a man named Tearakura was chief. Conflicts developed and, in the end, Tearakura, his two brothers, and one brother-in-law annihilated the remainder of the island's male population. Tongan and Samoan blood has been retained through women; but since descent, inheritance, and succession to titles normally are traced through males, the non-Uvean lines forever vanished as culturally recognized entities.

Anutans regard this as a watershed event and refer to it as *te taanga o te penua* ('the community's extermination'). The island's four major subdivisions, called *kainanga*, are attributed to Tearakura and his three loyal supporters. The lowest-ranking line would have died out within two generations, but its representatives were replaced by descendants of a Rotuman, Pu Raropita (Keve), who arrived a few years after the great cataclysm.[8] He was incorporated into the fourth *kainanga* before its indigenous members had departed the scene, and the present Kainanga i Rotomua consists of his progeny.

Throughout its history, Anuta has maintained relations with its neighbor, Tikopia. Despite occasional hostilities, most intercourse between the two islands has been friendly. Each community has always included migrants from the other. Intermarriage has been common, and young men have looked forward to the voyage across the 75 miles of open sea as a source of trade and adventure. The two islands' languages are mutually intelligible. Their cultures and social structure are similar, and the people see themselves as being closely allied when comparing themselves with the rest of the world. All persons on one island have kin on the other. And when Anutans travel to the central Solomons—a practice that has become fairly common— they are confident of finding food and shelter either with other Anutans or with their Tikopian relatives.

European Contact

The first written record of Anuta's sighting is from Captain Edward Edwards of the *HMS Pandora*. He observed the island on August 12, 1791, during his search for the *Bounty* mutineers and gave the isle its European name. During the nineteenth century, Anuta was visited periodically by European ships—mostly blackbirders and whalers—and a few islanders were induced to hire out their services to labor recruiters. An Anutan named Rangitauka is reputed to have reached the west coast of America, where he worked for several months; others found their way to Fiji and Australia where they labored for the sugar industry. None of these men ever made the voyage home, but tales were carried back by Tikopians, a few of whom did manage to return from overseas.

In 1871, some eighty years after Anuta's initial sighting by Europeans, Captain Albert Markham of the *HMS Rosario* landed on the island and provided our first extended account of the Anutan people. He identified the inhabitants as Polynesians, although he noted the atypical customs of betel chewing and making large perorations in the earlobes (Markham 1873:129–37). Women and children were nowhere to be seen, but from the number of men who came to greet the expedition, Markham estimated the population at two hundred. Like previous observers, he commented on the intensity of cultivation, listing mats, yams, taro, bananas, coconuts, and breadfruit among the island's products.

Most of the Anutans' contact with Europeans appears to have been friendly. However, traditions report two attacks on visiting ships. These incidents, motivated largely by the desire to obtain metal tools and other highly valued items, occurred during the late nineteenth century. The first raid caught the crew off guard, and the Anutans won an easy victory. The second ship gave more resistance, and Pu Tevava, one of the major instigators, was shot to death. The ship escaped and sailed to Fiji where the events were reported and a retaliatory expedition organized. Soon, a "man-o'-war" arrived, prepared for battle. However, an Anutan named Pu Pareaatai knew some English and asserted that the attacks had actually occurred on Tikopia. The sailors fired a few cannonballs into the forest as a warning of what would happen should such aggression be repeated. Then the interlopers did some trading and departed without further incident.

Vessels of the British Admiralty (1890:342, 1893:269) visited Anuta in 1872 and 1875. The sailors mapped the island and charted local waters. In addition to geographical data, they recorded some observations on the people, describing them as "timid, quiet, inoffensive . . ." (possibly due to their recent experience with the "man-o'-war"?) and noting, significantly, that "[t]hey appear to have neither pigs nor fowls. . . ."[9] In 1899 an individual protectorate status was proclaimed for the island, and during the early years of the twentieth century Anuta was incorporated into the British Solomon Islands Protectorate (Yen, et al. 1973:1).

According to Pu Nukumarere, my oldest informant in 1972–73, the man generally considered to be the most knowledgeable on the island concerning matters of Anutan history, and the islander who served as the first indigenous catechist, the church was established on Anuta in 1916. On May 16 of that year, John Wood, the bishop of Melanesia, arrived with three Tikopian missionaries aboard the *Southern Cross*. The bishop asked the leading men for permission to establish the church, and it was readily granted. When he left, the Tikopians remained behind to bring God's word to the local people. Spurred on by a devastating storm that hit in the same year, the population was soon completely converted. Anutans' understanding of Christian doctrine includes obvious remnants of their traditional religion, but they are extremely devoted to the Anglican Church. Attendance at services each morning and evening is expected of every able-bodied man, woman, and child. The mission has become a dominant feature in every aspect of Anutan life.

During the twentieth century, Anuta's contacts with the outside world gradually increased. The earliest administrative report on Anuta in the Western Pacific Archives in 1973 was dated 1935, and subsequent reports followed at intervals of many years. Beginning in the 1950s, the British colonial government attempted to send a local administrator once a year. Frequently, however, these trips were forced to turn back due to rough weather; and even after one arrives at Anuta, high surf often precludes landing. By the early 1970s, the government attempted to send a vessel approximately once a month, but with vast stretches of open sea taking a toll on small ships and urgent calls for help from more accessible islands in the eastern Solomons, it often was still three or four months between visits. For contact between visits, Anuta had a small radio, but it was difficult to hold lengthy conversations, and the instrument was out of commission entirely during more than half of my first stay.

In addition to government ships, the Church of Melanesia attempts to arrange annual visits by the mission yacht *Southern Cross*, but again the vicissitudes of weather take their toll. For two or three years prior to my arrival in 1972, the *Southern Cross* had been unable to land.

For decades the multinational Unilever company, which operated extensive coconut plantations in the central Solomons, arranged biennial visits by a labor recruiting vessel. Anutans eagerly looked forward to these visits, since they invariably brought back relatives who had been away for years. They provided others with a chance to leave the island, earn wages, and see the world. And they gave local people an opportunity to purchase flashlights, batteries, fishhooks, soap, and other European commodities in the ship's store. All of this was usually combined with grumbling about inflated prices and that the most desirable products tended to be sold out since Anuta was the vessel's last stop.

In addition to regularly scheduled visits, there are sporadic sightings of—and occasional landings by—vessels from foreign countries. These are usually fishing boats from Asia; in 1972, one Korean and two Taiwanese ships came close enough for some Anutans to board them. One of the vessels from Taiwan remained at the island for almost three days.

Around 1970, two American pleasure yachts visited Anuta and stayed for several days. During 1971, two oceanographic research vessels, one from the Soviet Union and the other from the University of Hawai'i, stopped by. The Russians would not permit any Anutans to board their ship, and they only stayed ashore a short time to trade for cowry shells. The Americans were rather more hospitable, and a half-dozen members of the research team spent the night on shore sleeping with Anutan families—an act that made a good impression on the willing hosts.

In October 1971 a research team from Honolulu's Bernice P. Bishop Museum landed on Anuta, and when the government ship did not return to pick the visitors up on schedule they remained for two months. They enjoyed their stay, and the Anutans certainly enjoyed having them. "Mr. Heni" (Douglas Yen), "Mr. Pat" (Patrick Kirch), and "Mr. Paul" (Paul Rosendahl) were favorite topics of conversation throughout the period of my 1972–73 investigation. Their sensitivity and generosity had a great deal to do with the cordial reception that the Anutans gave me and the enthusiasm with which they greeted my proposed investigation. Even during my most recent visit in 2000, a number of Anutans asked me to help them write letters to these researchers whose friendship with them has now spanned three decades.

Perhaps the most notable international visit occurred in October 1972, while I was on the island. The *Alpha Helix* from the Scripps Institution in San Diego arrived with a research team from the United States National Institutes of Health under the leadership of Carleton Gajdusek. Four years later, Gajdusek received a Nobel Prize in medicine for his groundbreaking work on an ailment called *kuru*, which he encountered in New Guinea's Eastern Highlands. *Kuru* is a transmissible spongiform encephalopathy, related to what we now call mad-cow disease. It was Gajdusek and his colleagues who demonstrated that this terrible degenerative disease of the central nervous system was caused by an infectious agent.

The *Alpha Helix*'s arrival coincided with extraordinarily rough seas produced by a hurricane several hundred miles away. With much difficulty, the researchers managed to get themselves and their equipment ashore, and they remained on the island for eight days while they conducted a medical survey of the entire population. The Anutans appreciated this team for the medical services they provided during their visit and for the willingness with which they shared their supplies and novel foods.

Since Solomon Islands independence in 1978, Anuta's isolation has changed only slightly. During the late 1980s, there was a period when all of Temotu Province was without a ship for the better part of a year (Feinberg 1990). As of 2000, two or three different ships occasionally called at Anuta, but visits rarely exceeded one per month, and several months could still go by without a visit. The old radio, however, had been replaced by one that was more powerful, reliable, and convenient, and the old hand-crank generator had been replaced by a solar panel. The new radio enables Anutans to communicate emergencies to governmental authorities in a timely manner. Unfortunately, that does not ensure the prompt arrival of a ship.

In light of this summary it may be said that Anutans, despite their relative isolation, have had a fair amount of contact in absolute terms—both with Europeans and with other Solomon Islanders. The consequences of international and interisland contact are perhaps most obvious in the sphere of material culture.

Living Conditions

Anuta forms a slightly elongated circle. Although volcanic in origin, its rounded hill rises only to a height of 212 feet (Yen, et al. 1973:1). The island's maximum diameter is one half-mile, and its total surface area has been estimated at .15 square mile, (Yen, et al. 1973:2). Considering these physical limitations, Anuta's population and ecological diversity are truly remarkable.

The resident population is relatively fluid since people come and go with almost every visiting ship. On the day before my departure from Anuta in 1973, there were 156 Anutans living on the island in addition to six Tikopians who had been in residence for two months and were planning to leave a few months hence. Residing overseas at that time were fifty Anutans: 21 in the Russell Islands; 22 in the vicinity of Honiara, the Solomon Islands capital; six children going to school on Tikopia; and one at school in the Santa Cruz Islands. In sum, there were at that time 206 persons who might reasonably be considered Anutans.[10]

Anuta's population is highly mobile. Of the Anutans living overseas at the time of my arrival in March 1972, eight returned to stay during my investigation. Fourteen persons who were present on my arrival had departed by the time I left. Thirty-three Anutans did not spend any time in residence during my stay, although several of them came for visits of a few days or less. Several other persons left after my arrival for periods of a month or more but returned home before my departure in January 1973. In addition, four live births, one stillbirth, and two deaths occurred during my period of residence. These data are summarized in table 2.1.

Table 2.1 Anutan population broken down according to island of residence.

	Anuta	Tikopia	Guadalcanal	Russell Is.	Other	Total
March 1972	162	10	17	14	1	204
January 1973	156	6	22	21	1	206

The island is ringed by a white sand beach, except where the perimeter is broken by sheer cliffs descending to the sea along the northern coast. The dwelling houses are located on this strand of beach, and they form a rough arc running from east to west along the southern shore (see figures 2.1 and 2.2).

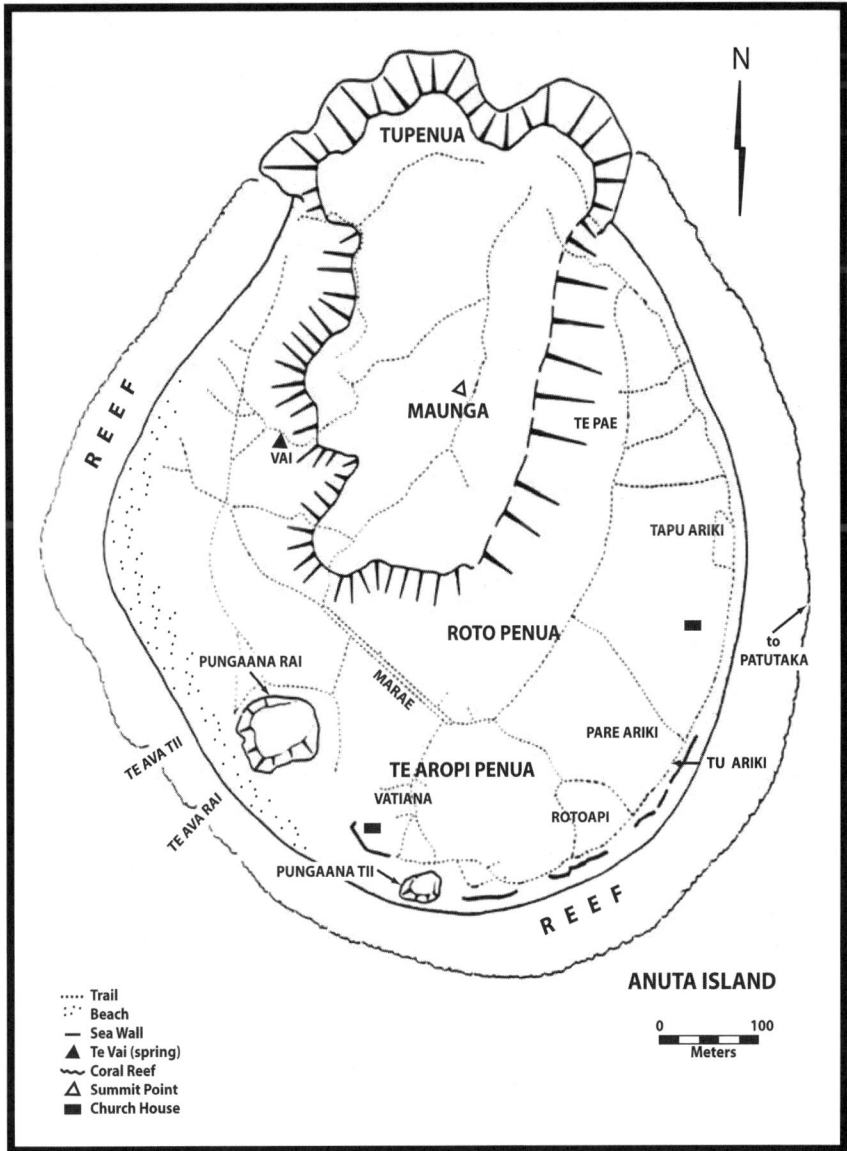

Figure 2.1   Base map of Anuta Island. (Adapted from Yen and Gordon 1973:27)

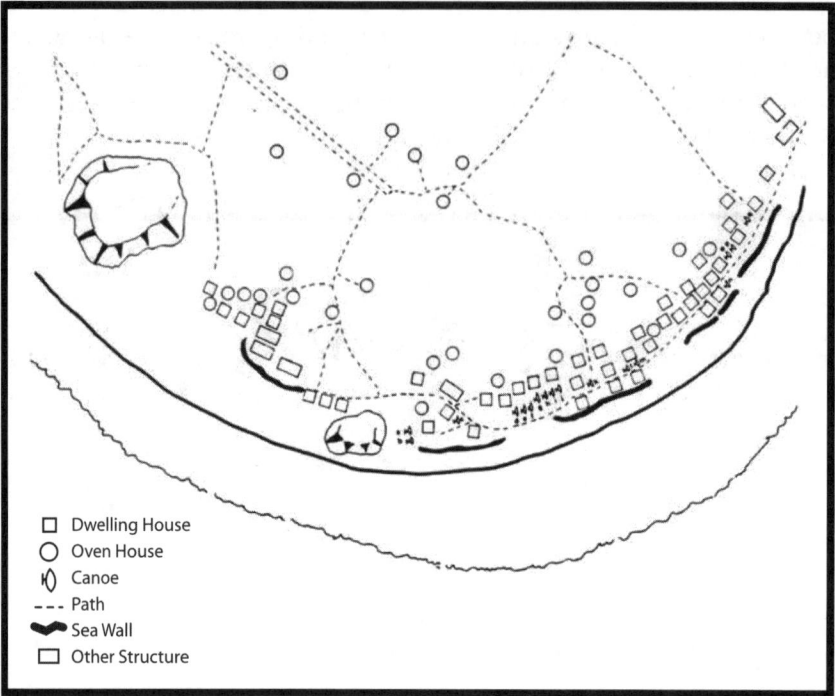

Figure 2.2 'Village' Plan.

Dwelling houses in 1972–73 were all built in the traditional style, as they are today with a few modifications. They are constructed of sturdy log frames and built close to the ground, without the aid of nails. Roofs slant at a steep pitch and are covered with coconut fronds. Anutans use leaves of the sago palm to thatch the walls. There are usually two low doors on the inland side as well as one at either end of the house, through which one must crawl on hands and knees. Inside, the floor is covered with coconut leaf mats on which one normally crawls about, standing only to get objects down from the low rafters which generally are used for storage space.

The houses are grouped into either two or three *noporanga* ('villages'), depending on the naming system that one chooses to employ. In aboriginal times there were two 'villages,' the easternmost being called Mua ('Front'), as it is closest to the point from which the sun rises in the morning. The more westerly is Muri ('Rear'). The church was constructed to the west of Muri in the early part of the twentieth century. A group of houses soon sprang up in its vicinity, and these houses were given a collective name, constituting them as a new 'village.' In the old system they were named for the church and called St.

Photo 2.2 Penuakena, house of the senior chief. The author and his family lived here during their 1983 visit to Anuta.

John, in contrast with the original units of Mua and Muri. In the new naming system, Mua and Muri are combined under the heading of Rotoapi and contrasted with St. John, which in this system is called Vatiana (see figures 2.1 and 2.2).

There are no obvious physical boundaries between the 'villages,' and they are not corporate social units. The word *noporanga* literally means 'dwelling place,' and this is really all they are—descriptive appellations indicating where people live.

A second church building called St. James was constructed east of Mua during the first few weeks of my 1972–73 study. Beyond that is a large cemetery, Tapu Ariki, which was used in pre-Christian times as a sacred *marae*—a place where chiefs and their assistants 'performed kava' to the major gods.[11] The most important ritual ground was a somewhat smaller area just inland from Mua called Pare Ariki. Anutans say that this is where Pu Kaurave's house stood until Ruoki-mata, angry at being unable to bury his father under the floor of his house as had previously been the custom, ripped down the building. From that time on, Anuta's dead were buried outside, and Pare Ariki became a chiefly cemetery. Since the church's establishment, it has become desanctified and is used for commoners as well as chiefs.

Along the beach on the southern tip of the island are two large promontories, Te Pungaana Rai to the west and Te Pungaana Tii in the east, rising to altitudes of approximately 60 and 45 feet respectively. They are covered with soil and cultivated, as is almost every piece of arable land.

Inland from the dwellings is a large, heavily wooded coastal flat, a kind of lowland plain which takes up approximately the southern half of the island; the northern half is occupied by the hill. On the western side of the hill is a spring, from which water for drinking and washing is carried down in aqueducts. In 1972–73, these were made from hollowed out areca palm and led to two locations so as to provide separate bathing spots for men and women. By the early 1980s, they had been replaced by metal—and now vinyl—pipes.

Around the center of the coastal flat Anutans have constructed a long, narrow dart pitch known as *te marae tika*, or simply Marae. Scattered around this area are between a half-dozen and a dozen large oven houses; smaller ones have been erected in the 'village' area near many of the dwellings. At the base of the hill on the eastern side are several large depressions called *nga rotopui*, which, according to legend, were dug by the first immigrants in order to collect drinking

Photo 2.3   Tapu Ariki Cemetery.

water before they discovered the spring. A well, known as Te Vai O Rimu, was also dug at one time in a depression near the beach. However, in heavy rains it tended to fill with dirt and garbage because of its unfavorable location. Thus, when the sea filled it with sand during the cyclone of February 1972, no one was inclined to dig it out again.

The remaining geographical feature playing a major role in Anutan life is, of course, the sea. The island has neither barrier reef nor lagoon, but it does have a rather extensive fringing reef surrounding all but its northern face. There is no opening or channel through the reef, not even the "mere fissures in the coral rock, not much more than the width of a ship's boat," reported by Firth (1954:95). There are two passages, termed Te Ava Rai ('The Large Passage') and Te Ava Tii ('The Small Passage'), just off Te Pungaana Rai near the southwestern portion of the island. Here the reef is at its narrowest, no more than about fifty yards from beach to breakers, and the bottom is relatively flat, making it one of the easier sections to walk on with bare feet. Moreover, it is on the leeward side of the island during the tradewind season, making the surf less dangerous than other sections. Nevertheless, the surf constantly breaks directly onto the reef along its entire length, and it is often difficult to enter or leave the island. The slope of the reef is such that water from both sides of the island comes together and runs out of Te Ava Rai, making the larger passage the desired exit. Entry must be effected through Te Ava Tii. Beyond the breakers, the bottom drops slowly, then levels off for several miles and eventually rises slightly before giving way to the *roto* or deep sea.

Off the southeast coast, at a distance of perhaps a mile from shore, are two large boulders: Te Patu o Veu, which is sometimes covered by waves in high tide, and the larger Patu o Mangoo, whose summit normally stands a good ten feet above the crest of the waves. Extending about three miles in all directions from the beach, Anuta enjoys a huge network of submerged reefs at depths ranging from 30 to 150 feet. A few miles further to the west and north and separated by a deep trench are two more coral banks, known as Te Aongo and Te Akau Motu. This reef system provides Anuta with remarkably productive fishing grounds, and it helps explain the island's population density. Finally, some thirty miles to the southeast is Patutaka, which, as a source of wild birds as well as travel and adventure, must be considered an integral part of the Anutans' physical environment.

Resources and Their Exploitation

Agriculture

I spent many hours participating in agricultural work with Anutans. I observed their activity and discussed with them many aspects of

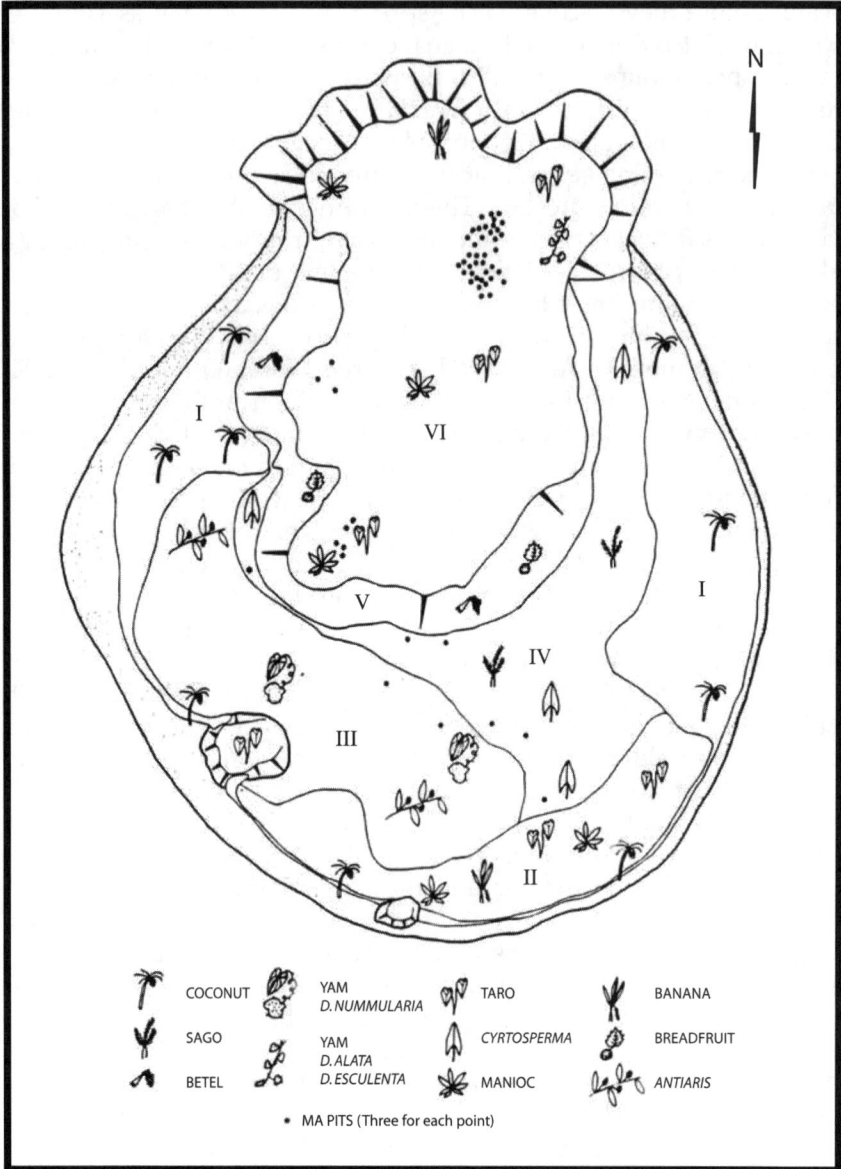

Figure 2.3 Map of Anuta showing the six agricultural zones. (Adapted from Yen and Gordon 1973:112).

this crucial endeavor. I am particularly indebted, however, to the work of Douglas Yen (1973), an ethnobotanist who preceded me on Anuta, and on whose work I will rely for the following account. My observations are presented where they either amplify or contradict Yen's findings.

Yen divides Anuta into six distinct agricultural zones based on the dominant plant species found in each one:

Zone I, "the strand belt," consists of the sandy strip encircling the island to the base of the cliffs. The dominant crop in this area is the coconut, which, with its many uses, is one of the most important products of Anutan soil. People drink the juice and either eat the flesh or shred it so that the cream may be expressed for use in cooking. They sometimes make the shells into water containers, although these have largely been replaced by tea kettles and glass bottles, which can hold more liquid and are less cumbersome. They split the shells in half for use as bowls and cups. The dried husks are used for wiping hands after meals, carrying sparks to kindle fires, and making sennit cord, which is still an important element in the Anutan economy. The leaves are used for thatch and for covering canoes when they are not in use as well as for making mats and baskets of various types. Anutans use the midrib to stir puddings, and they use the cloth-like bast as a filter in preparing turmeric dye. The strong, heavy, resistant wood is made into pillars and beams in house construction and for spears, war clubs, and arrowheads. Coconut proliferates in the other zones, but nowhere is it so dominant as along the strand.

In addition to the coconut, Zone I includes two types of pandanus palm: one (*te kie*) whose leaf is used for plaiting mats, and another (*te paa*) that bears an edible fruit. *Pipturus argenteus* (*te pau*) is a tree from whose inner bark Anutans fashion a type of cord that is used for making nets, and *Hibiscus tiliaceus* (*te kaute*) produces a decorative flower. *Calophyllum kajewski* (*te petau*) is a large tree whose wood is light yet durable, and from which canoe hulls are constructed. Leaves of *Cordia subcordata* (*te puko vai*), the island's most massive species of tree, and Polynesian arrowroot (*Tacca leontopetaloides*) provide vegetable greens. Yen's note that tubers of the latter plant are unused on Anuta corresponds with my experience.

Zone II shares with Zone I a predominance of coconut palm, but it is distinguished by the existence of small garden plots where sweet potato, taro (*Colocasia esculenta*), tobacco, and manioc are grown. In this area one also finds papaya, banana, sugar cane, and several larger species of tree.

Zone III consists of the forest which covers the coastal flat between the dwellings and the base of the hill. Yen found the dominant species here to be *Antiaris toxicara* (*te mami*), the tree from which Anutans make bark cloth. By my observation, it could equally well be identified as papaya. In addition, I found the areca palm, betel vine (*Piper betel*), and breadfruit tree primarily in this area. During a period of drought, taro and sweet potato may also be planted here on the theory that the forest might protect them from the sun's direct rays.

Coconut palms grow here in large number, as does the cordyline plant (*te tii*), whose leaf is used for body decoration and whose root may be eaten in a period of famine. Some yams (*Discorea nummularia*) are found in this zone, as are the Polynesian chestnut, the *vi* apple (*Spondias dulcis*), and some *Calophyllum, Cordia subcordata (puko vai), Terminalia,* and *Hernandia peltate (puko pakatangia)* trees. The last of these offers a soft light wood from which Anutans make canoe outriggers, model canoes, and church benches. Ground cover includes *Alocasia macrorrhiza,* whose root is occasionally employed as a taro substitute during times of scarcity.

Zone IV is the *"Cyrtosperma* Zone," characterized by large plots of *puraka (Cyrtosperma chamissonis)* commonly known as "giant taro" or "swamp taro," and sago palms. These are joined by the ever-present coconut palms and the large fruit tree *Burckella obovata.* This zone extends from the northern edge of Rotoapi to the base of the hill and includes the *rotopui* depressions where Anutans plant some of the largest plots of *puraka.*

Zone V encompasses the mountain slopes. Here Yen found the greatest concentration of breadfruit trees, areca palms, and betel vines. Many types of flowering and aromatic shrubs (*manongi*) appear

Photo 2.4   Terraced gardens on side of hill.

in this zone, as does the turmeric plant, from which Anutans make a ritually important dye and a spice that they use in flavoring certain types of pudding. A few large trees (e.g., *Calophyllum; C. subcordata)* also grow in this area.

Zone VI consists of the mountaintop gardens, in which manioc, taro, tobacco, and banana are the dominant crops. Many of these gardens are terraced with stone retainer walls of up to three feet in height, an unusual occurrence in Polynesia and one which is facilitated by a division of Anuta's limited land supply into definite plots that have remained highly stable through the generations.

Taro is Anuta's most highly valued crop. It is also fragile and easily damaged by excessive sun or moisture, so Anutans spend the greatest amount of agricultural time and effort on their taro gardens. The addition of the hardy manioc plant during the 1920s was a boon to the Anutan economy. It provided a new margin of safety in times of storm or drought and helped free workers from gardening so that their time could be devoted to other tasks. Other crops in this zone include the edible pandanus, a few small plots of yams, and coconut.

Additional crops are pumpkins (mostly in Zone II) and watermelons (occurring everywhere except Zone I), both relatively recent introductions. A few pineapples, also introduced by Europeans, grow in Zone III, and some ironwood pines, imported from Tikopia, appear in Zone II. A few Malay apple trees (*kapika*) are found in Zone V. Bananas grow everywhere except Zone I, but they are most common in wooded areas. The island's one orange tree was blown over in the cyclone of February 1972. I was told about a couple of lime trees, although they bore no fruit and I never saw them. The 1990s witnessed the introduction of several new plants, the most notable being lemongrass, from which Anutans have taken to brewing a flavorful tea.

This is far from a complete inventory of Anutan flora, but it includes most of the plant materials on which Anutans depend for their livelihood, and it demonstrates the remarkable variety of vegetable life which has been squeezed onto this tiny island. Almost every bit of land is cultivated. Even areas that look to the untrained eye like virgin forest are in reality carefully controlled. Useful crops are actively promoted and volunteer growth relegated to a secondary role. Yen (1973:125) describes Anuta's agricultural system as one of the most intensive in the Pacific, as well it must be to support its population on .15 square mile of land.

Anutan agricultural equipment is rather simple and limited in variety. It consists primarily of large steel machetes, metal axes which have replaced the stone and shell adzes of precontact times, large coconut-wood digging sticks, and long forked sticks for harvesting certain types of fruit.

Yen (1973:133–35) attempted to record the number of working hours spent by Pu Notau and his immediate family in various types of productive pursuit during the thirty-seven working days between November 3 and December 15, 1971. (Sundays were not counted because the church has forbidden all productive labor on the Sabbath except cooking for purposes of immediate consumption.) During that period, Pu Notau spent 101 hours in his gardens and 51 hours fishing. His wife, Nau Notau, spent a total of 116 hours gardening as opposed to ten hours fishing. Their eighteen-year-old daughter devoted 51 hours to agricultural pursuits and 11 to fishing, while their two younger boys (at school in Tikopia by the time of my arrival) spent a total of 16 hours in the gardens and 32 hours trying to catch fish.

Yen presented these figures to demonstrate that agriculture is by far the most labor intensive activity on Anuta, taking up twice as much time as fishing. The figures are misleading, however, in a number of ways. Pu Notau, as Yen (personal communication) recognized, was one of the best and most careful gardeners on the island. This was partially a matter of personal inclination, but it also was a reflection of his limited garden space, which meant that his family was forced to produce more food per unit area in order to feed itself. Moreover, agricultural work, although strenuous while in progress, is interrupted by frequent long breaks during which participants may sit in the shade to smoke, chat, and perhaps treat themselves to food or drink. On occasion almost as much gardening time may be spent resting as at work. Nevertheless, the figures do lead to two sound conclusions: substantially more man-hours are devoted to growing crops than to fishing, and the ratio of fishing time to gardening time is much higher for men than it is for women. The environment's productivity is indicated by the fact that even Nau Notau, the most diligent gardener of the family, spent an average of just over three hours per day engaged in agricultural pursuits.

Of gardening techniques, Yen (1973:123) notes that:

> The trees and perennial plants require the least attention. Harvesting with long poles seems to be the greatest labor investment in the care of fruit trees. The weeding, thinning, and occasional planting of *Cyrtosperma* are performed with a knife; a digging stick is used for making planting holes. The pollarding of *Antiaris* is done at early growth stages of the tree and is an activity incidental to other chores—picking off the young side shoots as one is walking through Zone III to other gardens, or to one's ablutions at *te vai* (the island's water supply). No transplanting of bread-fruit "suckers" was observed during our stay, for it was said that it was too dry, even though there was no regular season for such planting.

Other chores—such as the mounding of *D. nummularia* yams, and thin-ning banana stands and providing windbreaks for them—are difficult to describe for there seems little order, system, or periodicity to them. At the time we left, I knew all the yam plants in Zone III. Of the 41 plants, only seven had been offered any attention—they had been remounded. Certainly in my discussions in the gardens and houses, I could not record a sequence of procedure in relation to perennial-crop cultiva-tion. It was obvious from the review of the *Cyrtosperma* gardens of Zone IV, however, that some cultivators lavished greater attention on them than others.

Techniques employed to grow manioc and, especially, taro are more ordered and complex. The normal sequence of events is more or less as follows.

First the planter clears a garden plot of trees and brush with axe and knife, and if the ground cover includes a type of low fern (*Nephro-lepsis biserrata*), the area is burned to suppress the rhizomes. A week or so later taro planting begins. The gardener makes holes in the ground with a digging stick, and taro tops are placed in the holes. The loose soil then is gently packed by hand around the cuttings.

The sensitive taro does not stand up to weeds much better than it does to rain or uninterrupted sun. The plots must be weeded two to three weeks after planting and at regular intervals thereafter until the crop is ready for harvest. The weeds, along with grass brought in from elsewhere, are then used for mulching. Windscreens are erected on occa-sion, although this is more common with tobacco than taro. Some people are more diligent than others in their cultivating activities, and when cli-matic conditions are favorable, a few Anutans may do away with the mulching altogether. More industrious agriculturalists may put down as many as six applications of mulch before the crop achieves maturity.

If all goes well, in five to seven months the taro is ready for har-vest, and the corms, with stem and leaves still attached, are pulled out by hand. If the crop is to be used for immediate consumption, some corms may be left in the ground for over a month after they have matured. When it is to be stored as a fermented mash known as *ma*, an entire plot may be harvested and prepared within a matter of days.

After the taro has been harvested, it is time to plant manioc. The gardener pushes foot-long defoliated sections of manioc stem into former taro holes until the garden has again been filled. Weeding and mulching may be performed as with taro, but for the sturdy manioc this is not mandatory, and the mulching process may be largely ignored. In four to seven months, the plants mature, and the root is harvested with the aid of a digging stick. When this has been com-pleted, the cycle begins anew with the planting of taro, usually with-out any significant fallow period.

Alternating taro and manioc cultivation in a rotational sequence is the ideal procedure, and it is the one most frequently followed in practice. During the latter part of my stay, however, I recorded 182 manioc plots and only 77 taro gardens. The predominance of manioc over taro by a rate of more than 2.5 to one, considering the non-seasonality of the two crops, suggests that the ideal may stray quite far from actual practice. This is probably explained by the differential durability of the two plants.

I arrived on the island shortly after a devastating cyclone that destroyed most of the taro crop but left the manioc more or less intact. Before the island had a chance to recover, it was struck by a drought. This made taro cultivation problematic, and therefore, people tended not to plant it in large quantities. Moreover, nature is never completely reliable, and this makes overdependence on taro a dangerous luxury even in the best of times. Normal crop rotation may be interrupted in order to plant tobacco, yam, or banana, and such crops are more likely to replace taro than manioc. Finally, the reduced expenditure of labor entailed by manioc production is undoubtedly attractive to some people.

Anuta's climate is subject to noticeable seasonal variation. With a location of about 11°40′ south of the equator, it is generally exposed to the southeast tradewinds from April through October. During this period, brisk winds blow almost constantly from the southeast quadrant with considerable force. At this time, known as *te tonga*, it is frequently overcast and temperatures may be chilly, but it tends not to rain a great deal. In the *raki* or 'monsoon season,' which usually lasts from October through April, winds blow sporadically from the west. During this season the weather is unpredictable. There may be extended periods of clear sky and blazing sun, interspersed with protracted downpours. Sometimes the wind may fall off completely for days at a time, but it is also during the monsoon season that the island experiences its occasional cyclones. All this has an important effect on fishing and overseas travel, but Yen (1973:125) confirms my observation that there is little seasonality to the agricultural system:

> Unlike other Oceanic gardens, the finite plant-harvest time is more easily defined because of the storage process that both manioc and taro undergo, requiring total harvesting. Seasonality nevertheless is lacking … taro and manioc may be seen at all different stages of growth at any one

Table 2.2   Number of *ma* pits, broken down by variety.

Manioc	Breadfruit	Taro	Banana	Cyrtosperma	Burckella
112	76	11	10	5	3

time, so that there tends to be a continuity of supply of corms, and pres-
ervation is a spread out rather than a seasonal demand on the labor
entailed. Tobacco, bananas, and, rarely, yams may occur in the cycle,
interrupting its broadly annual pattern, as they may occupy the land for
up to—and in the case of bananas, more than—a year. The Anutans recognize October as the main planting time of these species, and
April-May as harvest. Were yams (*D. alata* and *D. esculenta*) dominant in
the agricultural scheme, seasonality would be more marked, as in island
Melanesia. The application of this pattern would confer a greater formality to the rotational cycle, for a preponderance of yam-planting would
inevitably cause a rearrangement of planting times for other crops—and
perhaps the intervention of a fallow—to the June-September period.

As it is, the Anutan crop rotation is one of the most intensive recorded
in Oceania, at least by this investigator. It is rivaled only by the irrigated
terracing systems for taro-growing, e.g., in East Futuna . . . for whether
one applies the criterion of short (in this case, absent) fallow period or
labor input, mathematical formulae are hardly necessary to contend
intensity for this sector of agriculture on Anuta.

By contrast, the perennial and tree crops require maintenance and cultivation on a casual basis only, and harvest is the main activity. The
anticipation of maturity of breadfruit, betel nut, and bananas is generally the result of walking from village to mountain gardens, and the
choice of pathway through Zone V is dictated by the siting of a person's
trees. Again, seasons are poorly marked, but breadfruit has two flowering periods, September-October and May-June, when often some fruit
from the previous flowering remains on trees. This, with varietal differences, accounts for the often-recorded claim that five to six harvests of
breadfruit may occur in a year. Seasonal variation is also recognized,
and years with "big winds" can drastically curtail breadfruit production.

The Anutan environment is generally favorable to agricultural
production, and the people make the most of it. With a 1972–73 population density of around 1000 per square mile, more food was available than the Anutans could possibly eat. Even in 2000, when a
government census had just placed the island's populace at 340, creating an astounding population density of over 2000 per square mile,
Anuta's gardens and fishing grounds kept the people well fed! On
occasion, however, natural disasters create periods of shortage. With
this in mind, Anutans store a certain proportion of their produce in
underground pits where it is subjected to a process of semianaerobic
fermentation. Such fermented fruits and vegetables, known as *ma*,
may be kept for years as insurance against famine.

Manioc, because of its abundance and its relatively mild taste, is
the most common material for making *ma*. Taro is a distant second,
followed by breadfruit, banana, *Cyrtosperma*, and *Burckella* in that
order. A single *ma* pit may be up to twelve feet deep and more than a

yard in diameter. I recorded 217 pits on the island. Of these, well over sixty were completely empty and many more partially so by the time I departed the scene, but thanks to the surplus from times of plenty and the practice of storing it for periods of hardship, no one went hungry in the wake of the cyclone that preceded my arrival.

Fish and Game

In contrast to the proliferation of vegetable life, the variety of animal species on Anuta is quite limited. The only nonhuman mammal to inhabit the island in precontact times was the omnipresent rat, to which cats were added some decades ago for the purpose of rodent control. Several years before my first visit, an Anutan brought a dog to the island, but the animal made a nuisance of himself by eating cats and chickens and threatening to bite people. One day when the owner was away, a group of irate neighbors rid Anuta of the pest. In the years since 1973, Anutans have tried two or three more experiments with dogs, but with similar results.

In the middle of the twentieth century, during Pu Teukumarae's reign as the island's senior chief, Anuta boasted a few pigs—apparently obtained sometime after the British Admiralty expeditions of the 1870s. However, they turned out to be more trouble than they were worth by eating people's food, destroying gardens, and creating a health hazard. Thus, they soon were banned from the island. In November 1972, toward the end of my first stay, two piglets were imported on the Levers' labor-recruiting vessel as presents for Pu Nukumanaia and Pu Nukutamaaroa. And during the 1980s and 1990s Anutans made a few more attempts at pig domestication. But by the time of my 2000 visit, these experiments were also abandoned under orders from the chiefs and their advisors.

Other terrestrial animals include several types of lizard, some coconut crabs and a few other varieties of land crab, spiders, centipedes, and a variety of insects. Birds are available in large numbers at certain times of the year, but their variety is also limited. Anutans hunt wild birds at times when it is difficult to obtain fish, and a supply of chickens was introduced from Tikopia during the 1950s. The chickens, which used to run free around most of the island, now tend to be confined to coops. They are used to provide meat at feasts when other sources of animal flesh are unavailable; the eggs are not eaten. Patutaka is a productive spot for hunting birds, but it is rare for there to be more than one or two voyages in a single year.

By far Anuta's most productive source of animal protein is the sea. Islanders exploit dozens of varieties of reef fish, as well as dolphin fish (*matimati*), bonito (*atu*), tuna (*varu*, *kakati*), shark (*mangoo*), barracuda (*paravao*), wahoo (*paramauni*), and large billfish such as sail-fish and marlin (*takura*), all of which abound in the offshore waters. Whales and mammalian dolphins sometimes appear and remain near the island for weeks at a time, but Anutans make no attempt to catch them. They refer to these aquatic mammals as *nga ariki o te moana* ('kings of the ocean') and say that, should someone become lost at sea, dolphins may appear and lead the sailor back to shore.

The island has no crocodiles or terrestrial snakes although Anutans are familiar with these reptiles from other parts of the Solomons. They occasionally encounter sea snakes (*unukorokoro*), which have an extremely venomous bite, similar to a cobra's. But they tend to be lethargic and pose no serious threat to the human population. Sea turtles (*ponu*) sometimes appear, but they are difficult to catch, and I never saw Anutans eat one. Octopus (*peke*) is common on the reef and is a preferred fish bait. Children sometimes spend their leisure time searching the reef for crabs, snails, and cowries and cook them on the beach. Spearfishermen occasionally pick up crayfish near the surf line on calm nights. Giant clams of the genus *Tridachna* (*nga toki*) are abundant in the ocean a short distance beyond the breakers. Limpets (*matapiu*) adhere to the cliffs on the north coast and at Patutaka, but they can only be gathered on unusually calm days. Sea cucumbers and starfish are present on the reef but generally go unused. At one point Anutans collected and dried sea cucumbers (*puroria*) in an attempt to establish a commercial export business, but it proved to involve a great deal of hard work for little payoff. An abundance of shells along the beach testifies to the existence of a small abalone-like creature (*te matapiri*), but I saw none of these animals alive. Pearlshell (*tipa*) and trochus (*karikau*) have not been found on Anuta for many decades, but they may be obtained from Tikopia.

Among Anutans' myriad techniques for catching fish, the most productive involve use of hook and line from a canoe. When canoes are not in use, they are covered with leaves to protect them from the sun and the rain.[12] They are stored well up on land in Rotoapi, where there is a sea wall to protect them from the waves and there are few trees to fall on them during a storm. When a canoe is taken out, the crew uncovers it, carries it down to the water, and, inside the reef, one of the fishermen paddles it around to the passage. While this is going on, other members of the crew search the reef for an octopus to be used for bait.

The crew loads its gear into the canoe in the vicinity of the passage, and it is ready to set off. The men push the vessel to the edge of the breakers, where they wait for a momentary lull in the surf. Someone gives a signal, and everyone pushes at once. When some momentum is achieved most of the crew hops in, and the men paddle with all their strength to get well out to sea before another curl has time to come up and break upon the craft. Meanwhile, one or two men in the stern continue to push as long as they are able to stand on the reef. Once the canoe is safely past the surf line, the men who stayed behind to push swim out and climb aboard. If the wind is right, the crew sets sail; otherwise, they paddle to the fishing grounds.

Beyond the surf for several miles in each direction, the ocean bottom forms a series of concentric rings with depths ranging from 30 to 150 feet. Scattered through this region are hundreds of coral heads and other marine features. The island's expert fishermen (*tautai*) have mentally recorded the locations of all these reefs and other features, as well as the types of fish that tend to frequent them.[13] The *tautai* locates the general fishing area by lining up with landmarks on Anuta and two large offshore boulders. Then the crew looks down to find the reef's precise location. Most fishing is done in 60 to 80 feet of water, which obscures details on the bottom. However, the sea is clear enough that it is usually easy to make out the dark patches that indicate the presence of a coral head.

With little wind and a moderate current, everyone may fish except the sternman, who continues to paddle to keep the vessel hovering over the desired spot. If the wind or current is fairly strong, it is often necessary to have the bowman assist to keep the craft in place.

Fishing equipment for these inshore waters consists of nylon monofilament line in the 60- to 80-pound test range, wound around some sort of spool and used as a hand line. Hooks are of European manufacture, replacing the bone, wood, and shell of earlier times. Anutans occasionally section lead bars and fashion them into sinkers. Owing to a scarcity of lead, however, many fishermen continue to make do with stones as they did in olden days.

Using this technique, known as *tau vae*, in inshore waters, four fishermen can expect to catch 50 to 100 fish in the one- to three-pound range. Fewer than 40 fish indicate a very poor day, while hauls of over 100 per canoe are not uncommon. On occasion, I have seen a canoe with two or three fishermen come back with more than 200 fish. However, for adventure and variety, and to avoid overfishing the inshore reefs, Anutans sometimes take canoes to the open sea in search of large game fish. If only one canoe is fishing on a particular day, it usually remains close to the island for the certain catch; if there are several vessels, one or more may go offshore in quest of the big ones.

For a trip to *te roto* ('the deep sea'), fishermen start out as they do when exploiting nearby reefs, except that they begin earlier because of the long trip ahead. Armed with the usual octopus for bait, they head for a reef in the direction of their destination, and there they fish the bottom until a supply of the normal reef fish has been obtained. Then they head out to the open sea, perhaps four or five miles beyond. Still employing hand lines, but now of about 150-pound test, with large hooks and no sinker, they chop up some of the fish they have caught on the reef, bait the hook, and let it float freely at the end of perhaps a hundred yards of line. Usually one person fishes at a time to avoid fouling the lines in case of a large strike. Anutans call this fishing method *pakataataa*.

After a large game fish strikes, it is pulled in by hand. When it is close to the canoe, someone grabs the tail. Should the fish be small enough, it is taken aboard and clubbed to death with a heavy stick (*te tuki*) brought along for that purpose. If the fish is too large to be safely pulled in alive, it is held by the tail and clubbed senseless before being brought aboard. By this method, Anutans commonly catch small sharks, tuna, and dolphin fish; at the upper end, I have even seen them land a six-foot shark and an eight-foot marlin.

Another method of fishing from a canoe is *taki* ('trolling'). One does not go out specifically to troll. But on the way to the fishing grounds, and again on the trip home, a light line with a small hook and a strip from the end of an octopus' tentacle is frequently dragged behind the canoe. Flying fish (*ttave*) and large needle fish (*aku*) are the commonest varieties to be caught in this way.

A very different type of canoe fishing is *rarama*, night fishing for flying fish. A canoe goes out well after sundown—perhaps as late as 10:00 or 11:00 P.M.—with a long-handled net and either a leaf torch or a flashlight. The light attracts flying fish, which leap from the water in the vicinity of the canoe, and the net handler scoops them out of the air. In contrast with some islands where an entire evening may be spent collecting flying fish to take home and eat, Anutans typically keep at it only until they have caught a few. They then head out to deeper water where they use the flying fish for bait to catch the larger species. Fishing at night is generally more productive than during the day, and when the fishermen get home the next morning they usually have a good catch to show for their efforts. Getting through the passage, however, tricky as it is during the day, is doubly difficult at night. Consequently, this kind of fishing is normally reserved for the tradewind season when the passage is at its calmest.

A canoe requires many months to build, and it takes years for a tree to grow large enough to be used for a hull. Therefore, if there is any question about the weather being too rough, canoes are not taken out, and fish must be obtained by other means. On perhaps a third of the days that I spent on the island, the passage was too rough to be safely traversed by canoe.

One of the most popular methods of catching fish when the passage is impassable by canoe is for a man to grab a small fishing line in his hand, tie a basket around his waist, throw some bait into the basket, and swim out to sea. Most Anutans have inexpensive diving goggles with which they can easily see the bottom and follow the terrain to one of the nearby reefs. Then, while floating in the ocean, hovering over some large rock, they fish the bottom. When a fish takes the hook, it is pulled to the surface. The fisherman bites his quarry through the head to kill it and places it in his basket.

By this method, known as *taukurakura*, one does not have the same flexibility of movement as in a canoe. One may swim to reefs up to a mile offshore, but a distance of several miles is impossible. Thus, the fish tend to be of a smaller variety. Still they are often caught in large numbers. A single fisherman catching fifty *vanevane* fish in three hours is not uncommon; and occasionally larger species are pulled in.[14] I have seen a two-foot shark landed by this method, and I saw one man use a slight modification to catch a five-foot barracuda.[15] A variant of this method, sometimes used by children or young teenagers, involves fishing for immature rock cod (*nepunepu*) and related species near the surf line. Anutans call this technique *taunepunepu*.

Yet another method of obtaining fish is to swim past the surf line with a homemade speargun, usually fashioned from rubber innertube material and a metal rod with one end sharpened to a point. Spearfishermen stay fairly close to shore since they must be able to dive to the bottom where the reef fish congregate, and the Anutans' diving range is only about 30 feet. However, one can sometimes spear a fish that will not bite a hook, and at the same time one may dive for clams which are fairly abundant at such moderate depths. This procedure (called *panapana*) was in common use during my first visit in 1972–73; more recently spearfishing beyond the fringing reef was banned in order to prevent the fish from developing a fear of humans.

An important mode of fishing on which there are many variations is *tiiti* ('fishing with a pole and line'). This method is most usefully employed when the sea is too rough to take out a canoe. Most commonly one ties a two- or three-fathom length of eight-pound test monofilament line to a bamboo pole, lashes a tiny hook to the end of it, and binds a small hermit crab to the hook with fiber from a banana leaf. The fisherman stands on the beach, casts the bait out as far as he can into the water, and slowly moves the rod in such a way as to pull the hook back toward shore. In fact, bound as it is with banana fiber, the "bait" cannot be eaten and acts more as a lure. Usually the fish caught by this method from the shore are very small, averaging perhaps only three inches in length. However, when they are running, they may be caught in considerable numbers, so that in an hour or two a man may catch enough to feed his household for the day.

Other *tiiti* variations include standing at the surf line at low tide with a larger hook and heavier line, or walking onto one of the rock ledges at the base of the cliff and casting into the surf. Sometimes a fisherman even carries a pole out to sea and casts while treading water or standing on a submerged boulder. These variants produce much larger quarry than does casting from the shore; fish in the three- to four-pound range are common.

While Anutans sometimes use spears in the ocean, they are most often employed on the fringing reef, either in communal fish drives during the day, or by lone fishermen or in small groups at night. Night fishing requires a spear, diving goggles, and a waterproof flashlight. When fishing in groups, at least one youngster is frequently included to carry the fish. When the tide is approximately at its midpoint, fishermen wade into the waist-deep water covering the reef. Bending over so that their heads are in the water, they walk along, shining their lights into crevices and under rocks. The light temporarily blinds any fish that might be there, and they become easy prey for an expert spearman. During such nighttime fishing expeditions Anutans also frequently capture crayfish, either by spear or by hand. Women sometimes fish the reef at night with scoop nets, on occasion with a good deal of success. Overall, however, this is not one of the more important methods of food acquisition.

Communal fish drives take many forms, but all work on the same principle: a large number of people surround the fish and frighten them into an area where they may be speared or netted. In the simplest variation, Anutans form a large circle around a rock on the reef flat when the tide is about half full. Then, shouting and beating the water with hands and sticks, the people close the circle. Frightened fish swim away from their pursuers, and as the circle closes they seek refuge beneath the rock. The fishermen then dive down and take them with their makeshift spearguns.

Another version has people form a line across the reef from the beach to the breakers and walk forward, again with a maximum of commotion. This time they frighten the fish into a weir created by piling stones in such a way as to produce a long passage that funnels the prey into a rocky enclosure, where they are netted or speared by hand. Yet another method is for fishermen to line up across the reef when the tide is low and move systematically in the direction of one of the raised ends which are totally exposed. As the fish are driven into ever shallower water, they lose room to maneuver and are easily netted, speared, or clubbed, after which they are picked up by hand.

Photo 2.5 Communal fish drive *(paangota)*.

In addition to the developed methods of catching fish, Anutans often improvise. More than once I have seen a young child reach his hand into a crevice in the reef, to emerge a few seconds later holding a fish. Anutan women do not regularly comb the reef for shellfish and only rarely fish with hand-held scoop nets, an activity which Firth (1963 [1936]:52–53, 65, 92, 124) reports to be part of Tikopia's daily routine.

This discussion of Anutan fishing casts doubt on the common assumption (e.g., Goldman 1970) that the absence of a lagoon implies a shortage of fish. Two canoes carrying a total of eight to ten men rarely have difficulty providing as much fish as the island can consume. On more than half the days I was in residence, the sea was calm enough to take out the canoes. When it was not, there were many less efficient but quite acceptable methods of acquiring fish for the community.[16] With respect to other sources of animal protein, however, the picture is not quite so bright.

The only terrestrial animals to be eaten on Anuta are several types of land crab, and this is only done by children for entertainment. Birds, on the other hand, are sometimes fairly plentiful, and they may be hunted as an alternative to catching fish. There are essentially two ways of catching birds—to sneak up and grab them by hand or with a noose (a method known as *tangotango*), or to net them with a long-handled net (*veu*). Both techniques can be employed in daylight, but they are far more effective at night.

Veu involves climbing a tree and waiting for an unsuspecting bird to come along. When the bird comes to rest on a nearby branch the hunter quickly nets it, pulls it in, and breaks its neck. The simplest version of *tangotango* is to see a bird dozing in a tree, climb up behind, and grab it. Unlikely as this may sound, I have seen it done successfully. A more productive method, however, is to wait in a carefully selected tree for birds to approach of their own accord. Yet another variant of *tangotango* is to use a noose on the end of a long pole to grab the bird. This is usually done with large species on the island's northern cliff face overlooking the sea or on the peaks of Patutaka. When all goes well, these techniques offer impressive results. On two occasions during my first stay, groups of five young men set out in the evening and returned the next morning with catches of about a hundred boobies, noddies, and other large birds.

As insurance against being faced with an important ceremonial occasion and not having animal flesh of any kind available, the Anutans keep a stock of chickens. These, however, are reserved for special situations.

Wage Labor and the Impact of the Outside World

Anutans depend primarily on their subsistence economy, as they have few potential sources of cash income. Commercial coconut production is unfeasible on account of the island's small size and remote location. Islanders may sell an occasional artifact to someone on a passing ship. A few experiments with commercial shark fin and *bêche-de-mer* production over the years have generated a modest income.[17] And two schoolteachers, as of 2000, were on government contracts. Wage labor overseas, however, is by far Anuta's most important source of cash and European commodities.

All adult males on Anuta, and many of their wives and children, have spent at least some time away from their home island. In a few cases, this experience has been limited to Tikopia, but the vast majority of adults have spent periods ranging from a few months to many years in Honiara, the Russell Islands, or both. Levers Pacific Plantations, for a number of decades, had an arrangement with the people of Anuta and Tikopia whereby the company provided free transportation to and from the Russell Islands for any man who committed himself to work for a minimum of two years. Moreover, a worker might be accompanied by several family members. When the Levers recruiting vessel paid its biennial visit to Anuta in November 1972, four Anutans (one man and three dependents) returned to the island to stay while thirteen (four men and nine dependents) left. In addition to these, a handful of Anutans were living in the Russells on a long-term basis.

In Honiara, the picture is similar. Prior to 1978, the colonial government's medical department normally paid the cost of transport for anyone who required hospital care, and the independent Solomon Islands government has tried to maintain that practice. Then, after a free trip to the national capital, people sometimes stay on.

Anyone who cannot provide a medical justification must pay ship fare. In 1972–73, the cost of a one-way ticket was thirteen Australian dollars. In 2000, the price was approximately 150 Solomon Islands dollars, the equivalent of about US$30. Some islanders must struggle to put together even such modest sums, but with assistance from relatives, passage is within the reach of most Anutans. In 1972–73, nine Anutans had permanent or semipermanent jobs in Honiara—three taxi drivers, two police officers, and four maintenance workers employed by the Town Council. By 1988, I counted 60 Anutans living in Honiara, and in 2000, despite a civil war that had devastated the Solomon Islands capital, a good 30 Anutans remained.

The opportunity for involvement in wage labor has affected Anuta in a number of ways. First, it provides a safety valve for an expanding population. Normally, the island's resources can still support the population. In periods of scarcity, however, having an alternative to the subsistence economy on the home island can make a major difference.

Anutans' geographical mobility and involvement in wage labor have affected their perceptions of the world in which they live. Their travels offer them experiences they could not have at home. Their conceptions of time and distance have been altered. Through their living, travel, work, and school arrangements, they have come to know people from other parts of the Solomons and many "European" countries.[18] In this process, they have developed an understanding of foreign customs and lifestyles, and they have increased their sophistication in thinking about and dealing with people outside their own immediate cultural sphere.

Anutans also have become acquainted with new items of material culture. With wages that averaged only about thirty dollars per month during the 1970s, what they could buy was limited.[19] Nevertheless, they did have the funds to obtain a small number of inexpensive items: metal tools, cooking pots, fishhooks, monofilament line, lanterns, kerosene, and European cloth. On Guadalcanal and (previously) in the Russell Islands, Anutans have their own taro, manioc, and sweet potato gardens; but they also enjoy hard tack biscuits, coffee, tea, sugar, and rice, all of which must be purchased. Fish is scarce in the central Solomons, which means that it too must often be purchased in a store. Anutans, like most other Solomon Islanders, particularly appreciate tinned mackerel because of its oily taste.

Wage workers sometimes send money or goods to relatives back home, and those returning to live on Anuta usually bring a supply of manufactured goods. They try to keep a little extra cash to cover the price of passage in any future attempt to leave the island, to help kin who wish to emigrate, or to purchase odds and ends from the occasional ship that happens by. Thus, most European goods are obtained either directly or indirectly through wage work.

The outside world also has had some impact on Anutan education, but this is still in its beginning stages. In the 1970s, the island had a school of sorts, but children were only brought to a "standard two" level of education (theoretically, equivalent to second grade in the American system); and even this is a generous evaluation. The regular teacher at that time had been crippled by polio and rarely went far from his house. Therefore, he had plenty of time to devote to his teaching functions, and he usually was conscientious about teaching the children for two or three hours a day. However, in June 1972 he left for Honiara to have a leg operation and be fitted with braces so that he would be able to walk. He did not return to Anuta until November, and when I departed the island in January 1973 he had not yet resumed his teaching functions.

The local catechist also occasionally taught school.[20] By his account, he once was fairly diligent about his teaching. Then the church decided that secular education should be the government's responsibility and stopped paying him. As he was not certified by the Education Department, the government also refused to pay his fee. Since he was no longer being paid, teaching came to occupy a low position on his list of priorities; and from that time on his school consisted of calling the children together for an hour or so when the spirit moved him, to provide elementary instruction in English vocabulary and to teach a few prayers.

The effectiveness of Anuta's school system may be gauged by the fact that only two or three men on the island spoke enough English to carry on a conversation with a visitor who knew no Pijin and no Anutan—and even their English was sometimes incomprehensible to me.[21] Another handful of men spoke passable Pijin, a form of pidgin English that has been, for over a century, the most widely spoken language in the Solomon Islands.

Church services were held in "English," and most adults were able to follow to some extent in their prayer books.[22] However, it was difficult for me to determine how much they understood of what they were reading. Unless I had a written text, many of the "English" prayers remained unintelligible to me even after a year of listening to them practically every day. But perhaps the best index of the islanders' difficulty with the English language is that after about five or six months all my conversations were conducted in Anutan, even when dealing with the best English speakers on the island.

By the time of my second visit to Anuta, in 1983, all of this had begun to change—a trend that has continued into the new century. As of my most recent visit, a well-trained Tikopian headmaster and an Anutan schoolteacher ran a well-organized school that took Anutan children through "standard six." Many children and young adults spoke, or at least understood, a good deal of English. Children often wrote their names or messages in the sand, and I occasionally saw people read for entertainment. Today, the head catechists and several assistants offer religious instruction for all of the island's children

Photo 2.6 Pu Nukumairunga, the radio operator, school teacher, and medical orderly in 1972–73 had been crippled by polio. In late 1972, he was fitted with leg braces and able to walk for the first time in years. The boy to Pu Mairunga's left was covered with skin fungus. His case was cured several years later, but fungal infections remain a major problem on the island.

every Sunday morning, and most Anutans now seem quite conversant with Christian doctrine and church procedures.

The major remaining effect of overseas contact has to do with health, and from this point of view Anutans have fared much better than many non-Western peoples. The ravages of introduced disease and the benefits of modern medicine have more or less balanced each other. Tuberculosis is the most serious infectious disease, but it rarely seems to affect more than one or two people at a time. There are occasional outbreaks of dysentery, but they are rarely severe except in infants. Hookworm exists, but it is also rare and not debilitating. One man—the schoolteacher in 1972–73—is crippled from polio, which he contracted during the 1950s. However, he is an immigrant from Tikopia and actually came down with the disease while away at school before he settled on Anuta. Sexually transmitted diseases were not considered to be an issue in the 1970s, but with increasing interisland contact Anutans have grown progressively more concerned about their potential spread.

Solomon Islands medical authorities report that Anutan mosquitoes do not carry the malaria parasite. However, Anutans often travel to other parts of the Solomons where malaria is endemic, and they are exposed during their travels. Therefore, although Anutans are unlikely to contract malaria on their island, many bring it home and suffer the consequences. This conclusion corresponds with Firth's report of a Tikopian epidemic of "influenza complicated by malaria" as far back as 1955 that claimed the lives of at least two hundred people (Firth 1970:386). It also corresponds with the findings of the *Alpha Helix* expedition (Brown, et al. 1976; Gajdusek, personal communication).

Trachoma, a potentially debilitating eye infection, occurs on Anuta, but the local form is relatively benign (Gajdusek, personal communication). Older people usually have reduced vision, at least in part because of this affliction, but I only know of one Anutan who was completely blind.

The most obvious medical problem is skin fungus. Hardly anyone is totally unaffected, and many Anutans are covered from head to toe. This problem is noted even in early administrative tour reports, along with a recommendation that the single most valuable service the government could perform for the island would be its eradication. Reports have continued in a similar vein, but the disease is still endemic.

In a tropical environment, untreated cuts and scrapes easily become infected. Usually Anutans simply wait for their immune systems to counter the infection, but in especially bad cases they sometimes seek the medical orderly for treatment.

Owing to Anuta's isolation from the outside world, visiting ships often leave epidemics in their wake. Anutans report little mortality resulting from such experiences, and they remain anxious to make contact with any vessel drawing near their shores, but twice during my first visit, the island was affected by moderately severe epidemics of upper respiratory disease. Each epidemic lasted from two to three months, and hardly a soul was spared by either one.

In the 1970s, medical facilities on the island were minimal. There was no hospital, nor was there a trained physician or nurse. The medical authorities supplied Anuta with some basic medications: aspirin; chloroquine phosphate for malaria treatment; salicylic acid ointment for skin fungi; antiseptic and antibiotic ointments for topical application to wounds to prevent bacterial infection; a hookworm expellant; some bandages; and a few vials of injectable penicillin (which, to my knowledge, were never touched). These were dispensed by a medical orderly known to colonial authorities as the "native dresser." This man listened to me one day with interest and surprise as I explained to him the germ theory of disease.

Anutans have only the slightest understanding of modern sanitary procedures. Sick people cough on each other and then handle food without concern. Islanders bathe frequently—in most cases twice a day—but rarely do they wash their hands before a meal. Cats run freely through the houses and are handled during meals. Spitting, a constant practice in this betel-chewing community, takes place indoors as well as out. Since one normally moves about inside by crawling on hands and knees it is easy to pick up microbes from the floor that are transferred to the food in the course of a meal. When someone gets sick others demonstrate their concern by going to visit, and visitors are usually offered food. For toilet facilities Anutans generally use the beach below the high water line, and the wastes are carried out to sea each time the tide comes in. Short of chemical processing, this may be as good a way as any to handle the problem; still it is less than ideal.

Anutans pay little attention to garbage disposal. People often leave the remains of a meal in the middle of a path or throw them out the back doors of their houses. Occasionally, some of the more responsible community members object to this procedure, primarily on account of the unpleasant odor. Most people, however, quickly return to their old habits if not periodically reminded.

In recent years, medicine has become a point of contention on Anuta. During the late 1990s, the chiefs determined that reliance upon medicine indicated a lack of confidence in the church, and they banished any government-sponsored medical program from the island. Traditional remedies and prayer are acceptable, but most Anutans regard them as inferior to Western medicines and medical techniques. Individuals who choose to bring their own medications from Honiara are permitted to use them, but the cost is prohibitive to most islanders. Anyone who becomes critically ill has the option of leaving the island for treatment in Lata (the provincial capital) or Honiara. The scarcity of shipping, however, makes reliance on external medical facilities problematic.[23]

Fortunately, from the viewpoint of infectious disease Anuta is a fairly healthy island—at least in comparison with other parts of the developing world. The major ailments—fungal infections, sores, and occasional dysentery—most likely predate European contact. Of the two deaths that occurred in 1972–73, one was due to a long-standing cancer, and the other took the oldest man on the island—a man who may have been approaching a hundred years of age. While not entirely free from introduced diseases, the Anutans have been spared the havoc that infection has wrought among so many peoples in the post-contact period.[24]

In sum, Anuta has experienced a moderate amount of overseas contact since the mid-twentieth century. This contact has produced some changes in religion, material culture, education, and the island's medical environment. Still, Anuta is among the most isolated islands in Polynesia, and its culture has remained remarkably intact despite a degree of Western influence. The Anutans have managed to integrate those changes that have occurred into a highly traditional social structure, leaving their basic symbols, understandings, and assumptions largely undisturbed. In the final chapter, I examine the key changes that have faced the island and the stresses that those changes have produced. First, however, let us turn to the Anutan cultural and social order as I found it 30 years ago.

Chapter 3

Kinship in Anutan Culture

From the time of anthropology's origins as an academic discipline in the late 1800s, its practitioners have devoted more time and energy to the study of kinship than just about any other topic. Kinship is widely regarded as a cross-cultural universal, which, if true, would make it possible to compare communities in terms of their kinship systems. Kinship terminology appears to vary in a fairly systematic way from one community to another. Anthropologists contend that many communities are organized in terms of kinship; therefore, in order to understand the economic, political, and religious systems, one must be grounded in the local views of kinship. And kinship reflects the way in which members of a community make sense of their universe, their understandings of what it is to be human, and the connections they perceive to exist among people as well as between people and the other beings that surround them.

At a very general level, anthropologists have asked three kinds of question about kinship: How do different groups of people define kinship; how do they organize their kinship universes, particularly as this may be discerned from an examination of kinship terminology; and what relationships exist between the patterning of kin terms and other aspects of social organization? In practice, we have focused most of our attention on the second and third questions while taking for granted that people everywhere have systems of relationship that more or less resemble what we call kinship in the English-speaking West. It is only fairly recently that anthropologists have taken seriously and addressed systematically the first question: as David Schneider (1972) put it, "What is Kinship All About?"

This chapter attempts to answer Schneider's question with respect to the Anutans. Do they have a kinship system? If so, how do they define it and distinguish it from other cultural domains? What makes a person a relative? What are the symbols that differentiate kin from nonkin, and what are the implications of this distinction? What kinds of relatives do Anutans recognize, and how are relatives of different kinds distinguished from one another? The answers to these questions, as I show in later chapters, will help us to understand other aspects of Anutan social structure—how Anutans define the groups responsible for production and consumption and how they assign order to everyday life.

On an island like Anuta, where everybody is recognized as being related to everyone else, the category "kinsperson" incorporates everyone who falls within one's social orbit. At the same time, "kin" are subdivided into a number of "classes," and every kinsperson must fall into one or another of those classes. In other words, one cannot simply be a relative; one must be a relative of a particular type. Finally, kin relationships are intrinsically dyadic. A relative is *someone's* relative; one is kin by virtue of having a certain kind of relationship *to another person*. Thus, kinship is a set of principles that hold together units at all levels of Anutan culture and society, from the most limited to the most complex. In this chapter, I delineate the nature of these principles; the remainder of this volume examines the ways in which the same principles differentiate the units into which Anutan society is divided and define the nature of their operation.

What Is Kinship?

To native speakers of American English, "kinship" refers above all to relationships based on genealogical ties, that is, connections we denote by the terms "blood" and "marriage." The term "genealogy" itself is somewhat problematic, as it is used with a variety of meanings, and the same writer may be inconsistent from one occasion to the next.[1] Some writers (e.g., Goodenough 1970a, 2001), use the term in a way that is sensitive to cultural differences in what we call parenthood. Most anthropologists, however, have followed the common Western view that kinship in the strict sense is primarily a matter of what Schneider (1968) called "shared biogenetic substance" and, secondarily, of marriage. Should kin terms be applied in.' the absence of such connections, it is assumed that they are being used as a kind of metaphorical extension. Therefore, terms like "fictive kinship," "ritual kinship," or "courtesy kinship" permeate much of the literature.

This assumption is implicit in the very title of Lewis Henry Morgan's pathbreaking book, *Systems of Consanguinity and Affinity of the Human Family* (1871)—the work usually cited as the first systematic study of kinship—and it was maintained through most of the twentieth century. A. R. Radcliffe-Brown, founder of British "structural-functionalism," asserted that "the unit of structure from which a kinship system is built up is the group which I call an 'elementary family.' consisting of a man and his wife and their child or children, whether they are living together or not" (1952:51). Meyer Fortes, a leading British functionalist, characterized the family as being predicated on "two facts" of life: the fact of coitus as institutionalized in marriage and the fact of parturition as expressed in parenthood (1959:149). For Marion J. Levy, kinship is a structure deriving from "an orientation to the facts of biological relatedness and/or sexual intercourse" (1952:2). Raymond Firth, who recognized a behavioral component in determining assignment to kin classes (Firth 1930a 1963[1936]:226–27), found in the end that kinship still "is fundamentally a reinterpretation in social terms of the facts of procreation and regularized sex union" (1963 [1936]:483). Harold Scheffler, a prominent American anthropologist, argued in 1970 that "adoption does not and cannot make people kin because it cannot establish genealogical connections between them; it makes them 'like kin' for some social purposes, legal and otherwise; it creates a fiction of kinship; not kinship itself" (1970:372). And Floyd Lounsbury, a leader in American cognitive anthropology of the 1960s and 1970s, noted with respect to the Seneca (Iroquois) that:

> . . . I have not included all of the meanings of the Iroquois kinship terms . . . . Not included, for example, are the moon in the list of denotata of the "grandmother" term, or the thunderers amongst the "grandfathers," or the earth as our "mother," or the sun as our "elder brother." Nor have I included the metaphoric uses of the "brother" and "cousin," "father" and "son," "elder brother" and "younger brother" terms, in ceremonial discourse, for divisions of the Longhouse and of the political confederacy of the Six Nations; or that of the "uncle" term for the Bigheads (certain masked dancers at Midwinter ceremonies) or, formerly, for prisoners at the stake. There is no difficulty here in identifying these as "marginal" or "transferred" meanings . . . . Metaphoric extensions can be expected for any lexical item. In the structural analysis of a semantic field, however, they are excluded. We have not intended to deal with all of the meanings of the Iroquois kinship terms

here, but only with those that fall within the field defined as genealogical kin. (1969a:206)

If kinship is an English word and Americans typically use it to
refer to people sharing genealogical connections, then a domain in
another culture must be defined at least in part in terms of genealogy
if we are to gloss it as 'kinship.' As Goodenough (1970a:74; see also
Scheffler 1970) correctly observed, "a terminology that involves no
properties of genealogical space is not a kinship terminology." Since
virtually every culture seems to have some conceptual domain that is
set apart, either in full or in part, on the basis of its genealogical character, 'kinship' has been an important category for ethnological analysis. Because this category as we are familiar with it in American
culture is defined in genealogical terms, however, many anthropologists make the unwarranted assumption that conceptual domains in
non-Western communities that are characterized by genealogical
bonds do not have other distinguishing features as well.

Anutan culture recognizes a domain that is defined largely in
terms of ties established through marriage and procreation. Within that
domain further distinctions are made, again largely on the basis of genealogical criteria. However, a person also may be included in both the
overarching category and any of its subsidiary classes by acting in the
appropriate manner. Moreover, those actions often serve as partially—
and in certain circumstances even wholly—independent variables. It is
this conceptual domain, which Anutans define through a combination
of genealogical and interactional criteria, that I call 'kinship.' Anutans
normally term the domain *kano a paito*, although, like many words in
their language, *kano a paito* covers a range of possible referents.[2]

My account of the Anutan kinship universe begins in a conventional way, by looking at the classes into which it is divided and the criteria according to which a person is assigned to one class or another. I
then examine the collateral "extension" of kin terms and the question of
polysemy—the possibility of multiple meanings. This brings up the
way in which immigrants are integrated into Anuta's kinship system
and into the community at large. In each case, the guiding principles
combine genealogical elements with a behavioral component that
enables the parties either to reinforce or alter their genealogically
ascribed relationship. With these discussions in mind, we can then
draw some general conclusions about the nature of Anutan kinship.

Kin Terms and Kin Classes

This section begins with an exhaustive list of Anutan kin terms
and some comments on their application. Initially, the definitions and

explanations are phrased in genealogical terms; this perspective will then be modified as we proceed through the discussion.

Terms of Reference

"Consanguineal."[3]

Tupuna can be translated roughly as either 'grandparent' or 'ancestor.' as it refers to any relative in the second or higher ascending generation. One may specify either *tupuna tangata* ('grandfather'; 'male ancestor') or *tupuna papine* ('grandmother'; 'female ancestor'). It may also be applied to collaterals of any degree. By "collateral," anthropologists mean relatives who are off to the side. In this case, collaterals would include the grandparents' (or ancestors') siblings and cousins, however distant.

Nuna has the same range of meanings as *tupuna* but differs in that it may be substituted for "Pu" in a person's proper name to indicate a relationship of respect. To call someone by name suggests familiarity. While such familiarity is permissible when dealing with members of the grandparental generation, the junior party may wish to show special respect because of the age difference. Thus, in 1972 a teenaged youth named Maraetanu (later known by the marital name Pu Nukuriaki) referred to his father's father either as Pu Nukumarere or Nuna i Nukumarere; and nine-year-old Robert Pakapu (now Pu Taumarei) referred to Pu Tepae as Nuna i Tepae. *Tupuna* is used with the possessive pronoun so that 'my grandfather' is *toku tupuna*, not *toku nuna*; and it may not be substituted for "Pu" in a personal name as is done with *nuna*. For lack of a better designation, I refer to this type of construction as a "kinship title."

Tamana may be glossed as 'father.' but it also includes the father's brothers and male cousins.

Tamai is identical in meaning and usage with *tamana* but is less frequently employed.

Mana is a title similar to *nuna*, but with the same set of meanings as *tamana* and *tamai*. Anutans may not utter their fathers' proper names (e.g., Pu Taumarei; Pu Parikitonga). If it is necessary to specify which of a person's *tamana* one is talking about, however, most islanders consider it permissible to use constructions such as "Mana i Parikitonga". The word may also stand by itself as a substitute for a proper name, so that one may ask, *"Mana ne karanga pakapeepeeki?"* ('What did father say?'). Like *nuna*, it may not be used with a possessive pronoun. Whereas one may say *"toku tamana"* or *"toku tamai,"* *"toku mana"* would be incorrect. This contrasts with Tikopia, where *mana* (or *mmana*) is simply an abbreviated form of *tamana* and is used in the same way as its lengthier counterpart. Tikopia's equivalent to the Anutan *mana* is *pa*.

Papa is a title whose usage is almost identical with that of *mana* except that it is most frequently heard from children. Youngsters also use *papa* at times to refer to the *tuatina* ('mother's brother'), but adults regard this as improper.

Taati is an English loan word (from "daddy"), which Anutans use as a title in virtually the same manner as *papa*. I never heard this term in 1972–73, but by 1983 it was common.

Patamaaroa is a title for an unmarried man who, by other criteria, falls into the *tamana* class.

Pae may be glossed as 'mother.' but also includes the mother's sisters and female cousins. Grammatically, Anutans use this term in the same manner as *tupuna*, *tamana*, and *tamai*.

Paapae is a title designating the same range of kin as *pae*, but whose usage follows the pattern of *nuna* and *mana*.

Maami is an English loan word (from "mommy") that Anutans use as a title in virtually the same manner as *paapae*. I did not hear this term in 1972–73, but by 1983 it was in common use.

Nau taka is a title for unmarried woman in a *pae* relationship with the speaker. This is the feminine counterpart of *patamaaroa*.

Nga maatuaa may be translated approximately as 'parents.' It is used in the plural (*nga* is the plural form of the definite article) and usually refers to one's "real" parents unless they are deceased or absent, in which case it generally applies to the persons who are acting in their stead. In other words, it normally designates a person's closest social 'parents.' who are most often—but not necessarily—also the biological parents. Anutans often use this expression with a possessive pronoun rather than the definite article, e.g., *oku maatuaa* ('my parents').

Tuatina refers to the mother's brothers and her male cousins. It is used both as a standard term of reference, in the manner of *tamana* or *pae*, and as a title in the fashion of *nuna*, *mana*, and *paapae*.

Makitanga refers to the father's sisters and female cousins. Like *tuatina*, it may be used either as a standard term of reference or as a "kinship title."

Taina may be glossed as 'parallel sibling' or 'sibling of same sex as ego.' but also includes cousins. For "consanguineal" relatives of one's own generation Anutans use proper names, and there are no "kinship titles." Like other Polynesian outliers, and in contrast with most kinship systems of the Polynesian heartland, Anutans do not differentiate terminologically between older and younger siblings of the same sex.

Kave may be glossed as 'cross-sibling' or 'sibling of opposite sex.' but it includes opposite sex cousins as well.

Tama may be glossed as 'child.' A man calls his own children and the children of anyone he refers to as *taina* by this term. For a woman, all "consanguineal" relatives of the children's generation are called *tama*.

Pota is synonymous with *tama*. Anutans readily identify this as an indigenous term, but it is seldom used.

Tei can probably best be thought of as a metaphor for *tama*. It literally refers to a flower that is inserted into a perforated earlobe, the implication being that a man is adorned by his children much as he is by his *tei*.

Kaoa is a metaphor for *tama*, comparable to *tei* except that the literal referent is a floral necklace.

Iraamutu may be glossed as a man's 'sister's child.' although it actually refers to the child of anyone he calls *kave*. There is no comparable term for a woman, who refers to her brother's child by the same term (*tama*) as she does her own.

Tama tapu means 'sacred child.' This expression has the same set of referents as *iraamutu*, but it is rarely used and is generally restricted to ceremonial contexts.

Mokopuna may be glossed as 'grandchild' or 'descendant' and applies to any relative in the second or lower descending generation. One may specify *mokopuna tangata* ('grandson'; 'male descendant') or *mokopuna papine* ('granddaughter'; 'female descendant'). The term's referents also include collateral relatives of all degrees.

Affinal.

Nopine means wife. This term has no other referent.

Matua means husband. This term also has no other referent.

Maa is *kave*'s spouse or spouse's *kave*. It may be roughly glossed as a man's 'brother-in-law' or a woman's 'sister-in-law.' although collaterals of any degree may also be included.

Tangaata is a "title" with approximately the same set of referents as *maa*, but has the same grammatical usage as *nuna*, *mana*, and *paapae* and may be used only by males.

Taina is the spouse's *taina* or *taina*'s spouse. May be roughly glossed as 'sibling-in-law of opposite sex.' but, like *maa*, it includes collaterals of all degrees as well.

Pungona roughly classificatory 'parent-in-law' or 'child-in-law.' This may include one's spouse's *tamana*, *pae*, *makitanga*, or *tuatina*, or the spouse of one's *tama* or *iraamutu*. If one wishes to specify sex and generation, the word *pungona* must be replaced by *pungoai* in the following manner:

tamana pungoai: 'father-in-law' (i.e., father, father's brother, or father's male cousin of either one's spouse or one's sibling's spouse);

pae pungoai: 'mother-in-law' (i.e., mother, mother's sister, or mother's female cousin of one's spouse or one's sibling's spouse);

tama pungoai: 'son-in-law' (i.e., husband, or husband's brother or male cousin of one's daughter or niece);

nau pungoai: 'daughter-in-law' (i.e., wife, wife's sister, or wife's female cousin of one's son or nephew). Unlike the preceding three forms, this construction generally is not used with the possessive pronoun.

Tautaupariki is generally used as a synonym for *pungona*, although in certain contexts it may denote any kinsperson in a restraint relationship, as described below.

Patamaaroa refers to one's 'unmarried son-in-law' (i.e., the unmarried brother or male cousin of one's child's, nephew's, or niece's spouse) or 'unmarried father-in-law' (i.e., the unmarried brother or male cousin of one's spouse's *tamana*). This is a title; if one wishes to designate a relative in this category by a standard reference term of the type that may go with a possessive pronoun, one uses *pungona, tama pungoai,* or *tamana pungoai,* just as for a married relative.

Nau taka is 'unmarried daughter-in-law' (i.e., the unmarried sister or female cousin of one's child's, nephew's, or niece's spouse), or 'unmarried mother-in-law' (i.e., the unmarried sister or female cousin of one's spouse's *pae*). This term is a title in the same way as *patamaaroa* and their usages are identical.

Te maatuaa refers to any male *pungona,* but it is a title which must be used in the same manner as *mana, paapae, patamaaroa,* etc. It may also be used in the plural to designate 'parents-in-law' just as a phonetically identical term is used to designate one's parents.

Anutan kinship terminology is indicated in a standard kinship diagram in figure 3.1. The major kin terms and lists of genealogical kin types to which they apply are listed in table 3.1.

Terms of Address

Anutans sometimes use different terms when speaking directly to a relative than when discussing him or her with a third person. Anthropologists call the latter "terms of reference" and the former "terms of address." Following is a list of kin categories which, for convenience sake, I have labeled with English glosses, and the Anutan terms by which relatives in these categories are addressed.

'Grandparent'; 'Great-grandparent.' Called *nuna* or by proper name.

'Father.' Called *mana, papa,* or *taati,* the latter two terms predominating among (but not restricted to) children.

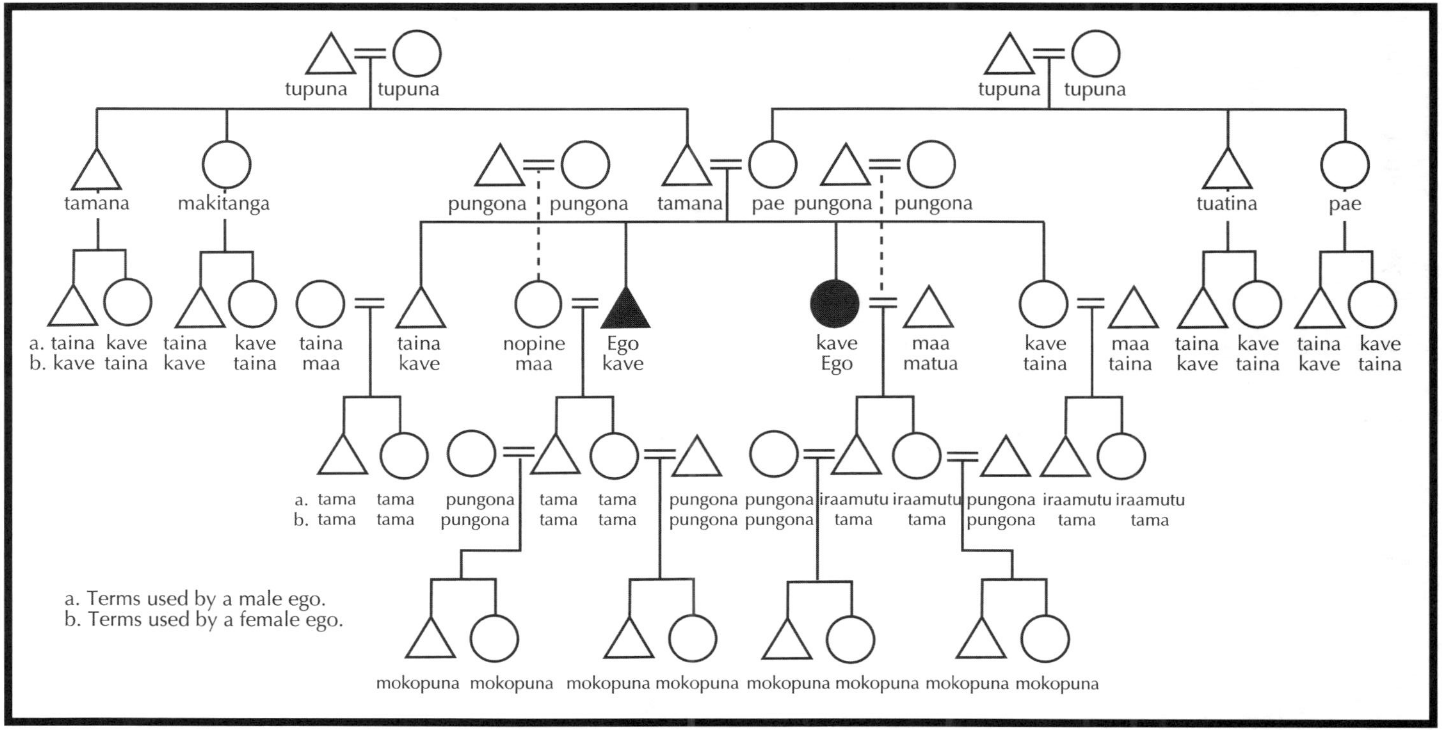

Figure 3.1 Diagram showing most commonly used Anutan kin terms and their usual application according to genealogical criteria.

Table 3.1 Anutan kin classes with their usual linguistic labels and partial extensional definitions in terms of genealogical kin types[a]

Anutan Term	Genealogical Kin Types
tupuna	FF, FM, MF, MM, FFB, FMB, FFZ, FMZ, MFB, MMB, MFZ, MMZ, FFF, FFM, FFFBS, MMMZD, etc.
tamana	F, FB, FFBS, FFZS, FMBS, FMZS, FFBSS, FMMZDS, etc.
pae	M, MZ, MMZD, MMBD, MFZD, MFBD, MMMZDD, MFFBSD, etc.
tuatina	MB, MMZS, MMBS, MFBS, MFZS, MMMZDS, MFFBSS, etc.
makitanga	FZ, FMZD, FMBD, FFBD, FFZD, FFFBSD, FMMZDD, etc.
taina	
a. male ego	B, FBS, FZS, MBS, MZS, FFBSS, FFBDS, FFZSS, FFZDS, FMBSS, MFBSS, MFBDS, MFZSS, MFZDS, MMBSS, etc.
b. female ego	Z, FBD, FZD, MBD, MZD, FFBSD, FFBDD, FFZSD, FFZDD, FMBSD, MFBSD, MFBDD, MFBSD, MFZDD, MMBSD, etc.
kave	
a. male ego	Z, FBD, FZD, MBD, MZD, FFBSD, FFBDD, FFZSD, FFZDD, FMBSD, MFBSD, MFBDD, MFBSD, MFZDD, MMBSD, etc.
b. female ego	B, FBS, FZS, MBS, MZS, FFBSS, FFBDS, FFZSS, FFZDS, FMBSS, MFBSS, MFBDS, MFZSS, MFZDS, MMBSS, etc.
tama	
a. male ego	S, D, BS, BD, FBSS, FBSD, FZSS, FZSD, MBSS, MBSD, MZSS, MZSD, FFBSSS, MMZDSD, etc.
b. female ego	S, D, ZS, ZD, FBDS, FBDD, FZDS, FZDD, MBDS, MBDD, MZDS, MZDD, FFBSDS, MMZDDD, BS, BD, FBSS, FBSD, FZSS, FZSD, MBSS, MBSD, MZSS, MZSD, FFBSSS, MMZDSD, etc.
iraamutu	
(male ego only)	ZS, ZD, FBDS, FBDD, FZDS, FZDD, MBDS, MBDD, MZDS, MZDD, FFBSDS, MMZDDD, etc.
mokopuna	FBSSS, MZDDD, FZSSSS, MBDDDD, etc.
matua	H
nopine	W

continued

Table 3.1 Anutan kin classes with their usual linguistic labels and partial extensional definitions in terms of genealogical kin types[a] (continued)

Anutan Term	Genealogical Kin Types
maa	
a. male ego	WB, WFBS, WFZS, WMBS, WMZS, ZH, FBDH, FZDH, MBDH, MZDH, etc.
b. female ego	HZ, HFBD, HFZD, HMBD, HMZD, BW, FBSW, FZSW, MBSW, MZSW, etc.
taina	
a. male ego	WZ, WFBD, WFZD, WMBD, WMZD, BW, BWZ, BWFBD, BWFZD, BWMBD, BWMZD, FBSW, FBSWZ, etc.
b. female ego	HB, HFBS, HFZS, HMBS, HMZS, ZH, ZHB, ZHFBS, ZHFZS, ZHMBS, ZHMZS, FBDH, FBDHB, etc.
pungona	WF, WFB, WFZ, WM, WMB, WMZ, HF, HFB, HFZ, HM, HMB, HMZ, SW, BSW, ZSW, DH, BDH, ZDH, SWB, SWZ, DHB, DHZ, etc.

[a] This table uses the following standard abbreviations:

F = father	S = son
M = mother	D = daughter
B = brother	H = husband
Z = sister	W = wife

'Unmarried father.' Called *maaroa* or *patamaaroa*.

'Mother.' Called *paapae* or *maami*.

'Unmarried mother.' Called *paapae* or *nau taka*.

'Mother's brother.' Called *tuatina* or *papa* (the latter "incorrectly" by small children), or by proper name.

'Father's sister.' Called *makitanga*.

'Sibling of same sex.' Called *taina* or by proper name.

'Sibling of opposite sex.' Called *kave* or by proper name.

'Child.' Called by proper name.

Man's 'sister's son.' Called by proper name.

'Grandchild'; 'great-grandchild.' Called by proper name.

'Husband.' Called by proper name.

'Wife.' Called by proper name.

'Father-in-law.' Called *mana* or *te maatuaa*.

'Unmarried father-in-law.' Called *maaroa* or *patamaaroa*.

'Mother-in-law.' Called *paapae* or *nau*.

'Unmarried mother-in-law.' Called *paapae* or *nau taka*.

'Son-in-law.' Called *te maatuaa*.
'Unmarried son-in-law.' Called *maaroa* or *patamaaroa*.
'Daughter-in-law.' Called *nau*.
'Unmarried daughter-in-law.' Called *nau taka*.
Man's 'brother-in-law.' Called *tangaata* or *tau maa*.
Woman's 'sister-in-law.' Called *tau maa*.
'Sibling-in-law of opposite sex.' Called by proper name.

In addition to the terms on this list, any term of reference, except a title, may be used as a term of address by prefacing it with *toku* or *taku*, the first person singular possessive pronoun. All titles, as should be evident from the above account, are used without the possessive pronoun as terms of address.

So far, kin terms have been presented as if their referents were strictly genealogical and could be adequately explained using English categories. I have used English glosses as a simple device to communicate the idea that an Anutan word, *tamana* for example, means something like our word 'father.' However, it does not mean exactly the same thing as father, and continued use of such glosses would perpetuate false impressions. For the remainder of this account, therefore, I will use American kin terms to indicate the genealogical kin types that these terms denote in English. Unfortunately, English has no convenient words or concise phrases that accurately delineate the precise meanings of Anutan kin terms. Therefore, when it becomes necessary to designate Anutan kin types or categories, I will rely primarily on the Anutan expressions. This procedure admittedly places some burden on readers unfamiliar with Polynesian languages. Fortunately, the number of terms is not great, and the gain in accuracy will more than offset the effort required to memorize a few new lexical items.

Criteria for Kin Class Membership

Anutans readily understand kinship diagrams and are capable of labeling the positions on such diagrams with the appropriate kin terms. I have gone through this procedure with them many times, and the rules on which they base their calculations are readily apparent. For "consanguineal" relatives, they are as follows:

1. In ego's generation, any relative of the same sex is one's *taina*, while any relative of opposite sex is *kave*.

2. In ego's parents' generation, calculation begins with *tamana* and *pae*. These are usually, but not necessarily, the child's biological father and mother, respectively. Anyone the *tamana*

calls *taina* is also one's *tamana*. Anyone the *tamana* calls *kave*,
ego calls *makitanga*. Anyone *pae* calls *taina* is also one's *pae*,
while anyone the *pae* calls *kave* ego calls *tuatina*.

3. In the first descending generation, a man's own child and the
   child of anyone he calls *taina* is his *tama*. The child of anyone
   he calls *kave* is his *iraamutu*. A woman calls any relative of the
   first descending generation *tama*. It is worthwhile to note that
   the calculations in rules 2 and 3 illustrate the conceptual
   equivalence of siblings, especially siblings of the same sex,
   made famous by A. R. Radcliffe-Brown, and his followers.

4. In the second and higher ascending generations, all relatives
   are called *tupuna*.

5. In the second and lower descending generations, all relatives
   are called *mokopuna*.

For affines, the picture is even simpler:

1. An affine of the first ascending or first descending generation
   is called *pungona*. This class may then be subdivided according to generation and sex.

2. In ego's generation, affines of the same sex are called *maa* and
   those of opposite sex are called *taina*. Husband and wife are
   terminologically distinguished from everyone else. In the distant past Anutans occasionally practiced polygyny, in which
   case all of a man's wives were termed his *nopine*.

At first glance, these criteria appear to be entirely genealogical.[4]
Such a conclusion, however, is illusory. There is a strong enough
genealogical element in Anutan kinship that as long as questions are
posed within such a framework, they can be answered in the same
idiom. However, such responses often are deceptive.

Prior to about 1980, Anuta appears never to have been inhabited
by more than approximately 200 people. In such an isolated population, there has inevitably been a great deal of island endogamy, or
marriage within the community. Consequently, every Anutan has
genealogical ties with everyone else on the island, and most people
are, in fact, related to each other in several different ways. The rules I
have enumerated provide a framework for the kinship system, but
they cannot by themselves determine which relationship will be
invoked in cases where there are several from which to choose.
Therefore, Anutans have a set of subsidiary principles that may be
brought to bear:

1. In most instances of multiple connections, one relationship is clearly closer than the others; and when this is the case, Anutans usually invoke the closest tie. If a man's brother, for example, marries their mother's second cousin, the man's connection to the couple's children will most likely be traced through his brother. Conversely, if a man's mother's sister marries his second cousin, his connection to the couple's children will probably be traced through his aunt (i.e., the children's mother). In the first instance, the children would be classed as ego's *tama*; in the second, he would call them his *taina* or his *kave*. These hypothetical conditions are illustrated in figures 3.2 and 3.3. Not infrequently, however, several possible relationships are equally appropriate on genealogical grounds, in which case new criteria must be invoked.

2. If two or more relationships are equally appropriate from the viewpoint of genealogical distance, other considerations may be invoked. The most often utilized is relative age. Thus, if

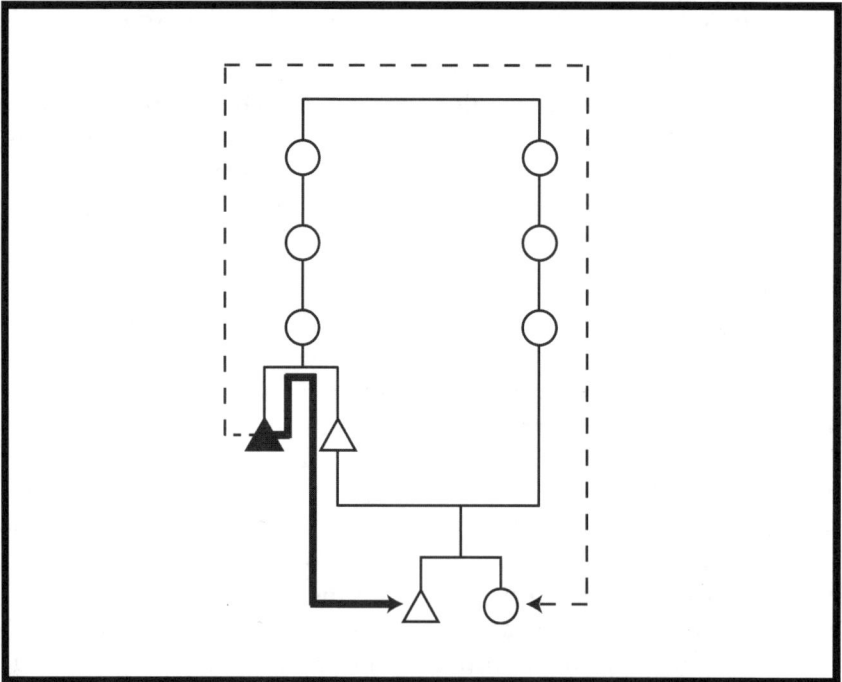

Figure 3.2 Calculation of effective kin relationship should ego's brother marry their mother's second cousin. Bold line denotes preferred connection; dotted line denotes inactive tie.

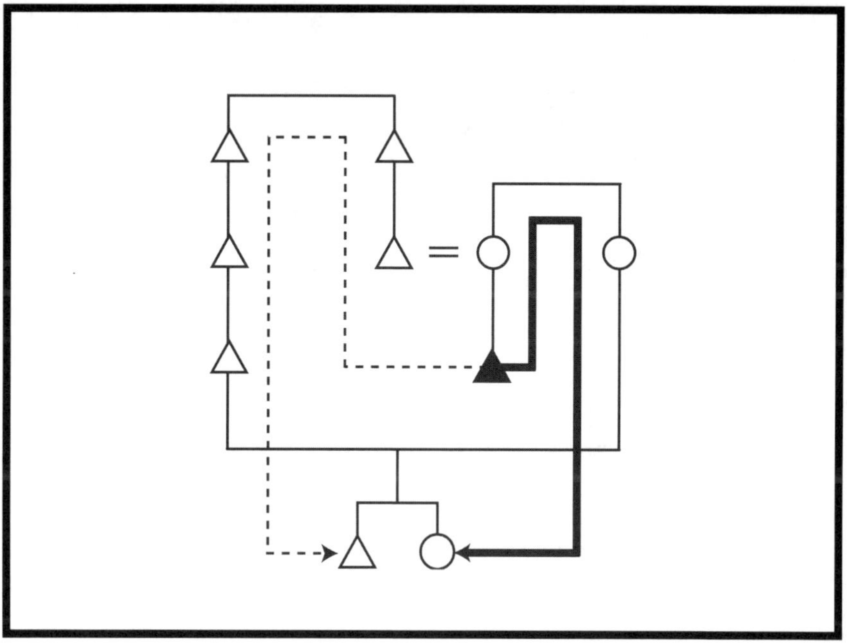

Figure 3.3 Calculation of effective kin relationship should ego's mother's sister marry ego's second cousin. Bold line denotes preferred connection; dotted line denotes inactive tie.

genealogical criteria make *tamana* and *taina* equally appropriate designations but the person in question (known technically as alter) is the same age as or younger than ego, the *taina* relationship most likely will be chosen.

A related strategy that Anutans commonly employ in problematic cases is to identify a child with the parent of its own sex. Thus, if a husband and wife are both first cousins of the same male ego, the couple's sons will most likely trace their connection to ego through their father and be classified as ego's *tama*; the daughters will most likely trace the connection through their mother and be classed as ego's *iraamutu* (see figure 3.4).

3. For native-born Anutans, a combination of genealogical considerations most often can establish the kin class to which one is assigned. However, if biological and genealogical criteria are indeterminate, social interaction is often decisive. A particular behavioral pattern is associated with each kin relationship. Each pair of individuals considers both past interaction

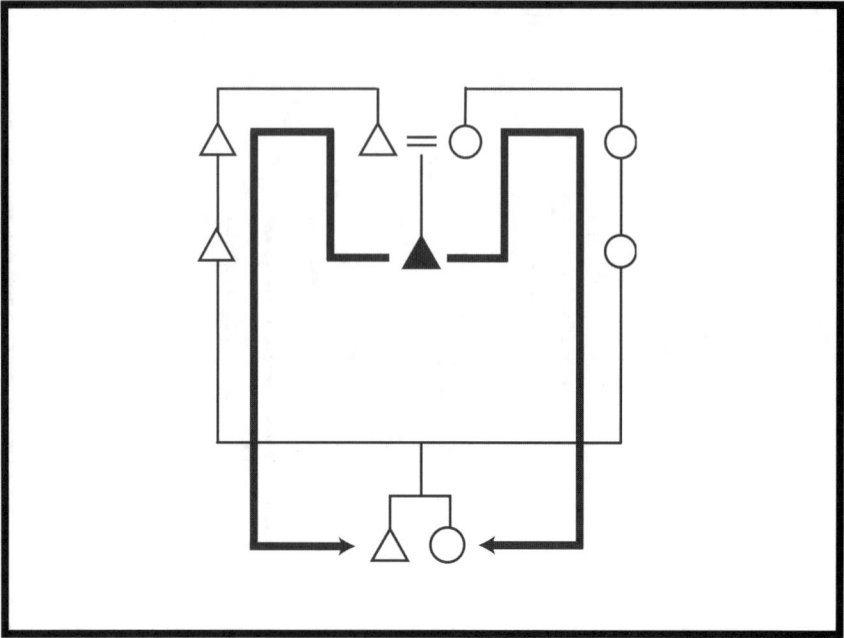

Figure 3.4 Calculation of effective kin relationship should a husband and wife both be first cousins of the same male ego. Bold lines denote connection most likely to be invoked between ego and each of the couple's children.

and what they want the nature of their future relationship to be when deciding how to classify each other. I will present a detailed account of the behavior appropriate to each kinship dyad in the sections on interpersonal relations within the extended family household (chapter 4) and kindred (chapter 5). Here I will illustrate how genealogical ties, past behavior, and personal preference may interact in shaping decisions regarding kin-class assignment.

Pu Tokerau and Pu Teaokena were full brothers, and Pu Pareaatai was, genealogically speaking, a distant *tuatina*. However, when the eldest children of this sibling set were born, certain ritual gifts known as *pai tuatina* (see chapter 5) were presented to Pu Pareaatai, converting him for cultural and social purposes into a 'close' *tuatina*. By Anutan standards, that should have made any marriage of Pu Pareaatai's children to any of Pu Tokerau's siblings a violation of incest prohibitions.

Despite this prohibition, Pu Pareaatai's son (later known as Pu Rengaru) married Pu Toke's eldest sister (Nau Rengaru). This led to a question of what the other siblings should call the older man. To continue referring to him as *tuatina* would imply refusal to accept the marriage as legitimate and underscore the importance of following the standard incest guidelines. To call him *pungona*, the normal designation for the father of one's sister's husband, would imply acceptance of the marriage as appropriate. Pu Teaokena began calling the older man *pungona*. Pu Toke, on the other hand, as Anuta's catechist, regarded himself as guardian of the community's moral integrity and expressed his opposition to the marriage by continuing to use the *tuatina* term. In the case of Pu Toke and Pu Pareaatai, the relationship was thus maintained as if the marriage had never taken place.

This type of situation is common on Anuta. Full siblings always share identical genealogies. Therefore, as brothers, Pu Tokerau and Pu Teaokena were in precisely the same genealogical relationship to Pu Pareaatai. Anutans, however, show little concern for genealogical consistency, and *tau paanau* or *tau kave* (people in a *taina* or *kave* relationship to one another) often use different terms for the same third person. This occurs most frequently when the *taina* or *kave* are relatively distant cousins, but even among siblings it is unexceptional.

4. Not only are extragenealogical factors invoked to resolve genealogical conflicts; there are instances where social considerations actually override genealogical ones. In the case just discussed, Pu Pareaatai was Pu Tokerau's sister's husband's "real" father, while he was only a rather distant uncle. Nevertheless, the *tuatina* relationship won out because Pu Toke's parents decided that they would make their *pai tuatina* offerings to Pu Pareaatai at the time of their children's births, and Pu Toke felt it important to follow through the logical implications of that action.

Another striking illustration is found in the case of Pu Tepae and Pu Rangateatu. There was no close genealogical tie of any sort between these two men, but Pu Tepae's first wife and Pu Rangateatu were first cousins. According to the obvious genealogical proprieties, Pu Tepae referred to Pu Rangateatu's brothers, Pu Tekoro and Pu Pareumutia, as his *maa*. When it came to Pu Rangateatu, however, he ignored the genealogical facts and called him *taina*. When I asked for an explanation, Pu Tepae simply said they had discussed the matter and decided that they would rather be *tau paanau* (in a *taina-taina* relationship) than *tau maa* (related as *maa*).

5. In sum, at least for persons born to Anutan parents, the basic model for assignment to kin categories is a genealogical one. However, the realities of social life in a population as small as Anuta's make adherence to a simple genealogical model impossible. Moreover, the rules that regulate interaction between persons in certain categories sometimes lead a pair of individuals to prefer a different relationship from that which is genealogically prescribed, and the kinship system readily accommodates such preferences. This is especially true when people in a warm, supportive relationship like *tau paanau* (*taina-taina*) or *tau tuatina* (*tuatina-iraamutu*) are suddenly put into more restrained affinal categories (as in the case of Pu Tepae and Pu Rangateatu), or when persons face the prospect of being placed in an affinal relationship because of a culturally inappropriate marriage (as in the case of Pu Tokerau and Pu Pareaatai). In such instances, the genealogical model may be breached and less genealogically appropriate relationships substituted. Furthermore, a relative who is classified on the basis of social rather than genealogical criteria is just as much a member of his or her kin class as one who meets all the genealogical qualifications. Hence, it is possible to trace more distant relationships through purely social as well as genealogical kin. Any *kave* of any *pae*, for example, may be classed as *tuatina* regardless of how the *tau pae* (*pae-tama*, roughly, 'mother-child') or *tau kave* (roughly, 'brother-sister') relationships were established. In this way, Anutans often place someone in a particular kin category because of his/her genealogical relationship with a linking relative whose position is based on purely social criteria. In general, the closer a genealogical relationship is, the more difficult it is to override on behavioral grounds. Finally, when one gets to the level of the nuclear family, the genealogical bonds are so strong that I have no case on record of their being overridden.

Intraclass Distinctions

Anthropologists have often assumed that when a single term applies to people occupying multiple genealogical kin slots, the term refers primarily to those with whom ego shares the closest genealogical relationship, after which it is extended metaphorically to include more distant kin. This has been termed the "basic member" or "extensionist" approach and is typified by the work of Radcliffe-Brown (1952:51–52), Malinowski (1929:525–31), Lounsbury (1969b), and many others.

The extensionist hypothesis may be contrasted with a "total class" approach. In the latter view, a category has no "primary" or "basic" members; rather, each relative within a class is equally a member of that class.[5] The Anutan data show that kinship systems need not conform neatly with either model, and that they may share attributes of both.

To speak of kin classes as such implies a degree of homogeneity. Yet, Anutan kin categories are subdivided in a variety of ways. Within each terminological category, Anutans distinguish between relatives who are described as *maori* and those who are *pakaapaapa*. The word *maori* generally means 'true' and is contrasted with *roi*, a 'lie.' *Pakaapaapa*, I was told, means 'outside'—although it is used only in kinship contexts, where it designates those falling outside the class of *maori* kin. The distinction superficially resembles that in American English between 'true kin' and persons who resemble kin in certain respects, yet fall outside the domain of kinship proper. It differs, however, in certain critical respects.

Anutans differentiate *maori* from *pakaapaapa* relatives in all named classes except *matua* and *nopine*, each of which for any given ego is represented by just one person—the husband or wife. Yet the criteria for distinguishing 'true' from 'outside' kin, at first glance, are not obvious. In a random group of four islanders, the first indicated that brothers are unequivocally *taina maori,* that first cousins may be thought of as either *taina maori* or *taina pakaapaapa,* and that second cousins are definitely *pakaapaapa.* The second asserted that *all* first cousins are just as certainly *taina maori* as brothers. The third said that patrilateral parallel first cousins are *taina maori,* he was unsure about cross-cousins, and matrilateral parallel cousins are *taina pakaapaapa.* The fourth stated "definitively" that only brothers are *taina maori;* first cousins are not. Cousins often disagreed, when asked separately, on how they ought to designate each other. Some Anutans included second cousins in the *taina maori* class, and a few suggested that there was a sense in which one might apply this label to any same-sex generation mates who can trace a connection to a common ancestor, however distant. One even insisted that the latter is *the* proper usage and maintained, when I pointed out that he was alone in his opinion, that he was right and everyone else was mistaken. Moreover, if one judges consistency on genealogical grounds, the same person may be inconsistent in use of these terms from one occasion to the next.

Much of the difficulty may be resolved by improving our translation of *maori* and *pakaapaapa*. While the former normally means 'true.' its kinship connotations are better approximated by the word 'near' or 'close.' The latter, by contrast, might then be rendered as 'distant.'

Genealogy is an important criterion in Anutan kinship for determining the 'closeness' or 'distance' of a relative, but the quality of social relations between individuals also affects the degree of closeness that Anutans feel for each other, and this is expressed in the language they employ. A man who feels especially close to his second cousin may refer to him as *taina maori*, while a first cousin with whom he is on bad terms may be relegated to *pakaapaapa* status. The status of a given individual may vary over time with the quality of interpersonal relations. A person who has just completed a cooperative activity may describe his partner as a *maori* kinsman, while the following day, when the two are engaged in separate pursuits, he may describe the erstwhile partner as *pakaapaapa*. An Anutan may characterize another as 'near' or 'distant' depending on immediate practical concerns. And if the investigator should pose a question in such a way as to emphasize solidarity, the designated relative is more likely to be labeled *maori* than if the issue is raised in negative or neutral terms. In any case, nearness and distance are not calibrated in measurable units. There are identifiable principles that one may invoke, but in the end each person must weigh all factors in light of the general principles and reach his or her own decision. This judgment factor partially accounts for conflicts of opinion.

As with assignment to kin classes, the designation of a relative as *maori* or *pakaapaapa* is based on a combination of genealogical principles and social interaction. For "primary kin," (i.e., the father, mother, brother, sister, son, or daughter), the genealogical component is sufficiently strong that I have no case on record of such a person possessing anything other than *maori* status. However, as one moves outward, the genealogical element is progressively weakened, and the behavioral component becomes increasingly important. Thus, a first cousin or a father's brother who is behaviorally distant may be classed as *pakaapaapa*, while even the most genealogically distant kin may be designated as *maori* should they act the part.

The *maori-pakaapaapa* division attests to a conceptual differentiation among kin within a single class. This, however, does not exhaust the issue. If Anutans are asked about their *tamana, taina,* or other relative without further qualification, they usually answer as if the question were posed specifically about the genealogically closest relative in the designated category. Moreover, true, full siblings (in the Ameri-

Kinship in Anutan Culture

can English sense) may be differentiated from their more genealogically distant counterparts by stipulating *nga maatuaa e tai* ('[they are of] the same parents'). Of paternal half-siblings Anutans say *te tamana e tai* ('the same father'), and of maternal half-siblings they say *te pae e tai* ('the same mother'). In contrast, even first cousins often say that their *maatuaa (tamana; pae) e kee* ('parents [father; mother] are different'), thereby indicating that in some contexts Anutan kin terms refer to primary "biological" relatives very much as do terms in American kinship. Hence, it appears that Anutan kin terms have at least two distinct types of meaning: one defined by a precise genealogical relationship with ego and the other referring to a category that may include a number of genealogical kin types.

This observation would seem to confirm the view that kin terms apply primarily to the genealogically closest relatives, and more distant ones are incorporated only later by a process of "extension." I would like, however, to suggest an alternate interpretation.

Most Anutan kin terms are used on two different levels of contrast. At the most specific level, there is no word for paternal uncle that may be contrasted with *tamana*, meaning father. Thus, if one were to ask an Anutan whether his father's brother is his *tamana*, the answer might be negative. Similarly, if one asks even first cousins, "*Koru tau paanau, nga maatuaa e tai?*" ('Are you two brothers with the same parents?') the answer is most likely to be no. In other words, despite the absence of a linguistic label, Anutans clearly have a conceptual category that includes collateral male relatives of the father's generation on his side of the family. This category contrasts with the father, who is called *tamana* in the narrow sense. On the more general level, *tamana* includes collateral patrilateral male kin of the father's generation as well as the father himself, and it is contrasted with such other labeled kin classes as *makitanga*, *tuatina*, and *pae*.

To sum up, then, Anutan kin terms have significance on two distinct levels. Both meanings are equally "real," and neither is logically derivative from the other. Historically, one meaning may have preceded the other, but such etymological speculation is irrelevant to the structure and meaning of Anutan kin terms. Functionally, each meaning has its own correlates and ramifications in Anutan social structure and organization. In their general sense, kin terms are an important factor in determining the nature of face-to-face domestic and economic activities, especially when it comes to regulating patterns of respect, honor, license, and restraint. In their specific sense, they are important determinants of rank, inheritance of supernatural power or efficacy (*manuu*), and succession to titles or positions of leadership, where it is necessary to calculate on the basis of one's precise genealogical position.[6] Where they are contrasted with other labeled kin categories, behavioral criteria are an important defining characteristic. Where they denote primary "biological" kin, the distinctive features of each type appear to be strictly genealogical.

Extragenealogical Kin

Up to now I have discussed the behavioral element in Anutan kinship as a means of invoking a distant relationship when others are closer and more appropriate on genealogical grounds. This is possible as long as one is dealing with persons born on Anuta, where everyone has some genealogical connection with everybody else. Every so often, however, visitors or immigrants arrive from overseas, and such people have no traceable genealogical relationship with anyone on the island. Yet, one cannot live in the community without being incorporated into the kinship system, and an immigrant is made kin not only in the general sense, but also in the more specific sense as outlined above.

The vast majority of immigrants to Anuta have been and continue to be from Tikopia. Tikopians are in a special category *vis-à-vis* the rest of the outside world, and the problem of integrating them is confronted in special way.

Since there has been a good deal of intermarriage between the two islands over the generations, many members of each community have genealogically related kin in the other. But the majority of Tikopians, whose community is much larger than Anuta, do not have such links. Irrespective of genealogical connections, however, every Tikopian *paito* ('lineage,' see Firth 1957, 1963[1936]) has a particularly close relationship with at least one Anutan household (*patongia* or *pare*). The term for this relationship is *tauranga*, a word that literally means 'anchoring point.' A resident of one island, upon landing at the other, immediately seeks out his or her primary *tauranga*, who will provide food and shelter. While living apart, the relationship is validated periodically through an exchange of gifts, and when in residence on the neighboring island, one functions as a member of one's *tauranga* unit. The visitor is assigned a definite kin relationship with each member of the *tauranga* unit, depending on gender, age, and generation. Then, on the basis of one's position in the *tauranga* group, his/her kinship status with respect to other community members is determined. An individual with two or more *tauranga* will probably also have more than one possible relationship with many residents of the host community. The visitor must then choose which of the alternative relationships to invoke, just as in the case of genealogical kin.

For immigrants from lands other than Tikopia, there is no foreordained point at which one enters the social system. The general principles, however, are much the same. I will draw initially upon my own experience to illustrate the process of creating kin in the absence of a genealogical connection. Then, after laying that foundation, I will build on it by citing other cases.

When I landed on Anuta, I was immediately placed in the house of Pu Tokerau and told that I was his *taina*. I was also the *taina* of his brothers, Pu Teaokena and the island's senior chief, Pu Koroatu. Pu Toke was Anuta's catechist and best English speaker; and by using English he was often able to make distinctions that could not be readily expressed in Anutan. In answer to the question of whether a very distant kinsman is a member of one's *kano a paito* ('kindred'), for example, his usual response was, "Yes, but in a different way." Yet he insisted, despite a good deal of rather skeptical questioning, that Pu Teaokena, the chief, and I were all his *taina* "in the same way." He asserted that I had all the rights and obligations—and had to abide by the same rules and prohibitions—as his brothers. He referred to me as his *taina, nga maatuaa e tai*, a phrase that Anutans normally reserve for true siblings in the English sense. The incest taboo forbade me to marry any of Pu Toke's close female relatives. If I should marry a woman from another *kainanga* ('clan'), my wife would join me in the Kainanga i Mua, following normal Anutan custom, rather than my going over to that of her people—despite her genealogical connection with her group and the absence of any such connection between me and mine. If we should have children, they would be members of my *kainanga* rather than the one from which my wife had come. Pu Toke asserted that all his gardens and other property belonged to me as well; and even if I left the island for years, I could always come back to claim my rightful share. If I did not return and married a woman from a different land, my children would still inherit rights to the Anutan property, which they would be free to claim at any time they wished to establish residence on the island. I was a *maru* ('executive official'; 'man of rank') by virtue of my fraternal relationship with Pu Tokerau and the chief; and my position as *maru* gave me the right to speak at the *pono* ('community assembly'). Pu Toke insisted that if the chief, his son, and his brothers should die, I would be next in the line of succession. Anuta has the words *kauapi* and *tama pakapiki*, which may be glossed as 'adopted child.' but my host was steadfast in his insistence that I was not his *taina pakapiki* (in fact, Anutans do not use such an expression); I was his *taina maori*, just as if I had been born to the same parents.

Still suspicious that Pu Toke might be trying to deceive me out of hospitality and concern that I should not feel out of place in what was obviously a strange new environment, I proceeded to pose the same set of questions to a general cross-section of the Anutan population, including the two chiefs, members of three of the four *kainanga*, persons of both sexes, and of ages ranging from about twelve to over sixty. In every case, the answers were identical, and in a culture that permits a great deal of flexibility in social relations, the unanimity with which my consultants spoke was remarkable.

This raises the question of "adoption" and whether, despite the lack of an Anutan term, I might be accurately described as Pu Tokerau's "adopted brother." To the extent that "adoption" implies a mechanism other than birth to become a relative without entailing that one mechanism creates a more "real" kinsperson than the other, such a designation might be appropriate. If an "adoptive kinsperson" is taken to be *like* a relative without actually being one, however, it would be misleading to describe my status as "adoptive".[7] While from a Western point of view I may have been Pu Tokerau's "adoptive brother," from an Anutan viewpoint I was his *real taina*. Because of this ambiguity, I prefer to avoid the word "adoption" in characterizing my position in Anuta's kinship system.

Clearly, I was not considered to be the same as Pu Tokerau's brothers in all respects. There were obvious differences in physical appearance, habits, skills, experiences, and speech patterns. But differences exist among native-born Anutans as well. These differences, obvious and relevant though they were for certain purposes, had no bearing on my membership in that class of persons to whom Pu Tokerau, Pu Teaokena, and the senior chief referred as *taina maori, nga maatuaa e tai*.[8]

Often the chief would joke with me in a rather undignified manner that seemed inappropriate to his chiefly status, but he explained that such behavior was permissible between himself and his *taina maori*. On the same grounds he repeatedly excused me from normal respect behavior that one owes a chief. Most recently, during my 2000 visit, I forgot to step aside for the chief as Anutans are expected to do when meeting someone of superior rank. He could have excused my oversight on several grounds. He might have said that I was not Anutan and was thus exempted from the normal rules of etiquette. Or he could have noted that I had been absent from the island for the better part of twenty years, making a few lapses understandable. In fact, he chose neither of those options but later explained that normal rules of respect do not apply to *taina maori*—even those of a chief.

The most dubious assertions about my status in the kinship system were those that placed me in the line of chiefly succession. Despite repeated assurances, I harbored doubts for many years. I imagined that my questions would go unresolved, as I neither wished nor thought that my friends' statements ever would be tested. However, something very close to the scenario I posited in 1972 has come to pass. The chief's only son has now been married for two decades and is childless. Two of the chief's three brothers have since died, childless as well. The last brother (Pu Teukumarae, also known as Frank Kataina, who had been absent from Anuta during my first visit) was married for a few years, had no children, is now divorced, and has no intention to remarry. Thus, in two generations, when Pu Koro-atu (the present senior chief) and Mataki (his son) are no longer on the scene, Anuta's chiefly line will be in real danger of extinction.

During a visit to Honiara in 1988, I asked a number of Anutans their opinions as to what would happen to the chieftainship if Mataki should pass away without leaving progeny. Pu Teukumarae observed that Mataki, as a dying chief, would have the right to name his successor. He speculated, however, that the line might be preserved by Pu Niukapu (Peepiti), a young man of Tuvaluan birth, whom Frank had brought as a teenager into the chief's household. If Pu Niukapu has a son, that son could be a viable candidate. When I pointed out that Pu Niukapu is really a Tuvaluan, Frank emphatically protested: "He came to live with me on Anuta and has followed the customs of Anuta. Therefore, he is an Anutan!"

This answer raised the old question of my place in Anuta's chiefly reckoning. When I was first told that I might be in the line of succession, the reasoning was similar to what I had just heard regarding Pu Niukapu. So I asked, half-jokingly, if my son, Joe, would not also be a likely candidate. Anutans knew Joe as a four-year-old from a five-month visit to the Solomons in 1983–84. That visit included one month on Anuta, during which we lived in the chief's house.

I was taken aback by the serious reply. Frank said Joe was not an option because the chief must reside on Anuta. But if he came to live permanently on Anuta, learned the language, and followed the island's customs, he might very well succeed Mataki as chief.

Some weeks after this initial conversation, Frank mentioned his hope that I some day would take Joe for a second visit to Anuta—to give him a chance to look afresh at the island and its customs and see what he thinks. I sensed that Frank had something more in mind, so I asked what he was thinking. He said he was thinking of *te noporanga* ('the seat'). I paused, then asked, *"Te noporanga ariki"* ('the throne')? He said yes and then proceeded to express concern about the absence of a chiefly grandson. If Mataki did not produce a son, *"te noporanga ariki ka reku ee rea"* ('the throne will indeed vanish'). Frank hoped that Joe might step in and rescue *te noporanga* by assuming the chieftainship upon Mataki's demise. This, however, would require him to have lived on Anuta for a substantial period, to have assimilated the language and customs, and to be equipped to handle the responsibilities. Therefore, he hoped that Joe, after his second viewing of Anuta, might like the place so well that he would stay. I asked whether this was his idea or if he had spoken with the chief about it. He responded that it actually originated with Pu Koroatu, and he seemed surprised that the chief had not brought up the subject during my previous visit in 1983.

I asked rather pointedly if he was serious about all of this. He replied that he was very serious! This, he asserted, is how Anutan custom works, and he even seemed a bit offended that I raised the question. He asked if my *toa* ('formal friend,' by whom he meant Pu Tokerau, his elder brother) had not explained all this to me. I admitted that he had but added that I had been somewhat skeptical. Frank admonished me for harboring such doubts and ended the discussion.[9]

I do not claim special merits for my fieldwork. My incorporation into Anuta's kinship system does not denote unusual competence or sensitivity. To the contrary, *anyone* coming to live on Anuta for an extended period *must* be made part of the kinship system. It is only as kin that Anutans deal with one as a part of their community. Anyone not incorporated into the kinship system is an outsider, a potential enemy, viewed at best with cautious regard, and certainly not to be trusted. Anutans work hard to avoid the tension that would be produced were such a person left at large on their small island, and one would have to be unusually offensive before they would consider rejecting his or her status as kin.

Government officials visiting Anuta are respected because of the power of the institution they represent, appreciated for the services (e.g., shipping, radio, and medical aid) the government supplies, and viewed with suspicion because of the threat to Anutan political sovereignty that the government presents. And shortly before I left the island at the end of my first study, when Anuta was visited by a Taiwanese fishing vessel, I was shocked to see the tactics employed by people whom I had found to be profoundly honest, friendly, and hospitable in extorting liquor, food, cigarettes, and money. Significantly, neither government officials nor the Taiwanese fishermen were addressed by kin terms. They were on the island for short periods, and no one attempted to incorporate them into the kinship system.

On the other hand, when the medical research ship *Alpha Helix* paid its visit (see chapter 1), several members of the scientific party remained on shore for a week. They were immediately incorporated into the kinship system, and long discussions followed in which Anutans debated what relationship the different members of the team bore to various islanders.

Similarly, the Yen expedition (see chapter 1) spent close to two months on Anuta, and members of the research team were all made into kin. By the way in which Pu Notau called Yen *taina* and followed out the implications of that relationship in every aspect of his behavior, the team leader was forced to reach the same conclusion I did, quite independently, as to his inclusion in the kinship system (Yen, personal communication).

In striking contrast is the case of Sione, a Tongan convict who stole a prison boat and drifted to Anuta around 1990. The Anutans refused to give him up to the Tongan authorities because they felt 'compassion' (*aropa*) for this "wandering sea bird," and they did not want to see him returned to prison. In his decade on the island, however, Sione refused to attend church with the rest of the community. He never learned to speak Anutan, and he made a habit of stealing food from people's gardens. When he began starting fights and beating children, the Anutans tied him up and placed him under guard in one of their houses. Eventually, he escaped in a canoe and sailed to Tikopia, where he was living at the time of my departure from the Solomons in November 2000. Significantly, Sione was not incorporated into any Anutan domestic unit, given an Anutan name, or called by kin terms. Unlike Pu Niukapu, the Tuvaluan immigrant, Anutans still call him "the Tongan."

The Conceptual Basis of Anutan Kinship

I have written in rather general terms of social interaction as a means to alter or reinforce genealogically ascribed positions in Anuta's kinship system. Before moving on, let us consider more specifically the behavioral properties that distinguish kin from nonkin and near from distant kin, as well as the relationship between these behavioral properties and the principle of genealogical connection. This requires us to examine one of the most pervasive and highly valued constructs in Anutan culture, the concept of *aropa*.

In different contexts, *aropa* may be translated as 'pity.' 'sympathy.' 'love.' 'compassion.' or 'affection.' although none of these words captures the full flavor of the Anutan concept. An Anutan who is away from home and misses another will say, "*Kau aropa ki ei*" ('I *aropa* to him'). Anutans often told me that they hoped I would remain on their island because, "*Kau aropa ki a te koe*" ('I *aropa* to you'). When one suffers a misfortune one again is told, "*Kau aropa ki a te koe,*" although with a rather different connotation. And an orphan is called a *tama pakaaropa* ('pitiable child').

In most contexts, *aropa* may be thought of loosely as connoting what English speakers call 'love.' However, there are major differences in context and expression. In America, when one utters the words, "I love you," it is supposed to reflect a deep emotional commitment and is reserved for special persons on special occasions. Anutans, on the other hand, frequently reiterate, *"Kau aropa ki te koe"* and explain their actions in terms of their *aropa* for one another. Moreover, as opposed to the West, where love and friendship are taken to be immaterial qualities valued as ends in themselves, on Anuta they must be expressed in material terms.

The concept of *aropa* is inextricably bound to giving and sharing. One cannot be on Anuta long without realizing the enormous importance placed on this aspect of social life. To anyone Anutans consider a member of their community, they are generous to a fault—through both the medium of formal ceremonial gifts and informal expressions of good will. One is constantly invited to meals. It is virtually impossible to speak with someone and not be asked to come and eat. No Anutan may sit down to a meal without offering food to anyone who might be present, and contrary to what has been reported on some other islands (e.g., Nukuoro; see Carroll 1966), visitors are expected to accept such offers as a matter of course unless there is some pressing reason for them to decline. If there is a limited amount of food, it is offered to visitors before the host takes any. On the other hand, while Anutans give freely of their own supplies, they are also free with their requests of others. All reasonable requests for material assistance should be honored, and to admire an object in the possession of another is often taken as a request for that object.

Acts of generosity may be designated by different terms depending on the context, but any gift (as distinguished from a trade or sale) may be termed *aropa* and viewed as the material embodiment of sentiments bearing the same name. An offering is often handed over with the words, *Toku aropa ki a te koe* ('My *aropa* to you'). Once, before I was aware of the significance, I asked an intermediary to relay my *aropa* to a friend on Tikopia in the same way that Americans might speak of sending our regards or our love. I was taken aback by the response, "Where is it?" until it was explained that sending *aropa* to someone overseas requires the conveyance of a material object.

The identification of *aropa* with sharing is seen in all aspects of Anutan life, but it is especially prominent with respect to the source of life itself, namely food. Anutans constantly offer food, and they encourage each other to eat with such persistence that I often found consuming to the point of physical discomfort easier than to refuse. On those few occasions when I was not feeling well and resisted all prodding, the hurt expressions made it obvious that more was involved than the physical act of refusing to eat. When Anutans offer food, they are offering not just sustenance but also *aropa*, and an intended recipient who declines to partake is symbolically rejecting the donor's 'love.'[10]

Anutan kinship must be understood in relation to *aropa*. When I asked how I became the *taina maori, nga maatuaa e tai* of Pu Tokerau and his brothers, I was repeatedly told that I had been placed in that relationship by virtue of "living in their house." This did not mean I slept in the same physical structure as they did. In fact, while my immediate host and I generally did sleep in the same building, the chief and Pu Teaokena each had a separate house, and Pu Teukumarae lived on a different island. The crucial point is that the brothers held all their property in common, in conformity with Anutan norms. Therefore, by sleeping in Pu Toke's house, I was also sleeping in that of the others. Moreover, their gardens were held and worked in common, food was prepared in common by them and their wives and children, and they ate together as a single group on formal ceremonial occasions. Anything belonging to one of them was available to the others at any time; and if a member of one nuclear family was hungry, he or she was free to take food from the other brothers' houses as a matter of course.

All objects belonging to one of the brothers automatically belonged to the others as well. This expression of *aropa* through sharing rather than giving (since one cannot give to someone what that person already has) distinguishes the extended family domestic unit. Ideally, brothers always should be members of the same domestic unit, and any immigrant or long-term visitor must be incorporated into one or another of these extended family 'households.' The immigrant's relationship to others of his or her generation within the same domestic unit is based on sharing in precisely the same manner as a biological sibling; and the transition from having all the rights and responsibilities of a brother to being classed as *taina maori, nga maatuaa e tai* is easily accomplished.

The ideological basis for incorporating a visitor in this way is expressed in terms of *aropa*. One should feel *aropa* for anyone with whom one shares a genealogical tie, and the closer the connection, the more intense the feeling of *aropa* should be. Yet in practice, these are semi-independent variables. A man may turn against his brother or feel a deep affection for someone with whom he has no genealogical tie, and in neither case is the person disqualified from kinship. In other words, there are two criteria for kinship status—genealogical connection and the expression of *aropa*—and in the absence of either one, the other alone may suffice.[11]

Aropa may result from pity for a traveler who is stranded in a strange new land, sympathy for someone who is far from home and separated from family and friends, or positive attraction to a pleasant personality. In the last analysis, however, other people's emotional states are unknowable, and professions of *aropa* are validated and judged on the basis of what one does rather than what one says or feels. *Aropa* expressed as willingness to share one's rights to property enables nongenealogically related persons to place each other in the same cultural category as primary kin.

While this conclusion seems compelling in important ways, it also leaves us with a paradox. Visitors from overseas who lack genealogical connections with any Anutan are made kin in even the specific sense, yet persons born into the community—who therefore start out with a much closer genealogical relationship—cannot be kin in the specific sense unless they already occupy that status by virtue of birth.

The solution, I believe, reflects a contradiction implicit in the principles on which Anutan social structure is based. For native-born Anutans, the opportunity to alter one's kinship status through mutual agreement and subsequent assumption of the appropriate social roles exists to a degree but is, nevertheless, limited by prior genealogical constraints. The closer the genealogical connection the stronger the bonds become and the more difficult they are to override through mutual agreement and altered behavior. When the ties become as close as those among primary kin, no room is left for redefining one's position. Visitors, however, have no prior genealogical constraints, and they are permitted to affiliate as closely as they wish with whomever they wish as long as the desire is mutual and their conduct is appropriate to the chosen position in the kinship system.

Once specific kin relations are established, determining one's status with respect to persons falling outside of the focal group becomes an easy matter; one simply uses the same terms as one's closest *taina* unless there is some reason for preferring a different designation in a particular case. In other words, one follows the same principles as do persons born into the domestic unit. Like any native Anutan, the immigrant must maintain bonds of *aropa* with kin who fall outside of the immediate group; but this is a collective responsibility taken on as a matter of course by the unit as a whole. We will now examine the domestic unit, its cultural construction, and its role in social life.

Chapter 4

Domestic Life

Patongia:
The Elementary Domestic Unit

Human beings differ from other animals in that we have a lengthy period of infant and childhood dependency. During the early years of life, a child cannot fend for itself; therefore, it must be fed, educated, and protected by older children and adults. Different communities arrange for such nurturance in a variety of ways, but every community must find some way to perform these tasks. The result is what anthropologists call domestic or household organization, or what most Americans term "the family."

The typical American vision of the family is rather narrow by world standards. The "proper" family—as pictured, for example, by politicians who bemoan the loss of so-called family values—is what anthropologists refer to as the nuclear family: a group consisting of a married couple and their unmarried children living together under the same roof. Nuclear families can be recognized in most communities, but they are not always central units of social organization. On Anuta, as in many communities outside of the Western world, the elementary domestic and socioeconomic unit extends well beyond the nuclear family, typically including certain uncles, aunts, cousins, nephews, nieces, and often a variety of more distant kin.

Anutans term their smallest discrete socioeconomic unit the *patongia* or *pare*. This unit may be loosely described as a 'patrilateral extended family.' I will gloss it as the 'household' on the basis of the intense sharing and cooperation that membership requires. Such a translation must be qualified, however, with the observation that members of the same *patongia* may occupy a number of dwellings dispersed throughout the island's village area. A more accurate, if cumbersome, translation is the 'elementary domestic unit.'

Children typically become members of their fathers' *patongia*, but several other means of gaining membership exist as well. When a woman marries, she joins her husband's household. An adopted child gains membership in both the natural and the adoptive parents' households. Every Tikopian *paito* ('lineage') (see Firth 1963[1936], 1954, 1957) has a special relationship with one or more Anutan *patongia*. Unmarried Tikopian immigrants automatically join the households of their *tauranga* (see chapter 3). A Tikopian man who marries an Anutan woman may either join his wife's domestic unit or bring his wife to join that of his *tauranga*. A Tikopian woman who marries an Anutan man and settles on Anuta normally becomes part of her husband's rather than her *tauranga*'s domestic unit. Non-Tikopian immigrants lack a preexisting relationship akin to the *tauranga* bond. Instead, they establish a *tau toa* ('friend') relationship (cf. Firth 1967:108–15) with someone on the island, through which they are incorporated into one or another of the indigenous domestic units.

Ultimately, the *patongia*'s composition must be understood in light of its cultural definition: it is that group which shares a common food basket at island-wide distributions. Such distributions occur at community feasts, when a canoe returns from a successful fishing expedition, and on a number of other occasions. In short, Anutans conceptualize the *patongia* in terms of economic rather than genealogical criteria.

In 1972–73, there were nineteen households on Anuta, varying in size from two to twenty persons. The nineteen households, broken down by 'clan' affiliation (see chapter 6) and listed according to their leaders' names and numerical size, are listed in table 4.1. In 2000, despite a doubling of Anuta's population, the number of *patongia* had only increased by two to a total of 21.

It is rare for all members of an Anutan household to live under a single roof. They may reside on opposite ends of the island, or even on different islands altogether. All Anutans living in Tikopia, Honiara, and the Russell Islands are considered to be members of one or another *patongia* regardless of whether they are expected ever to return home. The sole exception is women who have married men

Table 4.1 Anutan households in 1972, listed by clan affiliation, leaders, and numerical size.

Kainanga	Current Leader	Total Membership[a]
Mua	Pu Tokerau	19[b]
	Pu Maravai	15
	Pu Notau	10
	Pu Akonima	12
	Pu Raveiti	8
	Pu Paone	18[b]
	Pu Nukurava [Pu Ngarumea]	16
Tepuko	Pu Taramoa/Pu Tepuko	22
	Pu Parekope [Pu Nukumata]	16[c]
	Nau Tanukope	3
Pangatau	Pu Nukutamaaroa	17
	Pu Tuaapi	20
	Richard Maraetanu	11
	Pu Penuakimoana/Pu Pouro	21
	Pu Arataika/Pu Pareumutia	16
	Judah Mataamako	8
	Pu Nevaneva	5[d]
	Pu Rongovaru	17
Rotomua	Pu Maevatau/Pu Teraupanga	20

[a] These figures are as of January 1973. The total (274) is higher than that reported earlier (see chapter 2) for the number of Anutans due to the fact that many youngsters, either through formal adoption or informal affective bonds, have become members of more than one *patongia* and are, therefore, counted two or even three times.

[b] These figures exclude the anthropologist although during the course of his stay it is these units into which he was incorporated.

[c] This figure excludes Pu Parekope's father, Pu Teputuu, who died in December 1972.

[d] This figure excludes Pu Nevaneva s wife, Nau Nevaneva, who died during the early part of my study.

from other islands and are living overseas. These women have married out of their natal households, and, as their husbands are not members of the Anutan community, they do not gain membership in new ones by virtue of their marriages. Should such a woman return, she would have the option of being reincorporated, along with her husband and children, into her original household. Alternatively, if her husband is from Tikopia, she might affiliate with the unit of her husband's *tauranga*. In 1972, the only non-Anutans to have married Anutan women were from Tikopia, and even in 2000 there was just one exception to this rule.

Anutans say that members of a *patongia* eat together, although this may or may not be literally the case. In 1972, Pu Akonima, who lived in Mua, for example, ate regularly with his brother, Pu Rotopenua, who lived in Muri, close to the boundary of St. John. Meanwhile, Pu Paone and Nau Nukutapu ate separately despite being next door neighbors. Such considerations as health, the size of one's domestic unit, and the quality of interpersonal relations among its members determine the actual arrangements. The salient point is that members of the same domestic unit have an equal claim to household property, and they are entitled to eat any food under their household's jurisdiction, regardless of where it might be located. Even houses belong to domestic units rather than individuals; the house in which a particular person takes a particular meal is not culturally significant. However, when the entire island gathers for feasts the household usually does eat together physically. At such times, all household members sit on a common mat and eat from a common basket.

Economic Functions

The *patongia* is Anuta's primary productive, consumptive, and child-rearing unit. Gardens, houses, tools, food, and even European goods and money are owned by the household rather than its individual members. The household as a corporate unit controls most property and decides upon its use.

Gardens

Virtually the entire island is divided into plots of land, each of which is 'owned' by one household or another. Anutans recognize two main types of garden land: *i maunga* ('on the hilltop') and *i raro* ('on the coastal flat'). Many crops are especially suited either to highland or lowland cultivation (see chapter 2), and each household should have a number of gardens of each type.

Domestic units vary greatly in wealth, ranging from one with 56 gardens under its control to three others with but thirteen plots apiece. Table 4.2 lists the households along with the number of gardens of each type under its control.

Ownership is a problematic concept when discussed cross-culturally. The Anutan term that most closely approximates the English notion of 'ownership' is *pakarongo*, which means in other contexts 'to listen to' or 'to obey.' Lands are 'owned' by the household in the sense that it is they, under normal conditions, who control them. Anutans say that a garden plot 'obeys' a particular household, and it is that household which usually decides what crops will be planted, when the work

Table 4.2 Households as of 1972, and number of gardens of each type associated with each household.

Leader of Unit	Number of Garden Plots		
	i Raro	*i Maunga*	Total
Pu Rongovaru	33	23	56
Pu Tuaapi	27	27	54
Pu Maevatau	23	14	37
Pu Paone	24	13	37
Pu Nukurava [Pu Ngarumea]	21	11	32
Pu Tokerau	16	15	31
Pu Nukutamaaroa	14	17	31
Pu Maravai	16	13	29
Pu Nevaneva	15	13	28
Pu Arataika	16	11	27
Pu Akonima	16	8	24
Pu Taramoa	11	13	24
Richard Maraetanu	9	13	22
Pu Penuakimoana	12	10	22
Judah Mataamako	9	9	18
Pu Notau	10	3	13
Pu Raveiti	9	4	13
Pu Parekope [Pu Nukumata]	8	5	13
Nau Tanukope[a]	—	—	—
Total	289	222	511

[a] The case of Nau Tanukope is somewhat anomalous. She married a Tikopian and went to live on her husband's island for a number of years. During the early 1950s, they returned to Anuta where they were permitted to plant in the gardens of her brother, the second chief (this the *patongia* actively headed by Pu Taramoa at the time of my investigation), and two of her husband's three *tauranga* units—the groups headed in 1972–73 by Pu Nukurava and Pu Rongovaru. For unspecified reasons (probably irreconcilable personality differences), however, they were never fully incorporated into any of the groups, and after Pu Tanukope died, Nau Tanukope's ties with her husband's *tauranga* were dissolved. The Ariki Tepuko (the second chief) was not anxious to take the woman back completely, but neither could he let his sister starve, so he permitted her to continue planting on his lands and taking food from his gardens. They often used a single oven, but they ate in separate houses, and during food distributions each received a separate basket.

should take place, how it should be carried out, when the foodstuffs will be harvested, and, within certain limits, how they will be used. An Anutan may plant in someone else's garden—a practice known to economic anthropologists as usufruct—but only after permission has been obtained from the controlling household. The Anutan system differs from Tikopia, where uncultivated land may be planted by members of any 'lineage' (*paito*) with or without permission, provided only that a portion of the eventual crop is offered as compensation to the controlling group (see Firth 1963[1936]: chapter 10).

Crops requiring cultivation are generally at the disposal of the household that planted them. That unit may then use them for ritual exchanges, contributions to islandwide feasts, first-fruit presentations to the chiefs or the church, or its own consumption. Crops should not be taken from another household's garden without the owners' prior knowledge and consent. However, if the appropriator were extremely hungry, harvested a fruit or vegetable for immediate consumption, promptly informed the owners, and offered to recoup their loss, the owners could not easily complain.

The most important crops in this category are taro, which is ritually the most esteemed, and manioc. I never saw bananas or yams in a first-fruit offering, but in other respects those crops fall into the same class. I found sweet potatoes, pumpkins, sugar cane, watermelons, and many minor crops to be used strictly by the unit that grew them plus any visitor who might happen by at mealtime.

A second major class of crops from the viewpoint of land tenure is represented by the coconut (*niu*). Like those in the first group, the plant is under the control of the domestic unit on whose land it stands. Should one wish to fell a coconut palm that stands in someone else's garden, the owner's permission first must be obtained. The nuts, however, are common property. Anyone is free to take one

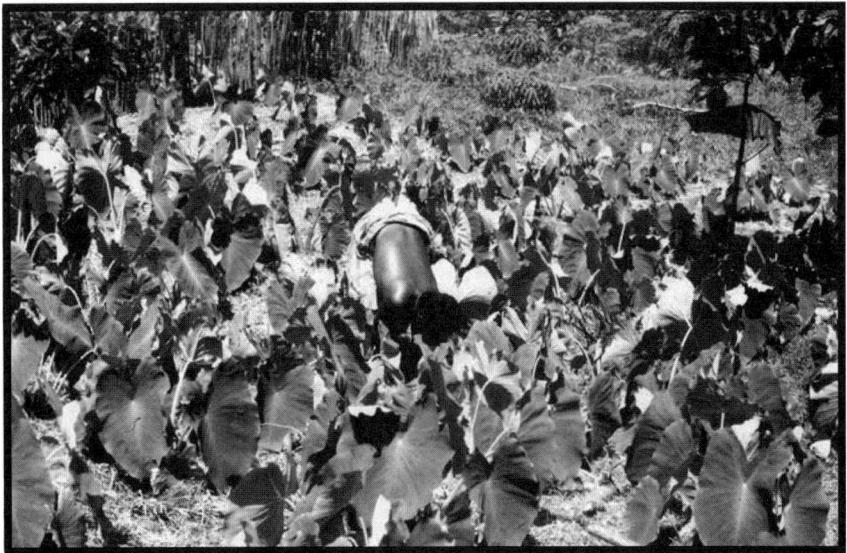

Photo 4.1 Woman cultivating taro in hilltop garden.

whenever he or she desires, regardless of the tree's location. An exception occurs when the chiefs place a taboo on the fruit, in which case it is off limits to everyone.

This system differs from neighboring Tikopia, where coconuts belong to the 'lineage' in whose orchard they are found. There one may take a nut from someone else's orchard without obtaining prior dispensation but must then leave the husks piled neatly near the tree and inform the owner at the earliest opportunity. On Anuta the nuts belong to all by intrinsic right, and there are no such constraints.

After the coconut, the most important crop in this class is papaya (*naaporo*). Papayas are abundant, and their fruit provides an important source of nourishment. The flimsy trunk, however, has no economic value, and chopping it down is not an issue. In one section of the island, near the spring, papayas may only be harvested by the household on whose land they are found. This, however, is a special case. Anutans enacted the rule because of a large stand of areca palms, the betel nut tree, that is located in the area. The chiefs were concerned that if people were free to roam through these gardens harvesting papayas, they might be tempted to steal betel nuts from other units' gardens.

Table 4.3 lists Anuta's major plant types according to their normal method of utilization and control. In addition, a number of shrubs and vines have economic uses but are unequivocally available to the community at large. In this category is the betel vine (*Piper betel),* grasses used for taro mulch, and a grasslike plant called *te tapatapaatunga,* whose pungent root is sometimes chewed in place of betel nut when the latter is unavailable.

Since gardens are the collective property of an entire household, inheritance normally is not an issue. Individuals are born and die or marry in and out, but the *patongia* is a corporate group that theoretically exists in perpetuity. The vast majority of gardens have been in the possession of their present owners from time immemorial (*mai mua rea*), and a garden's disposition only becomes problematic when a line dies out. In such a case, the lands are divided among those units with whom the last survivors held their closest ties.

A second and more common way in which a garden may change hands is through marriage. When a woman marries, her brothers sometimes donate a plot or two of land to be held in trust for their future *iraamutu*—their sister's sons-to-be. In 1972, I recorded 89 plots as having come to their present owners through a woman at some time in the past; and since only the more recent exchanges are likely to be remembered, this may be a considerable underestimate. By contrast, I discovered just a single set of gardens that was trans-

Table 4.3   Major plant types, listed according to their normal method of utilization and control.

A. Individual *Patongia*	B. Plant Belongs to Individual *Patongia*; Fruit Available to Entire Island
Taro	Coconut
Manioc	*Burkella*
Cyrtosperma	Papaya
Yam	*Vere* (a kind of nut)
Banana	*Rau Paopao* (a kind of tree)
Breadfruit	*Puko Vai* (a kind of very large tree
Sweet potato	whose leaf is used as a vegetable
Betel nut	green)
Sugar cane	*Paa* (pandanus species with edible
Turmeric	fruit)
Malay apple	*Pau Atonga* (a tree from whose bark
Cordyline	cord is fashioned)
Antiaris	*Kirivakai* (a tree whose light, hard
Kie (pandanus species whose leaf is	wood is used to make drop-line
used for plaiting ceremonial gar-	spools)
ments and sleeping mats)	Frangipani
Vati (a small tree whose leaf is used as	Hibiscus
a vegetable green in cooking)	*Rara* (a type of plant with fragrant
Puko Pakatangia (a large tree with	leaves which is used in bodily deco-
soft, light wood)	ration)
Calophyllum	
Pumpkin	
Tobacco	
Pineapple	
Watermelon	
Voia (a type of nut)	
Mapana (a type of bush with very fra-	
grant leaves; used in bodily adorn-	
ment)	
Ironwood	
Tau Unu (a type of large tree with	
hard but rather knotty wood; often	
used for canoe bailers and head	
rests)	
Sago palm	

ferred at the original owners' demise. In addition, a number of gardens were described as having been given to the household of a deceased man's *tuatina* as payment for having dug the grave, and islanders reported a few plots as having been given to a child by an adoptive parent.

Canoes

Next to gardens, the most important productive instrument is the canoe. In contrast with garden land, however, where each plot is owned by one domestic unit, a number of households typically share ownership in the same canoe.

More than a dozen men from different households may work together to construct a canoe. While they are working, these men also eat together as a group, not with their respective households. Most often, several *patongia* contribute food to the builders, and each household presenting food gains a share in the vessel's ownership. The *patongia* contributing the largest amount of food becomes the primary owner (*tapitonga*). The unit contributing the second-largest portion becomes the second ranking owner, and so on.

For most purposes, only the *tapitonga* is set apart. If the first two households contribute equal amounts of food, the position of *tapito* may be shared, as is the case with *Puinga*, Anuta's second largest and second most highly valued canoe. *Puinga*'s primary ownership is shared between the Api Taneanu and the household of the junior chief.[1] All the men in all the *patongia* who share ownership in a canoe are known as *taangata tau vaka* of that vessel.

Any number of households may share a canoe. In 1972, this number ranged from a few craft that were under the jurisdiction of only two or three domestic units to *Puinga*, in which 12 of the island's 19 households had a share. Every household has a share in at least a few canoes, and several are quite wealthy.[2]

The decision as to whether and when a canoe will be taken to sea is normally up to the *taangata tau vaka*, the greatest weight being given to the opinion of the *tapitonga*. A crew need not be restricted to the *taangata tau vaka*, but one could not put to sea over the owners' objection. The crew usually includes at least one of the *taangata tau vaka* since, if none of the owners were along to take responsibility, the fishermen would be held liable should the canoe be damaged in the surf.

Canoe fishing normally is done by community representatives on behalf of the entire population. When a crew returns, it divides the fish in the same manner as other kinds of food at island-wide distributions. In 1972, the fish were divided into 25 shares: one for each of the 19 households plus special portions for the units of the chiefs, the head catechist, and each of the assistant catechists. This arrangement was initiated by Pu Teukumarae, predecessor to the current senior chief, after the introduction of Christianity during the first half of the twentieth century. Prior to that time, fish were distributed only among the households of the crew and the *taangata tau vaka*.

Despite many changes between 1972 and 2000, Pu Teukumarae's system is still in effect with some slight modifications. During my initial study, only large canoes carrying crews of at least three or four men were taken out on fishing expeditions. In 2000, several small canoes were in regular use. If the fishermen procured enough fish to feed the entire community, they organized a general distribution. Otherwise, they kept the catch for themselves and their households. In addition, the distribution to the chiefs and catechists is no longer a routine occurrence but only marks special occasions, such as major religious holidays. In part, the changes have resulted from a population increase of more than 100%, to almost 350 people. The increased population makes it more difficult for one to take responsibility for the community's collective well-being and has generated a degree of atomism that did not exist earlier. Moreover, Anuta's communal ethos was at its peak in 1972–73 due to a food shortage produced by a violent storm early in the year. The senior chief determined that the best way to deal with the crisis was for the community to work together as a single unit, and he did everything he could to encourage island-wide sharing and cooperation.

Small-scale fishing rarely produces enough for general distributions. If a man goes alone to fish with pole and line (*tiiti*), to spear fish (*panapana*), or to swimfish with hook and line (*taukurakura*), the catch usually is brought home for his household. More often, however, fishermen go in small groups, the composition of which is usually determined by immediate convenience and personal compatibility. In such cases, the anglers divide the catch among themselves for their respective households. The division is based on need (primarily determined by the size of the domestic unit) rather than who caught how many fish.[3]

Bird hunting and women's scoop-net fishing on the reef are generally conducted according to the same principles as men's small-scale fishing. An exception occurs when birds are plentiful and an attempt is made to hunt for them in quantity. Twice in 1972–73 enough birds were captured for an island-wide distribution.

Houses, tools, and even articles most Americans would think of as personal in nature are not formally owned by individuals but fall under the domestic unit's jurisdiction. Such articles might be utilized predominantly by a particular person or group. For example, a house may be customarily occupied by a certain nuclear family, or a man may have a favorite knife that he routinely carries to the bush. However, a household's property technically belongs to all of its members and may be used at any time by anyone in the domestic unit without special dispensation from its customary guardian or user. The only exceptions are articles of clothing, sleeping mats, and headrests, which are off limits to anyone whose rank is lower than the normal user's. However, this is not a matter of property rights but a function of ritual honor and pollution.

Money, like other property, also is in principle under the collective control of the domestic unit. Catechists and schoolteachers may receive modest salaries from the church and the government respectively. They put these funds into their households' treasuries, to be used for ritual offerings of durable goods (*koroa*), to purchase supplies from passing ships, or to pay for passage off the island. However, Anutans obtain the great bulk of cash income from kin working overseas.

In theory, money earned in Honiara or the Russell Islands should be sent back home to help bolster the resources of the laborer's household. But living in a money-oriented environment requires cash expenditures, and temptations abound to spend cash on luxuries. A few Anutans have decided to remain permanently in the outside world and emulate the Europeans' style of living insofar as their finances and understanding permit. Yet even they retain close ties with their households back home, and a surprising proportion of their income finds its way to Anuta either in the form of currency or European goods.

Interpersonal Relations

The most constant and intense social activities take place within the *patongia*. Relatives within this unit are primarily responsible for teaching children how to think and act as competent Anutans. The following are descriptions of individual relationships within the *patongia*.

Mother-Child (*Tau Pae*)

During the period immediately following birth, an infant usually is kept at home and cared for by the mother. Other female relatives with child-care experience spend time with the mother and child to assist where necessary. Members of a church auxiliary group called the Mothers' Union visit the house, often staying overnight, to pray and assist in whatever way they can until the pair have become strong enough to start attending services.[4] Despite these varied contacts, however, the baby's closest bonds are clearly with its mother. This special connection often lasts throughout life, and many Anutans report their most intense emotional attachments to be with their mothers despite the island's classificatory kinship system.

As the child grows in size and strength, its more distant *pae*, primarily its mother's sisters and close female cousins, assume a more

Photo 4.2 Woman at work plaiting a pandanus mat in the company of her young son.

important role. Since upon marriage a woman joins her husband's unit, however, these individuals are not members of the child's household. They take an interest in the baby, devoting their time and energy to whatever extent they can, but they have responsibilities to their own domestic units. This places constraints on their contact with the child.

Both parents play a role in their children's discipline and education, but for the first few months, the mother takes prime responsibility. Children are called *koi kovi* ('still defective') until they learn to speak and *koi vare* ('still incompetent') up to the time that they start wearing clothes on a regular basis—usually at nine or ten years of age. Prior to that time they are viewed as irresponsible and unselfconscious; therefore, they must be guided, educated, and protected from themselves and their environment. In general, children are indulged, and physical punishment is rare. A child who becomes unruly and cannot be controlled by words alone may be slapped lightly on the top of the head. This is almost never done in such a way as to cause physical pain, but there are few things more demeaning than to be struck on the head, which Anutans regard as the most sacred (*tapu*) part of the body. Children learn this lesson early, and a light cuff is usually enough to reduce a youngster to tears.

A mother stands above her children in terms of honor and authority, and they must show her proper deference. They may not utter her personal name, turn their backs to her, stand while she is seated in their presence, or stretch out their feet in her direction. They may not strike her, while she is entitled to inflict physical punishment on them; and they are obliged to do her bidding. Still, the relationship involves indulgence and even camaraderie. Anutans agree on the propriety of a mother taking responsibility for her children's sexual education; and when a man decides to marry, his *pae* is often chosen as his emissary to deliver his proposal to the bride.

As children get older and learn the skills that they will need as adults, a sexual division takes place. Boys spend more time with their fathers, while the girls stay with their mothers or other female relatives, from whom they learn the arts of matmaking and caring for a household.

Young children have little status in Anuta's elaborate system of rank, but as they mature they grow into their ascribed positions. A mother outranks her children on generational grounds, and the respect a man owes to his *pae* must never be forgotten. On the other hand, as a boy grows into manhood his mother treats him with increasing deference because of the gender differential. A man should not call his mother by her proper name, but other indicators—such as stepping aside when meeting on a narrow path—operate in favor of the son. The reciprocal respect between a woman and her adult male offspring is distributed more or less evenly on both sides.

Father-Child (*Tau Tamana*)

In early infancy, child care is predominantly the mother's concern. When parents feel a child is old enough to withstand a man's less skillful handling, the father begins to play a role. Anutans place a high value on children, and men appear to lavish as much affection on them as do their wives. One sees fathers carrying children in their arms, holding them on their laps, and cleaning their messes. When the children have developed some strength and coordination, they may cling to either parent's back while the parent goes about his or her daily chores. Men speak of their children with obvious pride and often discuss how happy they are to have been blessed with offspring. Anutans say that it is difficult for a barren couple to be truly happy. After my departure in 1973, Douglas Yen (personal communication) told me of a meeting he had conducted at the urging of a number of Anutan men who wished to know how they might improve their chances of having children. Pu Raveiti once described to me in the most moving terms his sorrow at the death of his first three children and his joy at the survival of those who followed. And the senior chief impressed on me the pleasure he received from his son. In 2000 the senior chief, now in his 70s and widowed, appeared to derive his greatest satisfaction from having small children—whether closely related or not—visit him at his house, climb on his lap, and play with him.

When children are old enough to walk, they accompany their parents to the gardens and oven houses, where they learn—first by observation and later by assisting in increasingly important ways—how to carry out the duties conducted at those sites. Both boys and girls help their parents in gardening and fishing on the fringing reef, where they are usually assigned to carry the fish while they learn the art by watching the experts. By the age of seven some boys join their fathers in the crew of a canoe, where they bail water from the bilge while learning how to fish and paddle. When a boy is nine or ten, he may join his father swimming out to sea to fish on calm days. More specialized arts like carpentry depend on individual inclination, and one may learn from anybody who is willing to teach. Some craftsmen even told me they had no specific teachers but picked up pointers here and there by watching many different men at work.

While fathers and children show much affection, the relationship is dominated by an aura of respect. No one is more highly respected than the father and his brothers. One may not joke roughly with his *tamana*, utter his name, or discuss matters related to sex. It is inconsiderate for a man to stand in the presence of his adult *tama* while the latter is seated, or to point his feet or turn his back toward him, but the *tamana* is within his rights to do so. The reverse would be a severe breach of proprieties. One should never strike one's father, while the reverse is a much less serious offense. Striking one's child lightly in order to discipline him is perfectly in order until the youngster reaches the age of responsibility. All persons falling into the *tamana* category should act and be treated in the same way as the father, but rules pertaining to *tamana* outside of one's immediate household, especially *tamana pakaapaapa*, are not so stringently enforced.

A child generally sees and interacts more with his or her father than with other *tamana*, but within the domestic unit, the difference in intensity and frequency of interaction should not be great. Children may sleep and eat in whichever of their *patongia*'s houses they choose. A man who travels overseas may take a brother's child with him or leave his own children at home in a brother's care. If the child is young and the father is gone for a protracted period, the youngster may even develop a closer *tau-tamana* relationship with the father's brother than with the natural father. For example, in November 1970 Pu Maevatau left for two years to work for wages in the Russell Islands. His three year old son, Simeon (now married and known as

Pu Aramera), remained behind in the care of Pu Maevatau's half brother, Pu Teraupanga. Two months before my departure from Anuta, Pu Maevatau returned, but Simeon continued to spend most of his time with his accustomed guardian. Once or twice in response to my general questions about his *tamana*, Simeon, then five, began discussing Pu Teraupanga rather than his biological father.

The barrier caused by affiliation with separate domestic units was illustrated to me by Pu Paone. The greatest obstacle to his leaving Anuta to engage in wage work, he told me, was the absence of an appropriate man to look after his children. To entrust them to the care of their mother's brothers, Pu Tokerau, Pu Teaokena, and the senior chief might be an option.[5] To leave them with his patrilateral parallel first cousins Pu Notau, Pu Akonima, or Pu Raveiti, however, would be quite impossible, as they had divided their gardens, thereby fragmenting the *patongia* and severing all close ties.

The intimate connection with a father's brother who has remained in the same household, on the other hand, is illustrated by Nomleas (now known as Pu Penuaika), Pu Nukumanaia's eldest son. Nomleas told me that his *aropa* for his father and for Pu Tuaapi, his paternal uncle, was approximately equal since he "lived" with both— meaning that they all were members of a common *patongia*. Similarly, his *aropa* for his mother and Nau Tuaapi was approximately equal. His *aropa* for his mother's brother and father's sister was considerably less than for his parents because he did not "live" with them (i.e., they belonged to different domestic units). Anutans note that children who are given inadequate exposure to other members of their *patongia* while young might become attached to their natural parents to the exclusion of close collaterals. This, they say, is undesirable; Nomleas' was the culturally appropriate response.

Grandparent-Grandchild (*Tau Tupuna*)

After a child's birth, particularly if it is the parents' first, both the paternal and maternal grandmothers may come to assist the mother. Given Anutan culture's patrilateral bias, however, a person normally is in the paternal grandparents' domestic unit, so it is with them that one has the most intimate and frequent contact.

Grandparents sometimes take charge of their grandchildren for substantial periods, and they play a role in their grandchildren's discipline and education. However, they are more indulgent, and their disciplinary function is less pronounced than that of the parents. Their educational role is more likely to be directed toward matters of genealogy and traditional lore than the efficient execution of economic pursuits.

The relationship between grandparent and grandchild is predominantly one of close friendship and solidarity. They may joke and tease each other, use each other's names without restraint, and even discuss matters relating to sex. If there is any difference in rank, it is in favor of the grandparent. Thus we see the "title" *nuna*, which may be used as an alternative to the *tupuna*'s proper name, while for the *mokopuna* there is no such respectful term.

All relatives of the second ascending generation are classed with the grandparents as *tupuna*, and all relatives of the second descending generation are *mokopuna*. Interaction between *tupuna* and *mokopuna* within the same domestic unit is exceptional for its constancy and strength, although *tupuna* in the mother's natal household may be quite close as well. Relations with more distant *tupuna* are less intense and frequent, but prescribed patterns of interpersonal behavior do not differ fundamentally as to type.

Parallel Siblings (*Tau Paanau*)

Following Nayacakalou (1955) I use the expression 'parallel sibling' to refer to siblings of the same sex and 'cross sibling' to designate siblings of opposite sex. Parallel siblings or cousins of the same sex are referred to as *tau paanau* ('related through birth').[6] Their relationship is characterized by freedom and even license. Older siblings watch their younger brothers and sisters and help to teach them the ways of the world. Parallel siblings play together, tease each other, joke roughly, confide in one another, and openly discuss sexual matters. Anuta has a cultural preference for siblings to marry into the same domestic unit, but that does not occur with overwhelming frequency. Even when sisters grow up and marry into different households, however, they maintain a close relationship, often meeting to chat, plait mats, or fish together on the reef at night. Brothers remain members of the same domestic unit even after marriage. Thus, the social structure works in such a way as to promote greater solidarity among them than among their sisters. If one brother has a successful day of fishing, the others benefit; and if crops fail because one has not done his share in the gardens, the entire unit suffers. Brothers often work together in the gardens or at sea, and they should support each other in case of conflict with the outside world. Anutans, therefore, see an equivalence of siblings in social interaction as well as kinship terminology.[7]

An older sibling outranks juniors, and in theory they should defer to him. It is the role of the senior to order and his juniors to obey. Most kinship systems in the Polynesian heartland encode the hierarchical relationship between older and younger parallel siblings in their kinship terminology. Anutans have abandoned the terminological distinction, but they maintain the hierarchical order in cultural theory and social practice. Thus, an older brother may strike a younger on sufficient provocation, while the reverse should not occur, except perhaps in play. It is a greater breach of etiquette for a younger brother to stand while the elder is seated in his presence, to stretch out his feet in the direction of his elder brother, or to turn his back on him than for such behavior to be directed at the younger brother by the elder. In point of fact, however, differences in rank are minimal and emphasized only on formal occasions or in such situations as meeting on a narrow path, where it is a physical necessity that one or the other

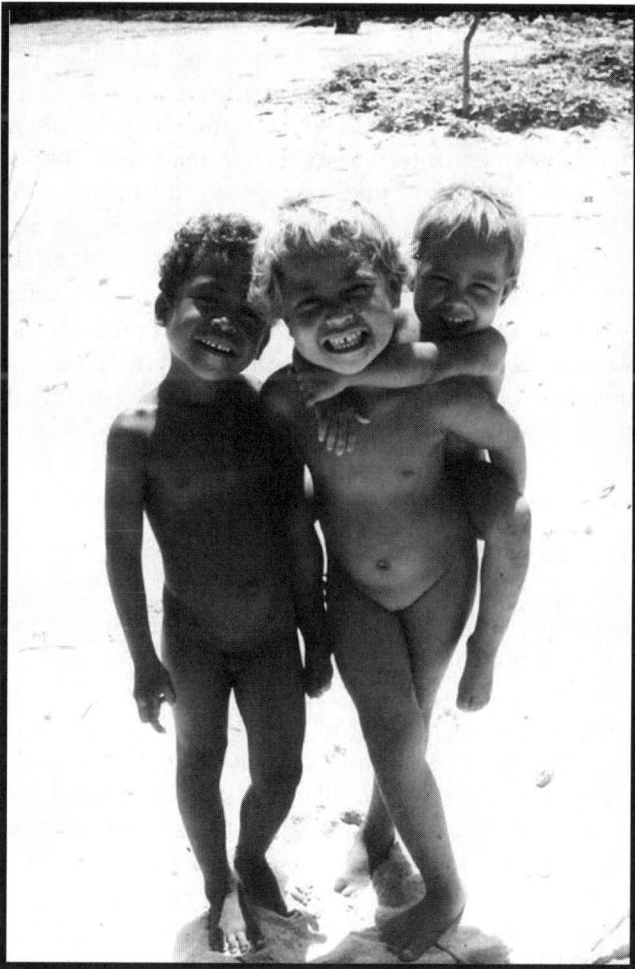

Photo 4.3   Children begin to care for younger siblings at a very young age. Here five-year-old Dorothy carries her sister, Vakangoto, on her back in the common Polynesian style.

party defer. Older siblings are expected to exercise authority over juniors who are very young, but in normal dealings only the eldest sibling of each sex is qualitatively elevated over all the rest.

The eldest son and eldest daughter of any couple are distinguished terminologically as *urumatua*; and there is a qualitative distinction between the firstborn child and those who follow. One may observe this distinction in several important rites of passage that only are performed for the first son and the first daughter. Among males, only the firstborn normally succeeds to leadership positions. Differences in ritual honor and political authority theoretically exist between any pair of parallel siblings, but they are rigorously enforced only for the *urumatua*. Even here, the free and solidary aspects of the relationship tend to be emphasized over respect and power.

While a close, friendly relationship among parallel siblings is the cultural norm, many Anutans fall short of the ideal. An illustration of cousins feeling greater fraternal solidarity than full siblings is provided by the children of Pu Nukumanaia and his brother, Pu Tuaapi. Pu Tuaapi's 12 year old son, Altaban (now Pu Rangitavake), told me in 1972 of how well he got on with Nomleas, Pu Nukumanaia's eldest son and a boy of about the same age. He then went on to tell me of his difficult relationship with Reuben (now Pu Rangituteki), his uncle's younger son, age six. Nomleas later told me that he felt the same way about Reuben as did his cousin. I found on later visits, as the three boys matured, that their relationship had normalized. For a number of years during childhood, however, Nomleas' relationship with his cousin was, for most purposes, closer than that with his brother.

Cross Siblings (*Tau Kave*)

Tau kave ('cross siblings') should exhibit mutual respect, but without the extreme restraint of the *tau tamana* relationship. A sister does not outrank her brother, nor does the brother fear his sister's curse, as has been reported for Tonga and Samoa. The pattern of brother-sister avoidance existing in much of west Polynesia is absent on Anuta—in fact, *tau kave* within the same household may even sleep on the same mat under a single blanket, since Anutans view sexual relations between them as inconceivable.[8] A man may not discuss sexual matters with his sister or other close *kave*, but a distant cross sibling is an appropriate marriage partner. In general, a man is expected to look after the interests of his close *kave*. In contrast with the practice in some Polynesian communities (e.g., Samoa; see Shore 1976), however, a man accused of violating a woman's honor should be dealt with by the *pono*, the island's 'governing council' or 'general assembly', rather than the brothers of the offended party. An Anutan woman should defer ritually and politically to her brother or male cousin unless she is considerably older and the *kave* is a small child or she is the firstborn of her sibling set (*te urumatua*) and the *kave* in question is "born behind." Cross siblings address and refer to each other by name, and there is no title which may be used as a substitute.

Husband-Wife (*Rumatua*)

As in the cross-sibling relationship, interaction between spouses is conditioned by the cultural fact that politically and honorifically Anutan men outrank women. Women may not sit on the (ritually superior) seaward side of a house. They may not stand while their husbands are seated, turn their backs or point their legs in their husbands' direction, use their husbands' headrests, or sit on the same sleeping mat during the course of normal daily affairs. Within the limits forced by these constraints, however, the relationship is one of solidarity, camaraderie, and intimacy. Ideally, the relationship is comfortable and loose; not fraught with the tension and restraint that marks the brother-sister or the parent-child relationships. The quality of marital relations may be best depicted by a series of illustrations.

I once asked Pu Tokerau about the basis for the status differential between men and women. As the island's head catechist, he was familiar with the Bible and responded that man was made from mud while woman was created only from a bone. I asked if this meant that mud is superior to bone, and he replied it is. His wife, who was sitting nearby, then ventured her opinion: "I think the bone is better." She often accused him in jest of being a weakling or a fool (both unfounded in fact), and these jibes were taken in the spirit with which they had been offered. Teasing and joking at this level is not only acceptable but looked on with favor as long as it is kept in bounds. When the husband offers a serious command, however, his wife is expected to give way.

One night I was visiting Pu Paone rather late, and while we chatted over dinner, his wife began to doze off in a corner of the house. When our meal was finished, he called his wife to rouse her, and after several attempts, he managed to obtain a grunt of acknowledgment. With his wife now half awake, he told her we had finished eating and that she should put the food away. She made no move to do so, indicating that she was too tired. Again he roused her and repeated his instructions, but with the same effect. After two or three more tries, each time posing his command in somewhat stronger terms than the time before, she finally capitulated and carried out his bidding. She then went back to sleep while Pu Paone and I continued our conversation. Perhaps twenty minutes later he wanted to get some items down from the rafters, and once again he roused his dozing spouse. She was no more anxious to get up now than she had been the first time, but after a few stern rebukes she gave in once more, got up, and took down the desired objects.

While a man should not flaunt his authority, my host was seen to be within his rights. Pu Paone was recognized as the 'wisest' (*poto*) man on the island at the time, and his behavior was universally held as a model for all Anutans to emulate. Significantly, his authority over his wife was not affected by the fact that Nau Paone was the sister of the island's senior chief.

Although in theory it is a man's right to lead and his wife's duty to follow, in short term matters relating to her spheres of expertise, she is often the decision maker. Moreover, in informal situations there is a great deal of individual variation, and many women exceed their normal sphere of jurisdiction. The Notaus, for example, often came to visit in my study. On a number of occasions, after several moments' pleasant chat, Nau Notau—an intelligent, assertive woman (who was also the sister of Tikopia's second chief, the Ariki Tafua), perceived that I was anxious to get back to what I had been doing before their arrival. On these occasions, she would strongly suggest to her husband that they should leave, and he readily followed her lead.

Anuta's major division of labor is between men and women. Adults may give young children simple tasks to carry out, such as carting water, relaying messages, or fetching hot coals to light a fire, but the youngsters' economic importance in the grander scheme of things is minimal. As soon as children are old enough to assume adult roles, however, they begin to do so—first as trainees under the tutelage of a senior relative; later as independent contributors to their household's well-being.

Agricultural pursuits are divided more or less equally between the sexes. However, heavier work like handling a digging stick tends to be allocated to men, while sweet potato cultivation in the Zone II house gardens (see chapter 2) is conducted exclusively by women. In fishing, as described in chapter 2, the division of labor is more pronounced. Only men fish in the ocean beyond the fringing reef or with a pole and line from shore. Women may participate in netting, spearing, or communal fish drives on the reef flat, but this occupies a small proportion of their time. A few men have acquired sufficient skill to help their wives at plaiting mats, but Anutans view this fundamentally as women's work. Conceptually, it is counterposed to ocean fishing, which, in the Anutan system of production, is the work of men.

The tasks involved in preparing food are shared between the sexes. Both take part in the harvesting processes and in preparing starchy fruits and vegetables for underground storage as *ma*. Cooking at home over an open fire is usually a woman's job, although a man may do it on occasion if he is hungry and no woman is around. Children sometimes capture birds or shellfish for impromptu picnics on the beach.

Preparation of oven food is a joint activity. Both men and women help to peel and cut the starchy vegetables and wrap them in leaves to be placed in the oven. Men usually grate coconut, extract the cream, and mix the puddings; women attend the oven itself, building the fire, arranging the stones, inserting the food, and removing it when done. In all of these pursuits, children and unmarried men and women assist as they are able. However, the greatest economic responsibilities fall on married people who generally take the initiative, set the example for the others, and end up doing most of the work.

'Adoption' (*Kauapi*)

Anutan children have a great deal of freedom to stay where they want, especially with close relatives. If parents are away from the island or deceased and no adult is left in a child's natal household, the youngster may move in with some other close relative on the basis of mutual agreement. After a boy's ritual circumcision, performed around the time of puberty, he may decide to stay with the *tuatina* who performed the operation. And if it should get late while a child is visiting at someone else's house, he or she may sleep there overnight without arousing great concern. Some of these arrangements are relatively permanent; others occur sporadically and are of short duration. They are all informal arrangements that may be terminated at any time by any of the participants.[9]

In addition to these informal arrangements, one may be formally 'adopted.' The child then is known as the adopters' *tama pakapiki* (literally, 'sticking' or 'adhering child') or *kauapi*. The first step in the adoption process is to consult and obtain the agreement of one's spouse. On the day the child is born, the couple must secure the baby's parents' consent. If the parents are amenable, the couple takes them presents of mats, bark cloth, and other durable goods to bind the agreement. They may take food as well, but this is not required. The procedure may be postponed for as long as a week after the infant's birth; beyond that time the child is no longer adoptable. The one case of which I am aware where this rule was breached caused considerable antagonism between the natural and adoptive parents.

During infancy, the child usually remains with the biological parents. When it is old enough to start eating semisolid foods, the couple who initiated the proceeding or members of their household prepare soft puddings known as *epuepu* or *pakavatia*, which they bring to the child as expressions of their *aropa*.[10]

One does not adopt a child who is already in one's own household, since such a child is already in the closest possible relationship. Rather, adoption is a means of formally bringing a child into a unit of which he or she would not otherwise be a member. An adopted child does not belong exclusively to the adoptive parents but is the household's *kauapi*, just as a person's own child is the *tama* of the whole domestic unit. Therefore, to make a *kauapi* of a child who is already in one's unit would be tantamount to adopting one's own child—the very concept is incoherent.

A *kauapi* becomes a member of the adopters' domestic unit, gaining the right to eat and sleep in any house belonging to that *patongia*. An adoptee is expected to spend a great deal of time with the adoptive parents, often accompanying them as they go to work at their ovens or in their gardens. Still, adoptees retain all rights of membership in their parents' households, and their kinship status remains unchanged in type. For example, if a boy is adopted by his mother's brother, he continues to call the adopter *tuatina*. While the kind of relationship remains unchanged, however, its closeness may be altered.

Through early infancy, a child usually is kept at home with the parents, but as soon as the adoptive parents are able, they take the youngster with them on a regular basis. Pu Aatapu once explained that he and his wife would take Vakangoto, their three year old *kauapi*, home with them as much as possible because they wanted her to get used to having them around. If they did not succeed at making her comfortable in their house while she was young, they recognized that in a year or two, when she was old enough to make her own decisions, she would not go to them. Some adoptive parents are less conscientious, and there are even cases where the *kauapi* relationship has been reduced to little more than a formality. This, however, is rare.

Although one does not adopt a member of one's own household, adoptees generally are fairly close kin. The offspring of one's *tama maori*, *kave maori*, or even *taina maori*, if the domestic units are different, are especially good candidates. The motivating factor in adoption most commonly is said to be *aropa* for the child and for its parents. Anutans readily acknowledge that children are desirable because of the help that they provide around the house—and later in the gardens, on the sea, and at the ovens—but this is seen as an expression of *aropa*, offered in return for the *aropa* the child has received in the form of food as a result of the *kauapi* relationship.

The *kauapi* relationship continues only until marriage. At that point, a man loses his position in his adoptive unit and becomes a member solely of his natal household. A woman loses membership in both her natal and adoptive units when she joins her husband's group. In many Pacific Island societies a barren couple may adopt a child in hopes that he or she will help to care for them in old age. Because the *kauapi* relationship has limited duration, care in old age is not an important motivating factor in Anutan adoptions.

'Formal Friends' (*Tau Toa*)

The *tauranga* and *tau toa* relationships are, like 'adoption', methods of bringing a person into one's domestic unit when such action would be barred on genealogical grounds alone. The *tauranga* relationship establishes bonds between Anutan households and their Tikopian counterparts so that when a member of one community visits the other he or she automatically is integrated into one of the indigenous units (see chapter 3). The *tau toa* relationship, however, is somewhat more complex and bears additional comments.

Toa is the Anutan version of *soa*, a common Polynesian word meaning 'friend.' Anuta recognizes two rather different kinds of *toa*. Both provide mechanisms for creating close fraternal bonds where they otherwise would not exist. One makes a native born Anutan into a close *taina*. The other makes a total stranger into a household member and, indeed, into a *taina, nga maatuaa e tai*—'true sibling of the same parents' (see chapter 3).

The first type of relationship is exemplified by Pu Aatapu and Pu Tokerau. They were born almost simultaneously, and their parents decided to emphasize that link by declaring them *tau toa*. They were encouraged to play together, spend time at each other's houses, exchange food and other presents, confide in each other, share adventures, and help each other in time of need. During childhood they may have been reckoned members of each other's households, although this point remains unclear from the statements I received. In any case, by the time of my investigation, they had both been married for some time and were clearly tied to different groups. Nevertheless, they remained close, often assisting one another in gardening, catching fish, preparing food, and other chores. On long canoe trips, such as that to Patutaka, they frequently traveled together. They maintained their *tau paanau* relationship despite Pu Aatapu's marriage to a close *kave* of Pu Tokerau's. Pu Aatapu classed Pu Tokerau's brothers, Pu Teaokena and the senior chief, not as *taina* but as *maa* on the basis of his marriage to their *kave*.

The second type of *toa* relationship is established when someone comes from overseas without a prior genealogical tie to anyone on the island and is integrated into the Anutan social system by means of incorporation into one or more domestic units. The visitor becomes *taina* (or *kave*) *maori, nga maatuaa e tai* with generation mates in the newly acquired household and is expected to function in that household as a true sibling, just as if the domestic unit had been entered through birth.

Authority Structure within the Elementary Group

At the head of each domestic unit is a leader, known as its *tapitonga* or *tapito*, literally, 'base' or 'source.' This is normally the unit's most genealogically senior male. Because the position is more instrumental than honorific, when the *tapito* becomes too old to exercise energetic leadership, he normally passes the position to a younger man. The recipient should be a lineal relative of the outgoing leader, which means that the successor normally is the former *tapitonga*'s eldest son. However, the old head may appoint a junior relative if he prefers to do so.

Instances where a junior man was made his unit's leader include the *patongia* of Pu Tuaapi, Pu Akonima, and Pu Tokerau. In the first case, Pu Nukumanaia, a generous and widely admired but modest, unassuming man, asked his younger brother, Pu Tuaapi, to serve as formal leader of their unit. In the second, Pu Notau, the eldest son, was visiting Tikopia when his father was lost at sea. Pu Akonima, the next younger brother, took over in his stead, retaining his position even after Pu Notau's subsequent return. Although I could obtain no explicit confirmation, this may have been a factor in the group's division a few years later.

Still more striking is Pu Tokerau's position as *tapito* in the senior chief's household. Although Pu Toke was genealogically second, he held ultimate authority in matters relating to the unit's internal workings, counting among his subordinates on a domestic level the island's most powerful man. This arrangement was determined by Pu Teukumarae, grandfather and predecessor to the present chief, probably because of Pu Tokerau's exceptional devotion to the old man in his waning years. Such an arrangement, however, is considered temporary. If the unit remains intact in subsequent generations, the leadership position should revert to the senior line.

Below the *tapito* men outrank women, and members of the first ascending generation outrank members of their children's generation. Grandparents and grandchildren are about equivalent in rank, although any differential works in favor of the older generation. Older parallel siblings are superior to younger ones in both honor and authority, with the firstborn male and firstborn female standing far above the rest. Among cousins, genealogical seniority comes into play, with the highest rank going to the eldest son of the eldest son, the lowest going to the youngest son of the youngest son, and the rest placed in between accordingly. Small children have little standing either in terms of ritual honor or political authority and are outranked by anyone who is many years their senior. The elderly, if they are senile or decrepit and can no longer depend upon themselves for their own well-being, may be equated in some respects with children.

Many of these factors are independent variables and may cross cut one another in a particular case at a particular time. As in attempting to distinguish 'near' and 'distant' relatives, the principles are clear. However, they are not divided into quantitatively measurable units, so that their application in concrete instances is subject to interpretation. The result is a measure of flexibility in daily life despite what look like rigid structural constraints.

Unit Segmentation

The *patongia* is defined as a group that takes its meals together from a single basket. Therefore, when a unit grows so large as to be unwieldy, or if personality clashes make cooperation difficult, it must ultimately divide. Division means, in economic terms, the allocation of property formerly held in common to each of the resulting units. Garden plots are distributed among the new households, and especially desirable plots of land are subdivided. In my inquiries into garden ownership, I often found several units holding plots that bore a common name. Further investigation showed that in some cases these were entirely separate plots which shared names as a matter of coincidence. In most instances, however, sharing of a common name reflected the subdivision of what was originally a single garden as a result of household segmentation. When this occurs, each of the new land divisions is assigned to one or another of the resultant social units.

As with gardens, houses and other property must be divided when a unit segments. Only canoes are not a problem—each of the new households retains a share in all the vessels that belonged to the original unit, since the food initially presented to the builder was given on behalf of them all. Should one of the groups created through the segmentation process provide food for a new canoe, however, other members of the original domestic unit do not obtain shares by virtue of that act.

Patongia division is recognized as an inevitable fact of social life, but it is regarded as unfortunate, and rarely will anyone admit to having caused it. Men often blame segmentation on alleged quarrelling among their wives. Sometimes they say simply that the group became too large and had to split. Others profess ignorance of the reason for the separation. I encountered but a single individual who admitted that his unit divided because he and his *taina* failed to get along. Such explanations are readily offered, however, by members of other units looking on from the outside. Division of a domestic unit occasionally takes place among brothers, but more frequently the rift occurs between cousins. It rarely takes place while a common male ascendant is alive.

Summary and Discussion

Anutan culture distinguishes the *patongia* as the elementary social unit. Despite some reservations, I have glossed it as the 'household.' It is defined in economic terms as the group that shares a common basket when food is distributed among the island's population; it is the unit that owns property, cooperates in production, and collectively looks after the welfare of its members. Admission into the *patongia* is gained primarily on the genealogical criterion of patrifiliation, but anyone who meets the fundamental requirement of eating (or having the right to eat) with the group on a regular basis is included on its roster. This may be accomplished through the formal processes of establishing a *kauapi*, *tauranga*, or *tau toa* relationship; or it may be done less formally by simply assuming the appropriate roles. Hence Ezekiel Taanaki (now Pu Ranigao), after his ritual circumcision, began living with Pu Nukurava, the *tuatina* who performed the operation. Ezekiel's brother, Solomon Manukapia (now Pu Raromanongi), spent much of his time in 1972–73 with his *tuatina*, Pu Akonima, since his father was deceased and his father's brothers had split from one another to form independent units, leaving Solomon's maternal uncle as his closest adult male relative. And Pakairipita, an unmarried woman in her thirties, had been living with her mother's brother, Pu Maevatau, from the time that her parents were lost at sea during the 1950s. In each case, the person was incorporated into the new unit and was considered when calculating how much food the group should get at general distributions. Ezekiel and Solomon retained their status in their natal group as well. Pakairipita, for all practical purposes, severed her ties with her natal household in the aftermath of her parents' death.

Leadership as well as membership in the domestic unit is determined by an interplay of genealogical and behavioral factors. A unit's most appropriate leader is the most senior male, but if this person is too old or otherwise not fully competent, he is expected to step down. By the time a man has reached his fifties or sixties, his eldest son has generally become a full adult with a wife and children of his own, and it is common to hand over the reins of power. The normal successor is the firstborn son of the unit's former head. This means that leadership should rest with the most genealogically senior competent male. Should the outgoing leader prefer someone in a genealogically less appropriate position to take his place, however, he is free to designate his chosen heir and override the genealogical principle.

Choosing a junior member to head a group is dangerous in that it may promote hard feelings between the leader and his senior relatives who have been made subordinate. The antagonism engendered by such an anomalous arrangement is sometimes a factor in promoting unit segmentation. If the *patongia* does hold together, leadership in the following generation should revert to the senior member of the most senior line. However, having tasted power, the juniors may choose to separate rather than submit to those who had been their subordinates. Thus, it is with reason that many Anutans look with disfavor upon assignment of leadership to a junior sibling. Yet, no one questions the right of an outgoing head to make such a decision, and in cases where the senior heir is unavailable (e.g., Pu Notau's absence from the island at the crucial time) or the junior is eminently more qualified on pragmatic grounds, a genealogically questionable appointment may be recognized as sensible and proper.

Aropa is expressed most intensely through sharing in the ownership, control, and utilization of material goods. Consequently, it receives its most constant and powerful expression within the household, as is amply demonstrated by repeated assertions of the correlation between *aropa* and the fact of "living together." Anutans consider it undesirable for units to divide, as this indicates a diminution of *aropa* among those who are party to the separation. However, division is recognized as an inevitable occurrence.

Aropa ideally varies in proportion to genealogical proximity, and we should understand the relative fragility of bonds connecting cousins as compared with siblings in this light. The domestic unit is conceptualized fundamentally in economic terms, and its maximum size is limited by the structural ramifications of its cultural definition.

These structural limitations also coincide with and reinforce the difficulty of maintaining strong emotional ties with a large group of people. Since the group cannot expand indefinitely, members must have some way of determining who is to remain inside and who will be excluded; and genealogical proximity provides a convenient criterion. On the other hand, *aropa* and genealogy are not always correlated in accordance with the ideal pattern, and cousins who maintain a common unit (as did Pu Paone and Pu Nukutapu for many years) are closer in all significant respects than brothers (like Pu Notau, Pu Akonima, and Pu Raveiti) who have seen fit to separate.

Chapter 5

Kindred and Marriage

Domestic groups may join together into larger units in several ways. One is through descent—a mechanism to be discussed in chapters 6 and 7. A second is through bonds established among individuals, bringing households together on the basis of their members' economic, ritual, and political relationships. Kindred and marital alliance fit into the latter category.

The term "kindred," in anthropological discourse, refers to a group of people connected to one another on the basis of their common attachment to a particular individual. Such a focal individual is known as "ego." Members of a bilateral kindred trace their connection to a shared ego through any combination of males and females within a fixed degree of genealogical distance. "Alliance," by contrast, usually denotes the establishment of relationships among independent social units through the exchange of personnel in the marriage process.

We in contemporary Western society are taught that marriage is an arrangement between two individuals based on personal attraction. Anthropologists, by contrast, recognize that such an understanding is unusual among world cultures. Often marriage partners are carefully selected by the families of the bride and groom; and frequently there is a certain type of relative whom one is expected to marry. Extensive ethnographic and historical analysis reveals that marriage is most commonly a mechanism through which social groups establish relationships of mutual economic and political support. Anuta is more typical than modern America in this respect.

The concept of alliance has been most productive in analysis of elementary kinship structures (Lévi-Strauss 1969[1949]). Such structures are found in communities that divide the opposite sex into clearly delineated classes of marriageable and non-marriageable persons. Elementary structures stipulate not only who is unavailable as a marriage partner (a negative rule based on the incest taboo); they also contain positive rules indicating the particular class of persons into which one *should* marry.

The Anutan marriage system is complex rather than elementary, as there are no positive rules but only incest prohibitions. Therefore, rather than producing a clearly defined exchange pattern, Anutan marriage creates an interlocking network of alliances among households. Similarly, the kindred organization, while apparently consisting of a set of individuals centered around a given ego, in fact, provides another means of bringing households into relationships of reciprocity and cooperation. Moreover, a man's in-laws are his child's maternal kin. Therefore, to whatever degree marriage cements a bond between two independent units, the tie is strengthened when the union has produced a child to serve as a focus of common interest. In other words, affinal and "consanguineal" kin are, at a certain level, distinct and counterposed. However, at another level they are kin of the same type, joined through a common relative by what Americans term "blood."

Ngutuumu ('Oven Sharers')

It sometimes happens that two or more domestic units decide to pool their resources and operate collectively in economic activities. They work together and share the produce of their gardens. They harvest and prepare food jointly. They eat together on the same coconut-leaf floor mat at island-wide feasts. And they often assist each other in sponsoring feasts or making ritual offerings. When such a relationship exists it is said of the domestic units, *te ngutuumu e tai* ('[they are of] the same *ngutuumu*'). Literally, *ngutu* means 'mouth' and *umu* is 'oven.' *Ngutuumu*, then, refers to two or more domestic units that share food cooked in the same oven.

Households in this relationship retain their distinct identities as separate units. Gardens, ovens, houses, and other forms of property continue to be controlled independently. While members of one unit use the others' property freely, this is only with the latter's approval. In general food distributions, each *patongia* receives a separate basket. Whether to merge their baskets or pool their food is up to them; but from the overall community's viewpoint, each household is an independent unit.

Households forming an alliance of this sort tend to be closely related through kinship, but this is not a definitive criterion. Thus, in the 1970s, Pu Paone shared his oven with the *patongia* of Pu Pareumutia (his mother's brother) and Pu Nukutamaaroa (his sister's husband). Yet he did not share a *ngutuumu* relationship with any of his father's brothers' children, with Pu Teaokena (his wife's brother, and the husband of his second sister), or with the units of Pu Tekoro or Pu Rangateatu (also brothers of Pu Paone's mother). Similarly, Pu Tokerau shared his oven with Pu Nukurava's household despite a fairly tenuous genealogical connection—Pu Toke was Pu Nukurava father's father's brother's wife's sister's son. By contrast, brothers who have divided their households rarely recombine; in fact, I know of not a single case where that has happened.

Personal attachment is an important factor in forming a *ngutuumu*. This probably accounts for the joining of the households of Pu Teukumarae, a former chief, and Pu Raropuko, the leading *maru* (see chapters 6 and 7) early in the twentieth century.[1] If fathers are close, their children are likely to spend a good deal of time together and will be encouraged to develop close relationships themselves. This combined with the inertia of tradition—established bonds are not dissolved without good reason—means that *ngutuumu* relationships tend to be passed on through the generations. The relationship between the units of Pu Nukurava and Pu Tokerau was established in the days of their *tupuna* (Pu Teukumarae was Pu Toke's paternal grandfather, and Pu Raropuko was the father of Pu Nukurava's father's father), and handed down from there.[2]

Finally, if one household becomes numerically decimated or does not have the material resources with which to carry on, it may ally with another domestic unit. This accounts for the relationship between Nau Tanukope and the junior chief (see chapter 4) and the earlier alliance between Pu Teaapua and the ancestors of the current Api Taneanu (for a discussion of the *api* see chapter 6).

In sum, the *ngutuumu* is an informal relationship, defined in terms of economic cooperation. It is a flexible, utilitarian arrangement, ultimately based on personal preference and mutual agreement. It is sensitive to genealogical relations, but these are often overridden by economic, demographic, or personal considerations. The *ngutuumu* is not a descent group since it is not ancestor-focused (see Goodenough 1955), nor is it ego-focused in the manner of the kindred. Still, 'oven sharing' provides a framework for independent *patongia* to operate together to fulfill their most important functions.

An Outline of the Kindred

The Anutan term *kano a paito* may be used with any of several referents. It can be applied in essentially the same manner as *api* and *pare* (see chapter 6) to indicate an ancestor-focused unit; it may refer to the aggregate of patrilateral kin; and it may be used with qualifications to designate kin on the mother's side as well as the father's.

Boundaries of the *kano a paito* shift with the context in which one is speaking. I have had Anutans tell me that any kinsperson, however related and however distant, is included in their *kano a paito*. At other times, I have been told that the *kano a paito* refers only to one's own domestic unit. Some Anutans assert that the mother's brother and assorted in-laws are excluded from one's *kano a paito*, while others insist that they are included—although with the reservation that "*te kano a paito e tai i te paai o te papine*" ('the *kano a paito* is the same [but] on the woman's side').

In other words, the *kano a paito* is not a group with constant borders. People disagree on who should be included and who does not belong, and even the same person may be inconsistent from one occasion to the next. If we conceptualize it in economic rather than genealogical terms, however, much of the apparent confusion disappears. When one asks Anutans why their domestic units have joined forces to form a *ngutuumu*, the most likely answer will be, "Because they are my *kano a paito*." In describing a ceremonial feast or ritual exchange, one is likely to explain that members of the *kano a paito* assisted with contributions of food and/or *koroa*—durable goods such as mats, fishhooks, paddles, or clothing. On different occasions a person might be aided by different relatives. Sometimes only one's closest kin may come to one's assistance; for more important rites, even the most distant relatives contribute. Also, a popular and influential person finds it easier to mobilize distant kin than someone who is less so.

Most important rites involve an exchange of food, and sometimes durable goods. A person, assisted by his or her paternal kin, usually constitutes one side of the exchange; the maternal kin comprise the other. Paternal kin express their *aropa* for ego through pooling resources, while ego and his or her maternal kin express their ties by means of reciprocity. Pooling (analogous to sharing at the level of the household) differentiates ego's "own" group from the "others," for whom reciprocal exchange constitutes the basis of interaction. Yet pooling and reciprocity, in a way, are aspects of a single integral process. Ego's group (ego and the body of paternal kin) pool their goods while the "other" group (ego's maternal kin) pool theirs. The two groups then come together and engage in ritual exchange.

As with other structural units in Anutan culture, the *kano a paito* is formed by an intersection of genealogical and behavioral principles. All kin are potentially members of one's *kano a paito*, but they are only such in fact when they act the part by cooperating with ego's *patongia* in the economic sphere, either by pooling resources or participating in a reciprocal exchange. Both forms of economic action are taken as expressing *aropa*, and I was told explicitly, "If you say that someone is of a different *kano a paito*, it means you do not *aropa* to him. If you say the *kano a paito* is the same, it means you *aropa* to him." It is no coincidence that the closest Anuta has to a generic term for 'kin' is *kano a paito*.

Firth (1963[1936]:213–17) describes the Tikopian *kano a paito* as a bilateral kindred. This designation also is apt for the Anutans as long as one remembers that there is a fundamental cleavage into ritually opposed sections. Moreover, one of those sections—*te paai o te papine*—only is included in the *kano a paito* with reservations.

Interpersonal Relations within the Kindred

The *kano a paito* brings together both a set of individuals acting on the basis of their ties to a common relative and the domestic unit to which the individuals belong and on behalf of which they act. First I will discuss the personal aspects of the Anutan kindred; then I will consider the forms of intergroup activity that are built around the different types of person.

Chapter 4 discussed the character of interpersonal relations among various types of kin. Relatives in all the categories discussed (except husband and wife) are found outside as well as within the bounds of the domestic unit. Interaction within the unit is particularly constant and intense, but more distant relatives should not be treated as qualitatively different. One may not deal with a distant *tamana* as frequently as with one's own father, and when such dealings do occur, the rules of etiquette may be enforced less strictly. Nevertheless, they exist and should be followed; any differences are of degree, not type. In addition to these kin classes, which are represented within the *patongia*, several others exist which by their very nature cannot be. They are as follows:

Tau Makitanga ('Father's Sister-Brother's Child')

The father's sisters and close female patrilateral parallel cousins may be in ego's own household. Upon reaching adulthood, however, they are expected to marry out—an event that often takes place before their brothers' children have been born. Therefore, even one's closest *makitanga* usually are in a different unit from oneself.

Anutans respect the *makitanga* and identify her with the *tamana*. Restrictions placed on freedom of interaction between the *tama* and *tamana* apply to the *tau makitanga* relationship as well, but in the case of a male ego they are modified somewhat by the sex difference. Therefore, in certain situations (e.g., when meeting on a path where one or the other must step aside), if the *tama* is an adult male the *makitanga* must defer. This contrasts with Tonga and Samoa where women outrank their brothers, and the respect due the father is intensified rather than diminished in dealing with his sisters or his female cousins.

A woman takes a great interest in the children of her *kave*. During the first few weeks of an infant's life, she may spend a good deal of time helping the mother. Even later, she spends much time with the *tau pae*, assisting the mother in her tasks or taking custody of the child for longer or shorter periods. Often a *makitanga* initiates adoption procedures. As in the *tau tamana* relationship, the prescribed restraint permeating relations between a *makitanga* and her *tama* is alleviated to some degree by strong ties of affection, which continually manifest themselves and are obvious even to a casual observer.

Tau Tuatina ('Mother's Brother-Sister's Child')

The mother's brother is part of the household that the mother left on marriage. It is structurally impossible, therefore, for ego and ego's *tuatina* to belong to the same domestic unit unless the child has been adopted. The *tuatina* is always "on the woman's side," and a member of this kin class represents the "other" group in ritual exchanges.

Along with the 'parallel sibling' relationship, relations with the 'mother's brother' are the freest and emotionally closest on Anuta. The *tuatina* and *iraamutu* may joke roughly and tease each other. Horseplay is permitted, and even striking each other is not forbidden. They have ready access to each other's property and are expected to lend mutual support.

A child tends to spend a great deal of time with the *tuatina*, visiting him at home and accompanying him at work. The maternal uncle plays an important role in teaching his sister's child skills that will be needed in later life as well as proper etiquette in interpersonal relations; and in the latter role, he is expected to discipline the child when necessary. This is particularly true when the 'nephew' is the "real" sister's son. The relationship in general is egalitarian and reciprocal. To the extent that a difference in honor and authority exists, however, it operates in favor of the senior generation. While the *iraamutu* is still a child, the difference is accentuated. This pattern differs from the anthropologically famous *fahu* relationship in Tonga, where the sister's son is said to be "above the law," and it is correlated with the fact that an Anutan man outranks his sisters. The hierarchical relationship between 'cross siblings' on Anuta also explains why the *makitanga* commands less deference than the *tamana*.[3]

Cross Cousins

Anthropologists distinguish several types of cousin. Among the most important of such distinctions is one between so-called parallel cousins (children of the father's brother or children of the mother's sister) and cross cousins (children of the father's sister or children of the mother's brother). This distinction is important to many of the people anthropologists study. Several types of kinship system distinguish terminologically between cross- and parallel cousins, and the two types of cousin are often treated differently as well. Usually parallel cousins are called by the same term that is used for siblings and treated in essentially the same manner as one's brothers or sisters, while cross cousins are often distinguished from siblings both terminologically and behaviorally. Among other things, this means that parallel cousins are usually prohibited as marriage partners, while cross cousins of opposite sex are often acceptable as marriage partners, or even actively preferred.

Anutans do not distinguish cross cousins of opposite sex from cross siblings or parallel cousins, either terminologically or in the rules that regulate their behavior. Sometimes, however, they place cross cousins of the same sex in a special category. They are known as *tau paanau pakapariki* ('parallel siblings in a bad—i.e., restrained—relationship'), and the deference one owes one's *makitanga* is carried over to her child.[4] Thus, a man may not discuss sex with, joke roughly with, verbally abuse, engage in horseplay with, or strike his *makitanga*'s son. The freedom one is permitted to exhibit toward one's *tuatina*, on the other hand, is also carried over so that the relationship is not reciprocal. A man, at least in theory, may hit or exhibit other forms of disrespectful behavior toward the son of his mother's brother should he so desire, and the recipient should accept his fate without protest. These comments theoretically apply with equal force to a woman and her female cross cousins.

While Anutans readily enunciated this view of the relationship between cross cousins of the same sex, I never witnessed such behavior. Indeed, I rarely observed any difference between the quality of interaction among cross- and parallel cousins. One consultant even claimed that the distinction between cross- and parallel cousins is not indigenous to Anuta but was imported from Tikopia. However, the presence of a distinct Anutan term (*tau paanau pakakovikovi*; see note #3) and the existence of the same discrepancy between theory and practice on Tikopia suggest that the distinction is one of long standing on both islands.

Tau Maa ('Parallel Siblings-in-Law')

The *tau maa* relationship is marked by respect and restraint. 'Siblings-in-law' of the same sex may engage in mild joking, but without sexual allusions. Practical joking is forbidden. *Tau maa* may not strike each other even in fun. They may not touch each other on the head or point their feet in each other's direction, and one may not stand while the other is seated in his or her presence. They may not turn their backs on each other when seated at close quarters or call each other by name. When using personal or possessive pronouns to address each other, they must use the dual form (*korua*) as a special index of affinal respect.

Tau maa, if male, are joined together by interest in a common woman (the *kave* of one and the wife or *taina papine* of the other) and her children (who are her husband's *tama* and her *kave's iraamutu*). Because of this, they share a common interest in each other's welfare and often assist each other in economic pursuits. When anyone requests assistance from his *maa*, the latter is supposed to be prompt and generous in his response.

Sisters-in-law and what I might call female cousins-in-law are also termed *tau maa*. Their behavioral requirements are similar to those in effect for brothers-in-law. A woman is the *makitanga* of her *maa's* offspring, and she may spend a good deal of time and effort in helping to care for her sister-in-law's children. She often takes mat-making material to the house of her brother's wife, where they spend many hours working together, and they assist each other in economic tasks. Despite the prescribed restraint which permeates this relationship, solid friendships may develop.

Taina Tangata-Taina Papine ('Cross Siblings-in-Law')

Both terminologically and behaviorally, the relationship between a man and his sisters-in-law or female "cousins-in-law" is modeled on the *tau paanau* relationship. Like parallel siblings and cousins of the same sex, they call each other *taina*; and their relationship is notable for its solidarity and freedom. They are free to joke and tease each other, and they even may discuss matters of sex. They refer to and address each other by proper names. Some Anutans say it is proper for them to use the dual form of the personal and possessive pronouns. However, it is not mandatory, and a few islanders even consider such usage incorrect as they feel it creates too much of a barrier. These relatives are preferred as marriage partners above all others.[5]

It may seem strange that siblings-in-law of opposite sex are called by the same term (*taina*) as siblings of the same sex. Tikopians, who have the identical practice, told Raymond Firth that they view a husband and wife as a unit. Therefore, a man calls his wife's sister by the same term that his wife uses (Firth 1963[1936]:231). Although Firth questions this interpretation, Anutan data lead me to view it as plausible. The Tikopian logic is further supported in the Anutan case by the fact that spouses address each other's parents by the same terms that they use for their own (*paapae*; *mana*; or *te maatuaa*).

Tau Pungona ('Parent-in-law and Child-in-law')

The *tau pungona* relationship is charged with restraint and respect very much on the order of the *tau tamana* or *tau pae*. This is seen terminologically in the use of *maatuaa* to designate one's parents and as a "title" or term of address for one's father-in-law. *Mana* and *paapae* are used to address the parents of one's spouse or siblings-in-law as well as one's own parents. Unlike the parent-child relationship, however, this one is reciprocal, with neither party inherently outranking the other and proper etiquette demanding that each side defer to the other whenever possible.[6] In general, restrictions on behavior between persons in this relationship resemble those applying to *tau maa*, except that they are even more rigidly enforced when different generations are involved. Economic cooperation is less in evidence among *tau pungona* than *tau maa*, as by the time the younger generation marries, members of the older generation generally have begun to reduce their level of activity.

Ritual Structure: Iki Nga Inati

Since the work of Arnold van Gennep in the early twentieth century, anthropologists have recognized that important changes of social status in most societies are marked by major ceremonies (van Gennep 1960[1908]). We term these "rites of passage" or "life crisis rites." On Anuta, all such ceremonies involve exchange of food, and often durables, among the various sections of one's bilateral kindred. In most ritual exchanges, one person in each section is singled out to represent that section, to serve as the primary center of attention, and to receive the principal presents. Both these focal persons and the presents they receive are termed *inati*, and the process is designated *iki nga inati* ('carrying the *inati*').

On most occasions, the *inati* are three: *te pai maatuaa* ('the making of parents' or 'the making of fathers'), *te pai makitanga* ('the making of father's sisters'), and *te pai tuatina* ('the making of the mother's brothers').[7] A critical feature of this arrangement, however, is that *maatuaa*, *makitanga*, and *tuatina* do not refer, in this context, to the biological father, father's sister, and mother's brother. Rather, the *inati* are structured in such a way as to maximize the diversification of connections among extended family households and reinforce ties within the *kainanga*, a unit that I will provisionally gloss as 'clan' (see chapter 6). Most notably, they reinforce the bonds between the household of the chief or clan leader and those of his constituents.

Normally the *pai maatuaa* offering is taken to the head of ego's clan, or rather, to the senior man in ego's father's generation who is in the clan leader's *patongia*. If this man is absent or deceased, his eldest available brother or son is substituted.

The *inati* cannot be carried to a member of one's own domestic unit, so if ego is a member of the chief's (or clan head's) *patongia*, the offering must be made to another household within the clan. Marriage to the child of one's own *inati*, moreover, is a violation of rules regarding incest and exogamy. Yet on occasion it occurs; and when it does, the present must be carried elsewhere to restore the proper order. Since Pu Paone's wife was the sister of the senior chief, for example, his children's *pai maatuaa* could not go to the chief's domestic unit. Neither was it taken to other members of the Api Taneanu—that is, the households headed by Pu Paone's patrilateral parallel first cousins, Pu Notau, Pu Akonima, and Pu Raveiti—since the division of one domestic unit into four occurred in the past generation, making their relationship too close as well. This left only the households of Pu Maravai and Pu Nukurava, the two remaining domestic units in Pu Paone's clan. As far as I can tell the choice between these two was arbitrary.

Personal attraction and antagonism provide a final basis for altering the *pai maatuaa* presentation. If ego's parents are angry at the unit to whom the *inati* would normally be carried, they may express their feelings by taking the presents elsewhere. This is rare in the first two clans, as such behavior usually would mean slighting a chief. In the Kainanga i Pangatau (the third-ranking clan and one of the two that is not led by a chief), it is more frequent. The Kainanga i Rotomua (the fourth and lowest ranking of the island's clans) has only one domestic unit. Therefore, its *pai maatuaa* offerings must be carried to a different clan. For several generations, they have been taken to the domestic unit of Pu Nukumarere and Pu Nukuriaki—one of the middle-ranking units in the Kainanga i Pangatau. Regardless of how the choice is made, however, the relationship is passed down in the paternal line. If A's *pai maatuaa* is carried to B, that of A's son is carried to the son of B, that of A's paternal grandson is carried to the paternal grandson of B, and so on. This relationship is maintained indefinitely until such time as it is ended by an inappropriate marriage or a personal feud, at which point a new and equally enduring relationship is formed.

The recipient of the *pai makitanga* offering ordinarily is the eldest sister of the *pai maatuaa*, although if this man has no sister or other close *kave*, the present may go to his eldest daughter or the daughter of his brother or male cousin—whoever is the most senior female to have been born into his domestic unit.[8]

The *pai tuatina* represents the mother's side and is normally the son of the man to whom the mother's *pai maatuaa* was presented, although, again, the pattern may be interrupted by personal incompatibility or a poorly chosen marriage. For example, the *pai tuatina* of the first chief's wife, Nau Koroatu, was given to Pu Pangatau. A sister of the chief, however, married her *inati* in the person of Pu Pangatau's brother's son. For that reason, the chief's line could no longer make *inati* presentations to that household, and his son's *pai tuatina* was given to another group.

The parents and their *patongia* have a degree of flexibility in determining where their children's *inati* gifts will be taken prior to the birth of their first child. Once that birth has been marked by the *pai paanaunga* ('birth recognition' ritual), however, the *inati* of all their children are set for the remainder of their lives. At all future rites of passage, the *pai maatuaa*, *pai makitanga*, and *pai tuatina* offerings will be carried to the same domestic unit—and, if possible, to the same persons—as they were during the *paanaunga*. The birth ceremony is performed only for a couple's firstborn son and firstborn daughter. In most other rites, junior siblings are 'stuck' (*pakapipiki*) onto a senior sibling or cousin, and the *inati* gifts depend on the oldest sibling. On occasions where a ritual relation must be invoked for a junior sibling directly, as in the exchanges surrounding a marriage, one follows the patterns set initially at the *paanaunga* of the firstborn.

Anutans have a form of what anthropologists call dual symbolic organization (see, e.g., Lévi-Strauss 1967, 1969[1949]:chapter 6; Needham 1973), meaning that they tend to organize their universe into sets of paired oppositions.[9] Such a cultural predilection does not sit easily with the *inati*'s tripartite structure, and the Anutans resolved this dilemma by creating an additional division of the kindred, known as the *pai tupuna*. The *pai tupuna* is presented to the parents of the *pai tuatina*, and in this way a second gift is added to the mother's side to counterbalance the two on the father's. The *pai tupuna* is not presented at the *paanaunga* ceremony, and at later ones it is optional, but the very fact of its dispensability accentuates its structural importance. In terms of practical consequences it is redundant, since the domestic unit receiving this gift would be presented with a *pai tuatina* offering in any case. Rather, the *pai tupuna* serves to maintain a conceptual balance in ritual exchange within the kindred. The ritual structure of the kindred as reflected in the *inati* is outlined in figure 5.1.

Life Crises

Thus far I have presented this account in highly schematic terms. In practice, different relationships are important in different rites. At times, focal relatives or other members of the focal relatives' households are critical. Sometimes all members of a particular kin class may play a collective role, while at other times the *inati* are central. Sometimes exchanges are limited to the paternal side, occurring only between ego's domestic unit and those of his or her *makitanga*. And on one occasion (as part of the rite surrounding a boy's circumcision), all the women of his kindred, *makitanga* and *pae* alike, work together in preparing food for presentation to the *tuatina*. The complexity and variation in Anutan patterns of ritual exchange will become apparent in the following summary of the island's major rites of passage.

Pai Paanaunga ('Birth Recognition')

Shortly following the birth of a couple's first son, and again after the birth of their first daughter (*urumatua tangata* and *urumatua papine*), a major rite takes place. This is known as the *pai paanaunga*, and Anutans say it is performed in honor of the mother and her child.

On the first night of an infant's life, the *makitanga* bring presents of *koroa* ('durable goods') for the child's parents. Then, for the next several nights, they come to stay in the baby's house in order to assist the mother while she regains her strength. All the baby's *makitanga*—

	Father's Side	Mother's Side
Central	*pai maatuaa*	*pai tuatina*
Peripheral[a]	*pai makitanga*	*pai tupuna*

[a] The *pai makitanga* is peripheral in the sense that she is not normally of the *pai maatuaa's* unit. The *pai tupuna* is peripheral in the sense that it is optional, but when included it always is presented to the same house as the *pai tuatina*.

Figure 5.1   The Ritual Structure of the Kindred.

distant as well as close—are free to participate in this activity, but no specific individual is required to attend. Sometimes one woman will be there every night throughout the period; in other cases, a different woman or group of women may participate each night as they distribute the responsibility. With the commencement of the *paanaunga* ceremony, this procedure comes to a halt.

The *paanaunga* rite requires a good supply of fish and vegetables. Therefore, its timing depends largely upon the weather. When an adequate supply has been collected, the populace begins preparing food. The households on the father's side work together as one unit; those whose closest tie is with the mother work together as another.

Once the food has been prepared it is brought to the house of the child, where the father and his close relatives begin a general distribution. Every *patongia*, each of the chiefs, the catechist, and each of his assistants is given a basket as in any normal distribution; but in addition the *pai maatuaa*, *pai makitanga*, and *pai tuatina* receive at least one basket apiece. These baskets are carried to the houses of the *inati*, but the contents are not consumed by the recipients' respective households. Rather, all the child's *tamana* eat together in the house of the *pai maatuaa*. All the *makitanga* eat in the *pai makitanga*'s house, and all the *tuatina* eat with the *pai tuatina*.[10] In the one *paanaunga* ceremony that I witnessed, 21 baskets of food were presented by the child's paternal kindred; ten by the maternal kin. The ten baskets from the mother's side plus nine from the father's were distributed among the 19 *patongia* that existed at the time. Two baskets for the chiefs, three for the catechist and his assistants, three for the crew of the canoe that contributed the fish, three for the three branches of the *inati*, and one for the mother of the infant all came from the gardens of the child's paternal kin.

Paangai Ika ('Fish Feeding')

Burying the umbilical cord, baptism, and weaning are all important events in a young child's life, but they are not marked by major feasts or ceremonial exchange. After the *paanaunga*, the next major ceremony is the *paangai ika* (*paangai* = 'to feed'; *ika* = 'fish'), which accompanies feeding the baby its first fish at about a year of age. Like the *paanaunga*, this ritual is performed only for the firstborn daughter and the firstborn son.

On the first day of the ceremony, the child's maternal grandfather (not the *inati*) or a member of the grandfather's domestic unit takes the baby up the hill for its first look at that section of the island. This is known as *te pakamatamata* ('the showing around').

In the meantime all the *patongia* of the island prepare oven food. In the evening the food is presented on the father's behalf to the man who took his baby to the mountain. Kin on the mother's side—at least one representative from each household—feast in the *tupuna*'s house while the father's relatives eat outside.

The following morning, the child's maternal kin return, and the feast continues. When the meal is over the host gives out durable goods (*koroa*) to his guests, who reciprocate with equivalent or slightly larger presents of their own. This exchange takes place among the child's maternal kin.

About a week after the first activities, the mother's kin gather to present fish and vegetable food to the child's father on the maternal grandfather's behalf. The father sends for his close relatives to join him in his house, and there is another feast—this a mirror image of the one the week before. The child's paternal kin eat inside the father's house, with others gathering to eat outside. No exchange of durables takes place, however, at this time.

Angaa ('Initiation')

At some point, each child is expected to go through a major cere-mony known as the *angaa*. There are several types of *angaa*, the most important of which is that done for the firstborn male and others who are 'attached' for purposes of the ritual. This is the *angaa pora koroa* ('the *angaa* of spreading goods'). Anutans say the father sponsors it to honor and demonstrate affection for his son. It may occur at any time in the course of childhood, although between the age of six and ten is typical. It lasts for an entire week, and in terms of time as well as material expense, it is the greatest ceremonial event in the life of a child. No *angaa* took place during the period of my initial research, but Pu Paone gave me a detailed account of the ceremony as typically performed for boys. The highlights are as follows.

The father and his *patongia* must prepare for many months, planting and cultivating so they might have the wherewithal to hold the feast. As the event approaches, members of the boy's domestic unit, assisted by the *kano a paito*, gather food and bake it in their ovens. While this is going on, the child's *inati*—in this case the *pai makitanga*, *pai tuatina*, and *pai tupuna*—send for all the child's *makitanga*, *tuatina*, and *tupuna* respectively to come and eat at the house where the cere-mony is taking place. The *pai tuatina* takes the child around to the houses of all the *tuatina*, and at each house the initiate is given pre-sents of durables. The child brings these back to the *tamana*'s house and then begins the circuit of his *makitanga*. They also present dura-bles, which the child brings back home.

When this is done the relatives all come together inside the house of the youngster's parents or some other *tamana* within the boy's domestic unit, and they begin the feast. The *tuatina*'s food is piled in the foremost portion of the house (*mataapare* [*mata* = 'face' or 'front'; *pare* = 'house']), the position of highest honor, and that is where they sit to eat. The *makitanga* gather around their food which has been piled in the rear (*tuaumu* [*tua* = 'back'; *umu* = 'oven']), the spot of lowest ritual esteem, while the *tupuna*'s food is at the (neutral) ends. There is no separate allotment for the child in whose honor the ceremony is performed. The primary initiate, along with any sibling who has been 'attached.' is seated in the center of the house and shares the supplies of all three groups of kin. The parents, assisted by others of the boy's *tamana*, remain at the ovens during these proceedings. They spend all day preparing food that has been taken from the gardens of the father and his *kano a paito*.

For the entire week, the feasting continues in the house of the *angaa*. The participants practice singing dance songs, and on the last two days of the affair, a dance takes place inside the house—an act which normally is *tapu* ('taboo'). On the final day, the dance begins inside the house and then moves inland to the ovens, where food has been prepared for the arrival of the party. There the relatives resume the feast. Before they leave, they are given large quantities of uncooked food, which they all take home, prepare, and in the evening bring back to the house of the *angaa*. Between the food presented by the *pai makitanga*, *pai tuatina*, and *pai tupuna*, plus that prepared by the father and his *kano a paito*, as many as two hundred baskets may be brought together. People feast outside the house, and the child partakes with each section of the kindred in its turn.

At this point, the *angaa* is finished, but there is a sequel. The *pai makitanga*, *pai tuatina*, and *pai tupuna* make return gifts of food to the child's parents. This is called the *aererepanga ki muri*.

Two varieties of *angaa* are held for girls. Both are simpler than the ceremony for a boy. The more complex of the two resembles the boys' *angaa* except that there is no gift of durables, and the distribution of raw food is not made. Moreover, there is no *pai tupuna* section. In the other version, the *pai tuatina* also is eliminated, and the participants are limited to the father's side—the girl's *tamana* and *makitanga*. This is a smaller, more modest affair, involving fewer people. It also differs from the others in that the dance does not take place, and it is most likely to occur when a scarcity of resources makes the more elaborate form impossible.

Anthropologists most often use the term "initiation" to designate a child's transition into adulthood. Initiation rites, thus, tend to occur around the time of puberty. The Anutan *angaa* generally takes place considerably earlier—clearly, a child below the age of ten is unlikely to be incorporated into adult society. Still, this procedure's complexity and the resources expended on it suggest that it marks an important transition. Significantly, it takes place after a child has passed the age where infant mortality is a grave danger, where the child has learned to speak well, and where one begins to show self-consciousness about one's state of dress and physical appearance. In Anutan terms, the child is no longer *kovi* ('bad') or *vare* ('incompetent'). Perhaps we may best understand the *angaa*, then, as initiating the child into full membership—even if not *adult* membership—in the Anutan community.

Vai Pa

Anutans mark a boy's return from his first voyage to Patutaka by a ceremony called the *vai pa*. Upon arrival at Anuta, one of the initiate's *makitanga* carries him on her back from the beach to her house, where he is washed with a warm infusion of fragrant leaves and presented with a welcome feast. One of the *makitanga* then invites him to her house, where he takes his meals for the next two weeks or so, until the rite is concluded by a feast called *te pakatavanga*, sponsored by the *makitanga's* clan to honor the young man. During the period that the initiate is eating at his *makitanga's* house, his own domestic unit repeatedly makes presents of food to that of the woman who has agreed to feed him. Often a boy's *angaa* is timed to coincide with his first fishing trip in a canoe. If not, an abbreviated version of the *vai pa* is performed to recognize and sanction that event.

Puru Nga Kere ('Circumcision')

Around the onset of puberty, a boy undergoes a rite of circumcision—a rite that Anutans term *puru nga kere*, literally 'cleansing the dirt.' Like the *angaa*, this ritual is performed primarily for the eldest son, while younger brothers and sons are 'stuck on' as appendages. There is no comparable rite for girls.

Sometimes the *angaa pora koroa* is postponed until the time of circumcision, in which case they are held together. Otherwise the ceremony consists of another type of *angaa*, known as *te pakavao*. I did not see this rite performed, but it was described to me by Pu Tokerau, Pu Pouro, and Pu Paone. The following is a summary of their descriptions.

The timing of the circumcision rite is determined by the youngster's age and the condition of his household's gardens. When a boy reaches eleven or twelve, he becomes eligible, but sometimes it is not performed until one is as old as fifteen. When preparations have been made and supplies are sufficiently abundant, the parents inform the man whom they desire to perform the operation. Normally this is the individual to whom the *pai tuatina* offering was carried in the *paanaunga* and any earlier *angaa*. However, if this man's competence is questioned, a substitute may be requested. In such a case, the substitute should be the most senior available competent man in the *pai tuatina*'s domestic unit.

The operation is performed outdoors. If it is being held in conjunction with the *angaa pora koroa*, it is done in the vicinity of the initiate's house; otherwise it is performed out in the bush. All the boy's *tuatina* may be present, and no one else is permitted to see the operation. Only two men touch the child, the *tipunga* ('surgeon') and one assistant.[11] The others stand around to watch and give encouragement.

While the operation is performed, the parents of the boy are busy making puddings. When this is done, the *tuatina* return to the initiate's house and eat. The parents present the *tipunga* with a new pandanus mat on which he will sleep in their house until the wounds have healed.[12] The boy's *pae* and *makitanga* lavish him with mats and other goods. This is called the *pare pae* ('house of mothers').

While the child is recovering from the operation, the *tipunga* remains at his side, and the boy's parents supply the pair with food. After a month or so, when the wounds have healed, the ceremony is ended with a rite known as *te panopano o nga nima o te tipunga* ('the washing of the surgeon's hands'). On this occasion, the whole island contributes food and durables to the *tipunga* on behalf of the boy's parents, and the parents 'wash' the *tuatina*'s hands with turmeric pigment—a symbolic cleansing of ritual pollution from the hands that have handled a defiling organ and been contaminated with blood.[13]

Aavanga ('Wedding')

As with other rites of passage, the marriage ceremony involves exchange of goods. The kindreds of two individuals rather than just one, however, are involved in the exchange. Moreover, this rite differs from the others in that a woman transfers her primary affiliation from one domestic unit to another. Here I describe the mobilization and alignment of kin and the exchange of goods in the marriage rites themselves. The structural implications of the marriage system for establishing alliances through the exchange of personnel will be considered in the following section.

There is no formal period of courtship on Anuta. Men and women are not expected to pair off into couples prior to engagement, and premarital sexual relations are forbidden by the church, although they sometimes do occur.

Boys and girls come to know each other as they play and work together during childhood and adolescence. When a man decides that he would like to marry, he consults with his parents about his proposed bride. If his parents approve he sends an emissary to the woman, bearing presents of tobacco, bath soap, cloth, or other goods. Most commonly, the emissary is the young man's mother or sister, although the father, brother, or other close relative or friend may go instead.[14] If the woman is amenable, she accepts the presents and may send return gifts for the man. The exchange of gifts is called *te pakakoroa*. At this point, the couple are formally engaged, and people refer to them as *tau toa*. This expression usually means 'friends' and can include a boyfriend/girlfriend relationship. In the present context, it has the more formal connotation of 'fiancés.'

The timing of the wedding rites is up to the parents of the bride and groom. On the designated evening, the parents of the man send word to members of their son's *kano a paito* on both the paternal and maternal sides to join them and the couple in their house. The groom's kindred then assembles, bringing gifts of durables—mats, canoe paddles, fishhooks, fishing line, and other non-comestibles—from each of their *patongia* to be presented to the bride's domestic unit. The woman's hair is cut short in the man's house by his *pai makitanga*, aided by the *pai makitanga*'s own close female kin. The bride is painted with turmeric pigment and then dressed in a ceremonial barkcloth skirt, provided by the groom's kin.

When all of these procedures are complete, the group of kin assembled in the groom's house goes en masse to the house of the bride's parents to present their gifts. This is known as *te maarai*, the term for a formal request. There they press noses with the members of the woman's kindred. After this the pair are called *te rumatua* ('a married couple').

In former days, Anutans say that they practiced a kind of "marriage by capture" similar to that described by Firth for Tikopia (1963 [1936]:chapter 13), and the *maarai* offerings were seen as atonement by the man's group for taking a woman from the bride's. Members of the man's group pressed their noses to the knees of members of the woman's group as a gesture of contrition, and all of this was done amid mock fighting that would, at times, get out of hand. The custom was abolished on the order of Pu Teukumarae, grandfather of the present senior chief, who insisted that a marriage ought to be a happy occasion, not one for quarrelling and combat. He also objected to the view that one group must abase itself by pressing their noses to the knees of the other—it was his decision that, henceforth, relatives of the bride and groom would press nose to nose as a sign of equality between the two groups.

Considering Anuta's size and the high rate of island endogamy, everyone is likely to be kin to both the bride and groom. Choices must be made, therefore, as to the side with which an individual and his or her domestic unit will affiliate when a wedding occurs. If someone clearly is related more closely to one party than the other, there may be little difficulty, but the matter often is ambiguous. A person who is related closely to both sides may go to one house and have another member of the domestic unit participate with the other. Alignment based on individual preference, stemming from the quality of inter-personal relations, may further complicate the picture.

The night of the *maarai* offering, the couple sleeps together in the house of the groom. The next morning they are married in the church, and preparations begin for the wedding feast. If the sea is reasonably calm, one or two canoes go out that afternoon to provide fish for the festivities; if the passage is too rough, the community holds a fish drive on the fringing reef. At the same time, vegetable food is har-vested and cooked to be donated to the feast. Each domestic unit con-tributes something, but a disproportionate amount comes from the gardens of the groom's *patongia*. The groom's eldest sister's husband is known as *te tokomatua*, and he plays a special role, along with the catechist and perhaps the chiefs, in organizing these activities.

The feast is held the next day. Then, for the next two to three weeks, each day a different household brings presents of food to the newly married couple. In theory the man's relatives are supplying him with food, and the woman's kin are supplying her. In practice, all food is accepted by the couple and shared with the man's household. This practice is called *te uke rongi* ('the basket opening').

Approximately one year after the wedding, a rite known as *te pakatataanga o nga ariki* is performed in honor of the chiefs. Each domestic unit on the island contributes food, but the bulk comes from the husband's gardens, with a slightly smaller quantity provided by the natal unit of the wife. A basket of food is presented to each of the domestic units, and large baskets of especially prized foods are given to each of the two chiefs. The population gathers in the vicinity of the chiefs' houses, where they take their meals for the next day or two until the ceremonial foods all have been consumed.

Pariki ('Funeral')

Most post-marital involvement in life crisis rites is either as a parent sponsoring a ceremony for one's child or as someone else's *inati*. Illness, of course, may occur at any point in one's life, and when it does, other households express their concern by sending food. Large parcels of the most esteemed foods are sent by the mother's brother, who spends a great deal of time with the victim, giving what emotional support he can during the period of recovery. Anyone about to leave Anuta for a lengthy period takes a ceremonial meal and receives presents from each of the island's domestic units. This is followed by a period of ritual wailing with representatives from each unit. When returning from a protracted stay abroad, one takes a meal in turn with each of the *patongia*. The major post-marital rite through which every Anutan will eventually go, however, is the funeral.

When an Anutan dies, word immediately is spread throughout the island. The community divides itself into several groups on what seems to be an ad hoc basis, and each group begins to practice a different funeral dirge to be sung in the house of the deceased. One after another, the groups of mourners file into the house, and each group spends about an hour wailing before it is replaced by another one.

Each household sends at least one representative to wail over the body, while other members prepare food that will be used to feed the mourners. After the various contingents have finished wailing, they proceed from house to house, partaking of the food that has been prepared, until they have eaten with each domestic unit but that of the deceased.

When the mourners have finished their circuit of the island, the corpse is painted with turmeric pigment, dressed in new clothes, and wrapped in several layers of pandanus mats and bark cloth sheets. It is carried to the church for a final service, and then on to the graveyard where the mother's brothers and their close kin have dug a grave in the sand, about six feet deep. The mourners gather around the grave and lay the body inside, the catechist recites some final prayers, fragrant leaves are tossed in as a gesture of farewell, and the grave is refilled with sand.

After the funeral is over, the domestic unit of the deceased gives presents of durable goods—and sometimes even property as valuable as garden plots—as compensation to the men who dug the grave. This transfer of property is known as *te punepu*. Awarding land to the mother's brother's household serves to counterbalance, at the level of cultural rules, the practice of a man presenting gardens to his (prospective) sister's son upon a woman's marriage. As a matter of social practice, however, the frequency of including gardens in a funeral exchange is low.

Kin on both sides may assist the family of the deceased in its *punepu* payments. The main recipient of these gifts is the mother's brother of the deceased rather than the *inati*. If the mother has no surviving brothers, or if they are too old or infirm to participate in digging the grave, the offerings are given to the senior active male in the mother's patriline. That man may then distribute the presents among the other gravediggers.

It should now be evident that every Anutan has a wide-ranging kindred which, on various occasions, may include the entire island's population.[15] The kindred is subdivided in many ways, and depending on the occasion, one or another of the subdivisions may play the leading role. While on one level, interaction among members of an ego-centered kindred is phrased in individual terms, it must be remembered that property is owned not by individuals but by domestic units. Therefore, when one acts in a ritual exchange, one is acting on behalf of the entire group. When one gives presents, they are taken from the *patongia*'s resources, and it may be any member of the domestic unit whose efforts are embodied in the product that is ultimately given. Similarly, the gift may be presented to a particular individual, but once it has been presented, it becomes the property of that person's unit as a whole. In this way each household has ties with every other, either through pooling of resources for purpose of exchange with another set of households or through the medium of prestation and counterprestation, which creates an intricate network of reciprocal exchanges. Since the kindred is ego-centered, and there are well over three hundred different egos in the population, each domestic unit is bound to be allied with every other via pooling on some occasions and reciprocity on others. In cases where a particular unit is equally close to both sides in an exchange, it may even contribute resources and send representatives to each side in the course of the proceedings. Thus, the kindred system ties together all the island's semi-independent elementary units by a flow of goods among them, through the mechanisms of reciprocity and redistribution. Through this flow of goods along largely genealogical paths, the *patongia* are brought together into a single kinship community, held together ideologically by bonds of *aropa*.

Marital Alliance

In many ways, the marriage system is an extension of the kindred. The marital bond creates a close relationship between the households of the husband and the wife. The marriage ritual involves a complex set of exchanges of food and durables as well as a shift in the allegiance of the woman from the domestic unit of her parents to that of her husband. As time goes on, a man's affinal relatives become his child's maternal kin—a fact that Anutans mark in their classification of the *tuatina*, along with the *maa* and the *pungona*, as being "on the woman's side."

Anuta does not have marriage classes or "sections," and the closest that it has to a positive marriage rule is a mild preference for a man to take a *taina papine* for his spouse. The closer the *taina papine*, the more appropriate the choice, and a man's ideal marriage partner is said to be the sister of his brother's wife. Such a marriage reinforces an alliance that has already been established, and it maintains the social and economic solidarity of sisters by bringing them into the same *patongia*. However, a man does not have a *taina papine* until someone of his generation marries. Up to that time, all female relatives in his generation are classed as *kave*. Thus, no positive preferences may be inferred from the alliance pattern of the parents' generation.

More important for Anuta are proscriptions specifying whom one may not marry. The rule is that close kin must be avoided. Close, however, is relative. Consequently, incest rules express degrees of impropriety rather than absolute prohibition. Marriage to a third cousin or anyone more distant usually does not arouse concern. Marriage to a second cousin is looked upon with disfavor, and to wed a first cousin is definitely taboo. In fact, I could find only two instances in which such marriages have taken place, and they are thought to be

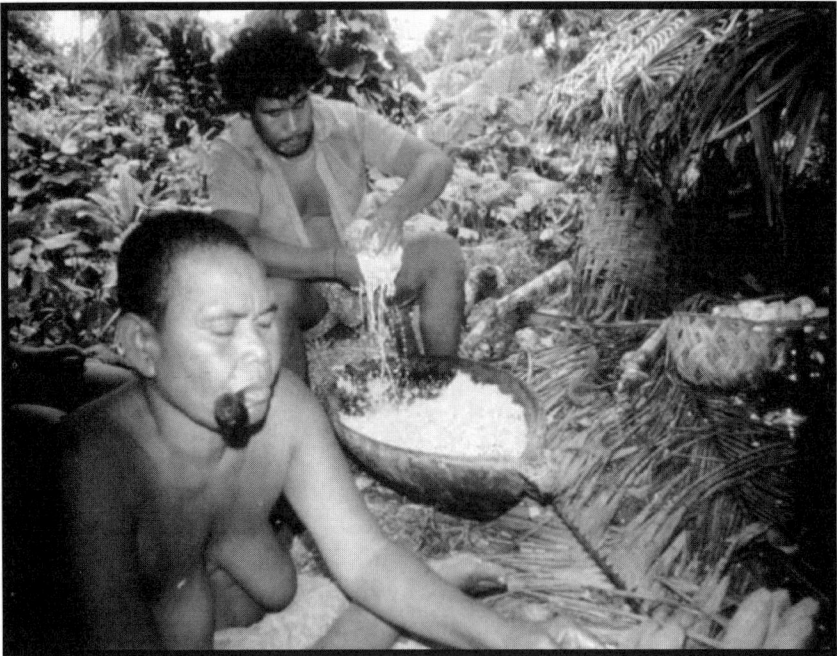

Photo 5.1 Domestic units connected by marriage are expected to provide mutual assistance. Here Pu Parikitonga (Harry Mataki) expresses cream from grated coconut while his father's sister, Nau Paone, peels bananas to prepare a pudding in 1983.

a serious breach of proper custom. In a famous case sometime during the 1950s, the son of the then junior chief almost exiled a couple to the ocean when a member of his clan married his father's brother's daughter. This was an especially egregious case because the couple, in addition to being first cousins, were members of the same domestic unit. At the last moment, the chief's son relented and allowed the pair to remain on Anuta, but the animosity has not been put to rest.[16]

Close extragenealogical kin are forbidden just as if they had a genealogical connection, and Anutans consider the idea of marriage to one's full sibling, the *kave maori, nga maatuaa e tai*, to be utterly absurd. The latter point was powerfully impressed on me by Pu Nukurava's response when questioned on this matter. After asking him about the possibility of marriage to various cousins, I inquired into the propriety of brother-sister marriage. His reaction was ten minutes of uncontrolled laughter followed by another five of chuckles as he fought to regain his composure. For the next two weeks or so, every time he saw me he would mutter with an air of good-humored bemusement, "Marry your *kave, nga maatuaa e tai!*" The Anutans' lack of concern about the possibility of incest between close *kave* is also evident in the fact, as noted above, that they are permitted to sleep on the same mat, and even under the same covers. Such close association between siblings or close cousins of opposite sex would be unthinkable in most of west Polynesia.

In addition to relatives who are excluded on grounds of genealogical closeness, one may not marry into the domestic units of the *inati, tauranga*, or *toa*. The child of one's step-parent is equally forbidden, and a prohibition against marrying into one's adoptive unit led to a well-known case of murder according to oral traditions.

The Anutans have what Lévi-Strauss (1969[1949]) called a complex rather than an elementary marriage structure. Nonetheless, alliance between groups of affines is important as a feature of the island's social life. In particular, it is central to the kindred system, drawing together an intricate network of domestic units into a set of working, cooperating, reciprocating, exchanging relationships. The prohibition against marrying close relatives means that each domestic unit is constantly reaching out to create new bonds with groups to which it does not already have strong ties of kinship. By tracing proximity bilaterally, it is assured that an individual will reach out to distant kin and reinforce the bonds that otherwise would be weakest. And since a man must seek a woman in some unit other than that from which his father took a wife, each generation must produce a set of alliances which differs from that of the preceding one.

The prohibition on marriage into the unit of one's *inati* may be seen from the same perspective. Since the *pai maatuaa* is always presented within one's own clan, and usually to the clan leader or chief, incest regulations force a degree of exogamy upon a unit that has no formal rule proscribing marriage among its members. In this way, bonds among the island's *kainanga* are reinforced through marriage, and the chief, who receives *inati* gifts from virtually all his clan's domestic units, is nearly always forced to marry out.

All Anutans have strong ties with their *inati*'s households—ties which are emphasized repeatedly throughout their lives without requiring the reinforcement of a marital bond. Therefore, to marry someone in the unit of one's *inati* would have the effect of creating what one might think of as a superfluous relationship and "waste" a marriage that could otherwise be used to substitute a close affinal connection for a distant "consanguineal" one. Since a man cannot take his wife from his own domestic unit, from those of his close relatives on either his father's or his mother's side, from those of his *inati* or anyone he serves as *inati*, from that of his adoptive parents, or from that of his *toa*, all the groups with which he would have close ties without the necessity of marriage are precluded. As a result, he is forced to marry someone from a group whose relationship to his own needs reinforcement, and the marriage system promotes the widest possible diffusion of powerful bonds among all the domestic units on the island. On the other hand, the number of units from which one should not take a spouse, combined with the community's small size, makes it is easy to see why incest rules must be put forth as relative constraints rather than absolute prohibitions.

Lévi-Strauss distinguished two common types of alliance that are compatible with elementary structures. Symmetrical alliance involves "restricted exchange," where two groups of people continually marry back and forth. In such a system, a man from "Group A" marries a woman from "Group B," and vice versa. Asymmetric alliance, by contrast, involves generalized exchange, where three or more groups continually exchange spouses in the same direction. This means that women from "Group A" marry men from "Group B," women from "Group B" marry men from "Group C," and women from "Group C" marry men from "Group A," thereby completing the cycle.[17] Symmetrical alliance systems tend to be egalitarian, while asymmetric systems tend to be hierarchical, with "wife takers" either outranking or being outranked by "wife givers."

From one perspective, Anutan marriage closely resembles a system of generalized exchange but on a diachronic rather than a synchronic plane. Due to the bilateral nature of incest prohibitions and the fact that a man's immediate affines are his children's close "consanguines" on their mother's side, the most appropriate source of spouses in one generation is among the least appropriate in the next. As the generations go by, this source gradually becomes more appropriate again, until eventually another marriage is consummated and the cycle starts anew. Unlike an elementary structure, however, this is a consequence of negative proscriptions rather than positive injunctions, and it takes place in the absence of clearly circumscribed marriage classes. It serves to maximize the web of marital alliances, but without a neatly delineated system in which Group A gives women to Group B, B gives to C, and C gives back to A.

The character of the Anutan marriage system as one of the complex variety is confirmed by the fact that neither side in an affinal alliance outranks the other. In fact, not only are wife givers and wife takers indistinguishable in honorific terms; they are not distinct at all. A man's sister-in-law is preferred as a prospective wife, but the direction of the marriage is not stipulated. Therefore, the marriage of a man and his sister to a woman and her brother is as acceptable and frequent as a pair of brothers marrying a pair of sisters. This is also correlated with the absence of a *fahu*-type relationship such as that found in Fiji and Tonga, where a man's sister's son is given extreme license and even sometimes said to be "above the law."

Lévi-Strauss (1969[1949]) characterized systems like that which I have described for Anuta as being of the "Crow-Omaha" type, and he suggested that such systems are transitional in the evolution of complex out of elementary structures. Most communities with Crow-Omaha systems, however, have a distinctive type of kinship nomenclature in which certain cross-cousins are called by the same term that ego uses for certain aunts or uncles.[18] Anuta's kinship system, like those of other Polynesian communities, emphasizes the separation of generations and lacks the distinctive Crow-Omaha type of kinship terminology. This suggests intriguing questions as to how the island's marriage system came to be what it is today. While this book's purpose is not historical reconstruction, a brief comparative note may provide the basis for some interesting speculation.

Tonga and Fiji, where cross-cousin marriage was institutionalized centuries ago, are large archipelagoes that until the nineteenth century were subdivided into frequently warring polities. Alliances had to be created among one set of groups in opposition to other sets for military purposes. On Anuta, over at least the past nine generations, there has been no need to establish well-marked military alliances among one set of units in order to oppose another. Rather than one group of domestic units being faced with the problem of over-

A ↔ B

Restricted Exchange

→ A → B → C →

Generalized Exchange

Generation 1:	A ↔	B
Generation 2:	A ↔	C
Generation 3:	A ↔	D
Generation 4:	A ↔	E
Generation 5:	A ↔	F
Generation 6:	A ↔	B

The Anutan System
(Complex Structure with Degrees of Impropriety)

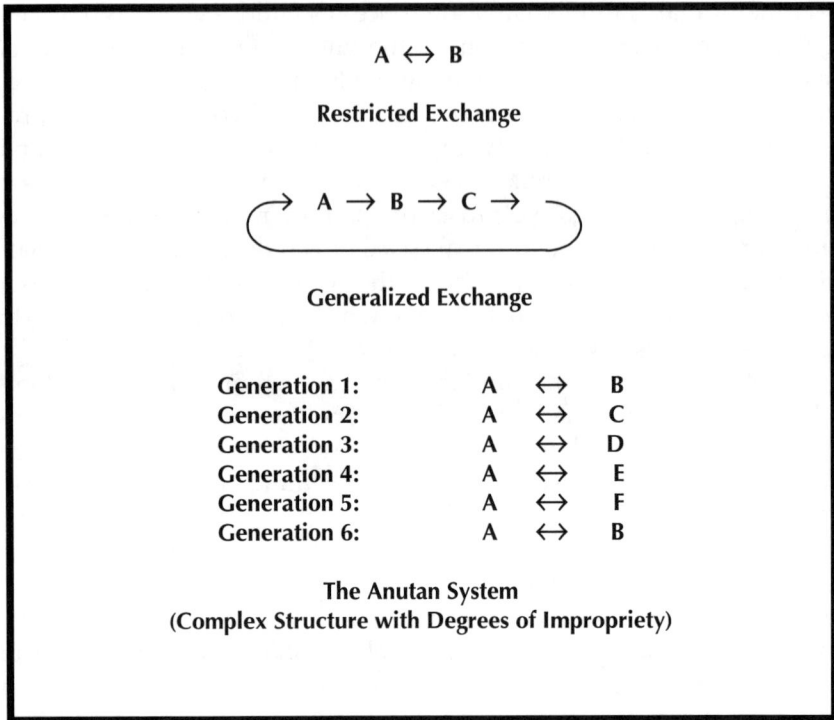

Figure 5.2 Comparison of the Anutan marriage system to restricted and generalized exchange with respect to the exchange of women.

powering or being overpowered by another, the issue has been how to bring all the households into close working relationships, to maximize the bonds of kinship among the entire population, to maximize *aropa*—on both a sentimental and an economic plane—and, in this way, to minimize potential conflicts within society at large. Restricted exchange would pair units with each other while reinforcing the distinction between each pair and everyone else. Generalized exchange would create cycles of greater scope, but the cycles might still be relatively independent of each other and become isolated atoms within the larger social setting. A complex marriage system on a tiny island, however, creates an intricate alliance network, ramifying through the social structure, always strengthening the weakest and most distant bonds wherever they may be.

Chapter 6

Descent Categories and Descent Groups: Pare, Api, and Kainanga

'Hearth' and 'House'

When it becomes necessary to identify someone's social position by reference to a named unit, one usually is said to be a member of "the *Api* _____." *Api* normally means 'fire.' but when used to designate a group of kin, a better translation might be 'hearth'—a group of people bearing a relationship to a common oven or fireplace.[1] The blank may be filled in by the name of the head of a domestic unit, a house in which its members sleep, or any important ancestor in the male line. Thus, the expression may apply in theory to any group of men who share a common patrilineal ancestor plus in-marrying women, unmarried sisters and daughters, and anyone who has been incorporated through adoption or establishment of a *tauranga* or *tau toa* relationship. It may refer to a group as limited as the *patongia* or to persons whose connection goes back as far as nine generations, to the so-called Chiefly Brethren (Te Paanau Ariki)—a group of siblings reputed to have exterminated most of the island's population and established the contemporary social order. In the latter case, it becomes synonymous with the *kainanga*, the group that I have to this point translated as 'clan' (cf. Firth 1957). Commonly *api* refers to a group that falls somewhere in between, but it is never traced back farther than the generation of the Chiefly Brethren.

In a sense, it is possible to say that a man is a member of as many *api* as he has patrilineal ancestors dating back to the time of the Chiefly Brethren. If one wishes to specify only the household of Pu Akonima, for example, one might say "Te Api Tungaaporau," Tungaaporau being the name of Pu Akonima's house. By contrast, if one is speaking of the units of Pu Notau, Pu Akonima, Pu Raveiti, and Pu Paone as a single collectivity, one says either "Te Api Taneanu" (Pu Taneanu being the father of the three brothers and paternal uncle of Pu Paone) or Te Api Pokotutai (after Pu Pokotutai, Pu Taneanu's elder brother and leader of the domestic unit when it was still a single *patongia*, before these two men were lost at sea). Similarly, I have heard the term Te Api Pangatau used to designate: the domestic unit headed by Pu Nukutamaaroa; Pu Nukutamaaroa's line, going back to Nau Ariki, elder sister of the Chiefly Brethren; or (very rarely) the entire Kainanga i Pangatau.

Except when used in such a way as to correspond with the domestic unit, *te api* tends to designate a category of people rather than a corporate group. By "descent category" I mean a conceptual set including all those people who may be distinguished from the remainder of humanity on the basis of a commonly recognized shared ancestry. A group, by contrast, is a concrete reality—a set of people who do something together. Rarely do all people who share common descent actively cooperate, and rarely are potential contributors to a group's well-being denied membership because they lack the appropriate descent links. A "descent group" by these criteria, is a type of corporation in which most members are also part of a common descent category.

Pare ('house'), when used to designate a social group, is almost synonymous with *api*. It may denote the people of a single domestic unit, as when it was explained to me that there is, at present, but a single *pare* representing the line descended from Nau Ariki in the Kainanga i Pangatau. More often, however, it is used to indicate a relationship between two or more households or between a household's current representatives and their patrilineal ancestors. Thus, the most common explanation for how a garden or a house site came to be the property of its present owners is that it has belonged to *te pare nei mai mua rea* ('this *pare* from long ago'). Unlike *api*, *pare* is not used as part of a name. One would not say, for example, Te Pare Taneanu. Like *api*, its exact meaning in a given situation must be inferred from the context.

A third term related to *te pare* and *te api* is *te vaa*. The best gloss for this is 'line.'[2] Like *pare* and *api*, it can include any set of persons with a common ancestor. Consequently, cousins may be said to be either of the same or different *vaa*, depending on which ancestor is invoked on the particular occasion. Unlike *api* and *pare*, two persons may be said to be of a single *vaa* even if they only can trace a connection on the maternal side, although it then is qualified with the stipulation *i te vaa o te papine* ('in the female line'), in a manner reminiscent of the *kano a paito*. It is not a corporate group, but rather a category of people. One is said to be either of the speaker's class or of a different one depending on whether the speaker wishes to emphasize closeness to or distance from the individual in question. This is calculated in genealogical terms with the reservation that outsiders who have been incorporated into the kinship system in the specific sense (see chapter 3) are also included.

Kainanga

A more definitively bounded group than the *pare* or *api* is the *kainanga*. In many respects, Anutan *kainanga* are analogous to Tikopian units of the same name (see Firth 1963[1936]: chapter 9, 1957), but there are also important differences.

Anuta, like Tikopia, has four hierarchically ordered *kainanga*, each one owing its existence to one of four *tapito* ('sources' or 'founders') who lived in the distant past.[3] Anutans state that their *kainanga* originated approximately nine generations ago, when Tearakura was the senior chief. In two separate incidents, the other 'houses' (*pare*) plotted against the chief, but he, his two brothers, and one brother-in-law thwarted the insurgents. Tearakura and his brothers are the Chiefly Brethren (Te Paanau Ariki), mentioned briefly at the start of this chapter.[4]

When the fighting subsided, these four were virtually the only males remaining on the island. The highest ranked *kainanga*, known as the Kainanga i Mua, is said to be descended from Tearakura. The second-ranking Kainanga i Tepuko traces its origin to Tearakura's younger brother, Pu Tepuko, also known by the personal names of Kavekau and—less frequently—Tearavave. The third-ranking Kainanga i Pangatau is descended from Tearakura's two sisters, Nau Ariki and Nau Pangatau, both of whom were married to the same man, Pu Pangatau. And the lowest ranking Kainanga i Rotomua is attributed to Tearakura's second brother, Tauvakatai, who was also the youngest member of the sibling set. The Kainanga i Rotomua derives its name from Tauvakatai's son, Pu Rotomua, said to be among the most powerful warriors in Anuta's history.

Males and unmarried females normally claim connection to their *kainanga*'s founder through a line of men. Anuta has no explicit rule

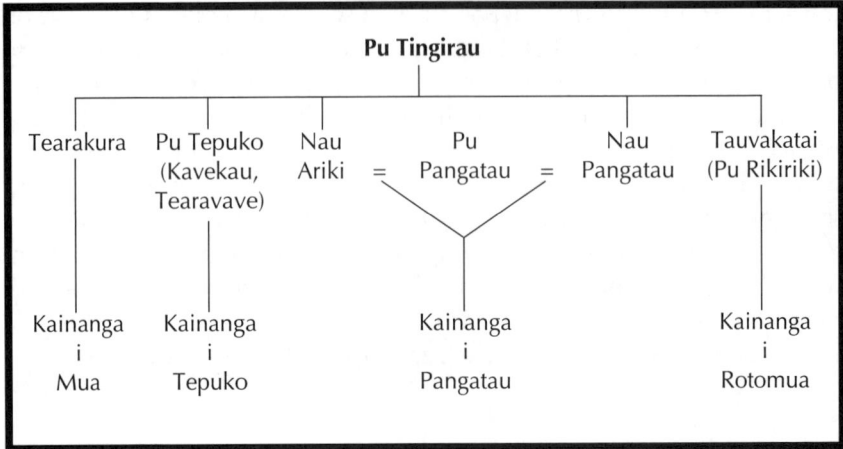

Figure 6.1   Founders of the Four Anutan *Kainanga*.

requiring marriage outside the *kainanga*, but when such a marriage takes place, the woman joins her husband's *kainanga*. An adopted child belongs to both the natal and adoptive parents' *kainanga* until marriage, at which point one normally loses membership in the adoptive *kainanga*. An immigrant is usually incorporated into the *tauranga*'s or *toa*'s *kainanga*. Alternatively, should the immigrant be a man who marries an Anutan woman, he may join the *kainanga* of his wife. In other words, one is incorporated into a *kainanga* through the same mechanisms that determine *patongia* membership. One may think of *kainanga*, therefore, as a group of domestic units whose leaders share patrilineal descent from a common ancestor. Only in this way does it make sense to say that a man in the Kainanga i Mua, his wife from (that is, whose parents are members of) the Kainanga i Pangatau, his *kauapi* from the Kainanga i Tepuko, his *tauranga* from Tikopia, and his *toa* from America share common descent from a single *tapito* in the generation of Tearakura.[5]

Even with this understanding, the concept of patrilineal descent must be qualified in order to make it applicable to the *kainanga*. A man who comes from overseas and is incorporated into the kinship system not only gains status in a *patongia* and *kainanga*, but he may be invoked to link a contemporary *patongia* to its *kainanga*'s founder in the absence of a biologically connected ancestor. This is illustrated by the Kainanga i Rotomua which would have died out a half dozen generations ago were it not for this procedure.

Tauvakatai's paternal grandson, Pu Pokotutai, had no male offspring, so if its continuation were absolutely dependent on patrilineal descent in the conventional sense the Kainanga i Rotomua would have become extinct. Fortunately, while Pu Pokotutai was alive a Rotuman canoe landed at Anuta, and one crew member was incorporated into the Kainanga i Rotomua as Pu Pokotutai's *toa*. He settled on the island, took a local woman for his wife, was given the Anutan name of Pu Raropita, and the couple had a son who perpetuated the line. Therefore, it is through the intervention of Pu Raropita, the Rotuman, that the Kainanga i Rotomua survives today. Significantly, no Anutan has ever cited this man's immigrant status in explaining the reason for his descendants' low rank or for the fact that their *kainanga* has no chief. Pu Raropita was fully integrated into the kinship system, and Anutans never seem to have raised the idea that his status might be compromised by his foreign birth. Tauvakatai, not Pu Raropita, is identified as the *kainanga*'s founder, and the lack of genealogical continuity is thought of as irrelevant. This is not patrilineal descent in the usual sense. However, if we consider the matter in Anutan terms and recognize that from their viewpoint there is no significant distinction between genealogical kin and immigrants who have been incorporated into the kinship system, it is perfectly reasonable that they should not insist upon a biological connection with their "patrilineal ancestors." In the same way that I have used "kinship" to denote a system that differs from the rigidly genealogical phenomenon that many Americans associate with the term, one may generally refer to the relationship between a domestic unit and its *kainanga*'s founder by the term "descent." Problematic situations occasionally arise, however, even with a loosened understanding of "patrilineal descent." This is illustrated well by the case of Pu Rongovaru and his *patongia*.

Approximately a dozen years before my initial study, Pu Rongovaru had a falling out with the man who later was to become Anuta's junior chief. In order to voice his protest, he withdrew his *patongia* from the Kainanga i Tepuko. Since then, members of Pu Rongovaru's household have cast their lot with the Kainanga i Pangatau, have participated with the latter *kainanga* in economic pursuits, and have renounced the honor and authority to which they would be entitled as members of the higher-ranking group. Because of these occurrences, their formal position is ambiguous. Depending on the context, members of Pu Rongovaru's household may identify themselves, and be identified by others, as members of either the Kainanga i Tepuko or the Kainanga i Pangatau. Pu Rongovaru's brother, Pu Aatapu, told me that when his son reaches adulthood, it will be up to him whether to return to his father's original *kainanga* or to remain with the newly acquired one. But after another generation or two, should his son pursue the latter course, all ambiguity would be removed and Pangatau asserted—consistently and without qualification—to be their *kainanga*.

To put the matter more schematically, Pu Rongovaru's putative disrespect for the man who would become his chief and the latter's threat to banish him to the ocean, meant a serious breakdown of *aropa*. At the same time, Pu Rongovaru established bonds of *aropa* with the Kainanga i Pangatau through the pooling of resources and labor in island-wide activities and by renouncing his former status in the higher-ranking *kainanga*. Change of *kainanga* membership is not a simple matter, and it requires that the realignment be maintained over a period of generations. In the long run, however, *kainanga* affiliation is determined by an interplay of genealogy and *aropa* as expressed in social interaction. As in determination of kinship status and *patongia* membership, it is even possible under certain circumstances for genealogical factors to be completely overridden by the quality of social relations.

Firth (1963[1936]:324–29) characterized the Tikopian *kainanga* as a 'patrilineal clan.' and there is something to be said for such a characterization of the Anutan unit as well. It is defined by a relationship to a *tapito* or 'founder' who is reputed to have lived about two hundred years ago, and the relationship is based ideally on a principle of patrilineal descent. Although there are a few Anutans who can trace the genealogical connection between themselves and their *kainanga*'s founder, such persons are rare. Therefore, 'clan' is arguably a more appropriate gloss than 'lineage.' To call the Anutan *kainanga* a 'clan.' or even a 'descent group.' however, several important qualifications must be made.

As in Tikopia, but unlike most groupings that anthropologists have called 'clans.' the Anutan *kainanga* are not exogamous. In this respect, however, Anuta's *kainanga* do not differ from most Polynesian descent groups. And while Anuta has no explicit rule enforcing *kainanga* exogamy, the prohibition against marrying one's *inati* makes it difficult to find an appropriate marriage partner within one's own *kainanga*. In fact, only six out of 59 marriages that I recorded during my initial study were between members of the same *kainanga*. Therefore, while the Anutan groups differ somewhat from the typical 'clan' on grounds of exogamy, this does not appear to be a major problem. If we can gloss such Polynesian units as the Tikopian *kainanga* or the Maori *hapū* as 'clans.' the Anutan *kainanga* ought to qualify as well.

More troublesome than the problem of exogamy is the question of descent itself. In particular, an immigrant from overseas is capable of linking a contemporary *kainanga* with its 'founder' just as if that person were an unequivocal patrilineal ancestor; and in certain circumstances, as in the case of Pu Rongovaru and his *patongia*, even extant genealogical proprieties may be overridden.

Descent groups in most Polynesian communities are of a type that anthropologists term cognatic or nonunilinear. In other words, one may invoke any combination of male and female links in establishing a connection with the group's founding ancestor. By contrast, female links may not be invoked to claim membership in an Anutan *kainanga*. When Pu Rongovaru withdrew from the Kainanga i Tepuko he affiliated not with Mua, the *kainanga* of his mother, but with the Kainanga i Pangatau. Nor is there any suggestion that seven generations ago, if Pu Raropita had not arrived on the scene, the Kainanga i Rotomua could have been perpetuated by an Anutan woman. Yet, one finds an evident anomaly in that Anutans often identify Tearakura's sisters, Nau Ariki and Nau Pangatau, rather than their husband, Pu Pangatau, as the founders of the Kainanga i Pangatau. Consequently, the first link between this *kainanga* and its founders must have been matrilineal in nature. The Kainanga i Pangatau's early history, however, seems to have had no effect on the present nature of recruitment to that descent group.

If "descent" is defined in such a way as to include extragenealogical kin who have been incorporated through a mutual expression of *aropa*; if it is recognized that the entities bound together through ties of common "descent" are domestic units rather than individuals; and if it is remembered that, even so, the rule of patrilineal descent is not absolute, we may be justified in designating the *kainanga* as a 'patrilineal clan.' Since use of this label must be so highly qualified, I have chosen in most of my publications to use the Anutan term or the more neutral designations 'unit' or 'group.' For convenience, I use 'clan' as a gloss for *kainanga* in this book; however, I must caution the reader to bear in mind the translation's notable limitations.

Internal Structure

Anutans distinguish two types of clan: those with chiefs (known as *ariki*) and those without. The senior chief stands at the head of the Kainanga i Mua and is called Te Ariki i Mua ('The Chief in Front') or Tui Anuta ('Lord of Anuta'); the junior chief heads the Kainanga i Tepuko and is designated Te Ariki i Muri ('The Chief in Back'), Te Ariki Tepuko ('The Chief of Tepuko'), or Tui Kainanga. The Kainanga i Pangatau and the Kainanga i Rotomua have no chief.

Firth (1954:97) reported erroneously that Anuta has two *kainanga*, Mua and Muri, headed by the Ariki i Mua and the Ariki i Muri, respectively.[6] His confusion resulted from an assumption that the Anutan *kainanga* are structurally identical to their Tikopian counterparts, where the concepts of *kainanga* and chief are so closely linked that one is unimaginable without the other. I also began my investigation with this model in mind, and only after some time did I realize that the terms in which I posed the question were inappropriate for the Anutan situation.

At the time of the community's putative extermination there was but a single chiefly office, held by Tearakura. Before his death, Tearakura proclaimed his desire to be succeeded by Pu Tepuko, his brother, rather than his son. After Pu Tepuko's death, the chieftainship returned to the senior line in the person of Kavataurua, Tearakura's eldest son. However, in order to give due honor to descendants of Pu Tepuko, who had been his elder brother's first lieutenant and served for a time as chief himself, the Anutans divided the office. The question is, consequently, not how there can be two chiefless clans; rather, it is why a second chiefly post was added to the one that had sufficed to rule the island for six prior generations, through the time of Pu Tepuko's demise.

Ideally, chiefly status is determined on the basis of genealogical seniority. The Ariki i Mua should be the most senior male in the Kainanga i Mua, and the Ariki i Muri is the most senior male in the Kainanga i Tepuko. Seniority is traced exclusively through males, so that a chief is normally his predecessor's eldest direct male patrilineal descendant, which, in most cases, means the former chief's eldest son. If the eldest son has died, is away from the island and not expected to return, or is incompetent, however, he may be passed over in favor of his eldest available brother.

There are many cases of chiefs who have attained their positions due to the deaths of their elder brothers, the most recent being the present Ariki Tepuko, whose elder brother was lost at sea many years ago. On the other hand, oral traditions attest to only one case of an elder brother who was passed over strictly because of unsuitable behavior. Tearakura's great-grandfather, Toroaki, had three sons: Pu Raatu, the eldest; Pu Rongomai, the second; and Pu Pongi, the last. Pu Rongomai was a trouble maker and challenged Pu Raatu to fight to the death—partly over control of a garden and partly just to prove that he was the greater warrior. Pu Raatu refused to fight his brother. When he left Anuta some time later on a voyage that brought him to Tikopia and then to Tonga, he announced his desire that Pu Pongi should take his place and succeed to the chieftainship when their father died. Pu Rongomai, he declared, should be disqualified because of his unfraternal behavior and lack of respect for his elder brother.

Once again Pu Rongomai defied Pu Raatu's wishes, and when their father passed away, he claimed the chieftainship. No one attempted to prevent his succession, but shortly after assuming office, he became severely ill. Anutans interpreted Pu Rongomai's illness as resulting from his disobedience. The usurper, upon this realization, decided that the chieftainship was not worth the price and abdicated. Anutans view Pu Rongomai's brief reign as illegitimate, and his name is not included in chiefly genealogies as they are presently recited.

Firth notes that Tikopia has but one aberrant case in which a dying chief announced his successor. On Anuta, overt decisions to contravene the normal succession patterns are not nearly so rare. I have just noted the case of Pu Raatu, a legitimate successor who decided to leave home before his installation as chief and announced prior to his departure that Pu Pongi, the youngest of the brothers, should take his place. Tearakura, before the end of his life, proclaimed that Pu Tepuko, his brother, rather than Kavataurua, his son, should succeed to his position; and other than a few mild protests by Pu Tepuko himself, no one challenged this decision. In the next generation, the chieftainship was returned to the senior line in the person of Kavataurua; after Kavataurua's death, the Anutans created a second chiefly title for Pu Tepuko's descendants. A few generations later at the suggestion of a departing chief named Pu Koroatu (Matakiapo), Pu Maapai—a man of an entirely different line—succeeded to Anuta's senior chieftainship. In the following generation the title reverted to the established chiefly line. Had Pu Maapai's sons objected, however, there would have been room for debate. The latter case suggests some of the problems in determining a successor when the deceased chief has no son or no son of sufficient age to hold office.

If a deceased chief has a son or grandson who is too young to assume office, Anutans, unlike the Tikopians, are usually quite happy to appoint a regent and wait for as many years as necessary for the child to reach the age of responsibility. The senior chief, in response to my query as to what would happen should he die before his son reached adulthood, told me that his brother would not be made *ariki*. Rather, he would "watch the island" (*mamata ki te penua*) until the chief's young son was old enough to assume the office. When Pu Parikitonga, the present chief's great-grandfather, died in the early 1900s, Pu Raropuko, the leading executive official (*maru*), "watched the island" for several years until Pu Teukumarae was ready to take over. In fact, in contrast to Tikopia, Anutans seem to feel it somewhat unbecoming for a man to succeed to the chieftainship too soon after his predecessor's death. Two or three years elapsed between the death of Pu Teukumarae and the succession of his grandson, the present chief, although the latter was in his twenties at the time. And the present Ariki Tepuko took office more than a year after his father's death despite his obvious qualifications and more than forty years of age.

If a chief has no patrilineal male descendants, succession becomes problematic. Generally, the title should go either to the eldest surviving brother or the eldest son of the eldest brother to have male offspring. Such pragmatic considerations as the respective ages of the potential candidates should also influence the final choice. In addition, the case of Pu Maapai illustrates that it is possible for the chieftainship to pass entirely out of the senior line under certain circumstances. However, if the chieftainship is passed to a junior line because the former chief's descendants are unavailable or not yet of sufficient age and maturity, in the following generation the title normally reverts to the senior line. This is illustrated by the passage of the chiefly title from Tearakura to Pu Tepuko and back to Kavataurua, and from Pu Koroatu to Pu Maapai and then to Pu Koroatu's elder brother's grandson, Pu Parikitonga (Katoakataina). The most recent example of such a succession pattern begins with Pu Teputuu (Rangioa), the great-grandfather of the present Ariki Tepuko. Pu Teputuu was the eldest son and in line to become chief, but while still a young man he traveled to Tikopia where he stayed for the remainder of his life. Thus, he forfeited his right of succession to his younger brother, Pu Parekope (Arikimeemea). On Pu Parekope's death, he was followed by his son, Pu Tepuko (Rangirua). While Pu Tepuko dwelt in the chiefly office, Pu Teputuu's son, Pu Orokope, returned from Tikopia. In the following generation, the chieftainship was returned to the senior line in the person of Pu Orokope's son, Pu Pareumata (Ikipure), father of the present junior chief.

In cases like these, the principles are clear, but the outcome cannot be assumed. Pu Pareumata had no trouble gaining the chieftainship because Pu Tepuko had no sons to contest it; if he had, they could well have put up an argument as to why the office should have been theirs, and the outcome of such an argument would not be foreordained. After a lapse of just one generation, if the senior contender is qualified, he will probably secure the title. As the number of generations increases, however, the claim of the junior line becomes increasingly strong. The ultimate decision always results from an interplay of genealogical factors and conscious agreement, validated by appropriate social action—particularly action that demonstrates generosity and compassion, i.e., behavior indicating that one is a man of *aropa* and has sufficient spiritually-derived power (*manuu* or *mana*) to exhibit the *aropa* that he feels.

Both the principle of maximizing interdependence among the clan's domestic units and the possibility of overriding genealogical considerations when circumstances make it necessary are illustrated by the process of installing a chief. No chief was installed in office during

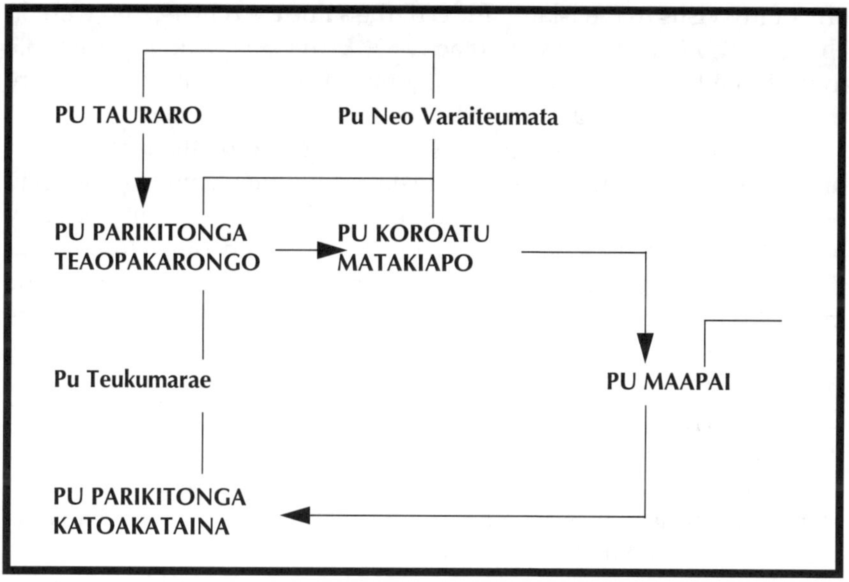

Figure 6.2 A case of irregular succession in the Kainanga i Mua. Arrows indicate succession path. Chiefs appear in capital letters; non-chiefs in lower case.

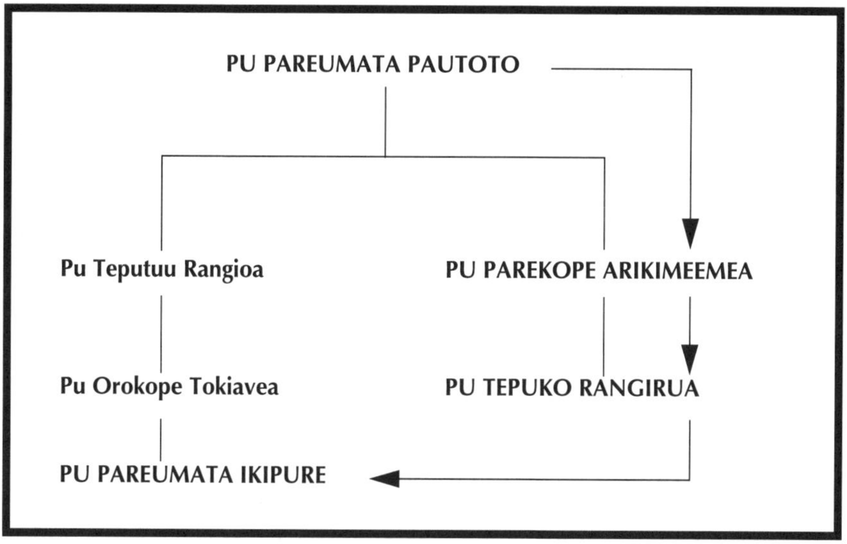

Figure 6.3 A case of irregular succession in the Kainanga i Tepuko. Arrows indicate succession path. Chiefs appear in capital letters; non-chiefs in lower case.

any of my visits to the island. Indeed, the same two chiefs who were in charge in 1972 are still alive and active 30 years later. And I was unable to elicit the kind of detailed oral account of the installation procedure that I would have liked. Nonetheless, the principles are clear.

Unlike Tikopia where a new chief is installed by the leading men of the other clans, on Anuta he is installed by men from his own clan but a different *pare*. When Pu Pareumata (Ikipure) died in the early 1960s, Pu Rongovaru's *patongia* had already split and joined forces with the Kainanga i Pangatau, and they were not about to place in office the man who had driven them from their natal *kainanga*. Pu Parekope, the chief's patrilateral parallel first cousin, had not yet separated from the Ariki Tepuko's domestic unit, and there was no adult male in Nau Tanukope's household who could have served to elevate the new chief. In addition, Nau Tanukope, as Pu Tepuko's sister, was too closely related for a member of her unit to serve in that capacity. Hence, it seemed that there was no one to install the new chief, and people began to speculate that there could never again be an Ariki Tepuko.

The leading men of the Kainanga i Mua, however, objected to this idea. Pu Tokerau along with Pu Teaokena (brothers of the Ariki i Mua) took it upon themselves to elevate Pu Tepuko to his chiefly status. Anutans recognized that this was not procedurally correct. However, the legitimacy of Pu Tepuko's claim to the office, the authority of Pu Tokerau and the Kainanga i Mua, the strength with which the tradition of having two chiefs was inculcated into the Anutans' scheme of values, and a recognition of the exigencies of an extraordinary situation were such that no one objected to the new *ariki*'s manner of installment, nor did anyone refuse to recognize the legitimacy of his position.

Both politically and honorifically, the chiefs sit at the heads of their respective clans. A chief may freely order his subordinates to fish, work in the gardens, or fire up an oven for purposes of ritual exchange or celebration. Anyone wishing to leave the island in search of education, adventure, or employment first must obtain his chief's permission. And when the clan acts as a unit, it is under the *ariki*'s leadership.

Anuta has no special chiefly language as do some Polynesian islands; but everyone must show the greatest deference in other respects. No one may stand in an *ariki*'s presence if the chief is seated. No one may touch any part of his body, especially his head, except on his direct instructions. Shouting or raising one's voice in the chief's presence, playing, or engaging in rowdy activity in the vicinity of his house is forbidden. Anyone who meets a chief while walking on a narrow path should step aside until the chief has passed. When a distribution of fish or vegetable food takes place, in addition to one pile or basket for each of the island's domestic units, a special portion

Pu Kaurave[a]   Pu Taupare[b]
| |
Ruokimata   **Toroaki**
                        |
                     Pu Pongi
                        |
                     Pu Tingirau

Tearakura   **Pu Tepuko**
| *(Kavekau; Tearavave)*
Kavataurua   **Pu Matauea**
| |
Pu Kirei   **Pu Teputuu**
(Tuitenepu)   *(Arikiteuku*

Pu Tauraro   Pu Neo[c]   **Pu Pareumata**
(Manongimaupa)   (Varaiteumata)   *(Pautoto)*

Pu Parikitonga   **Pu Koroatu**[d]   Pu Teputuu   **Pu Parekope**
(Teaopakarongo   *(Matakiapo)*   (Rangioa)   *(Arikimeemea)*

Pu Maapai   Pu Teukumarae   Pu Orokope   **Pu Tepuko**
(Porongai)   (Tearaamanu)   (Tokiavea)   *(Rangirua)*

Pu Parikitonga   **Pu Pareumata**
(Katoakataina)   *(Ikipure)*

Pu Teukumarae   **Pu Tepuko**
(Abraham Vakaraakeikitepoe)   *(Silas Aranganima)*

Pu Parikitonga
(Edwin Porautatua)

Pu Koroatu
(Jacob Tearaamanu)

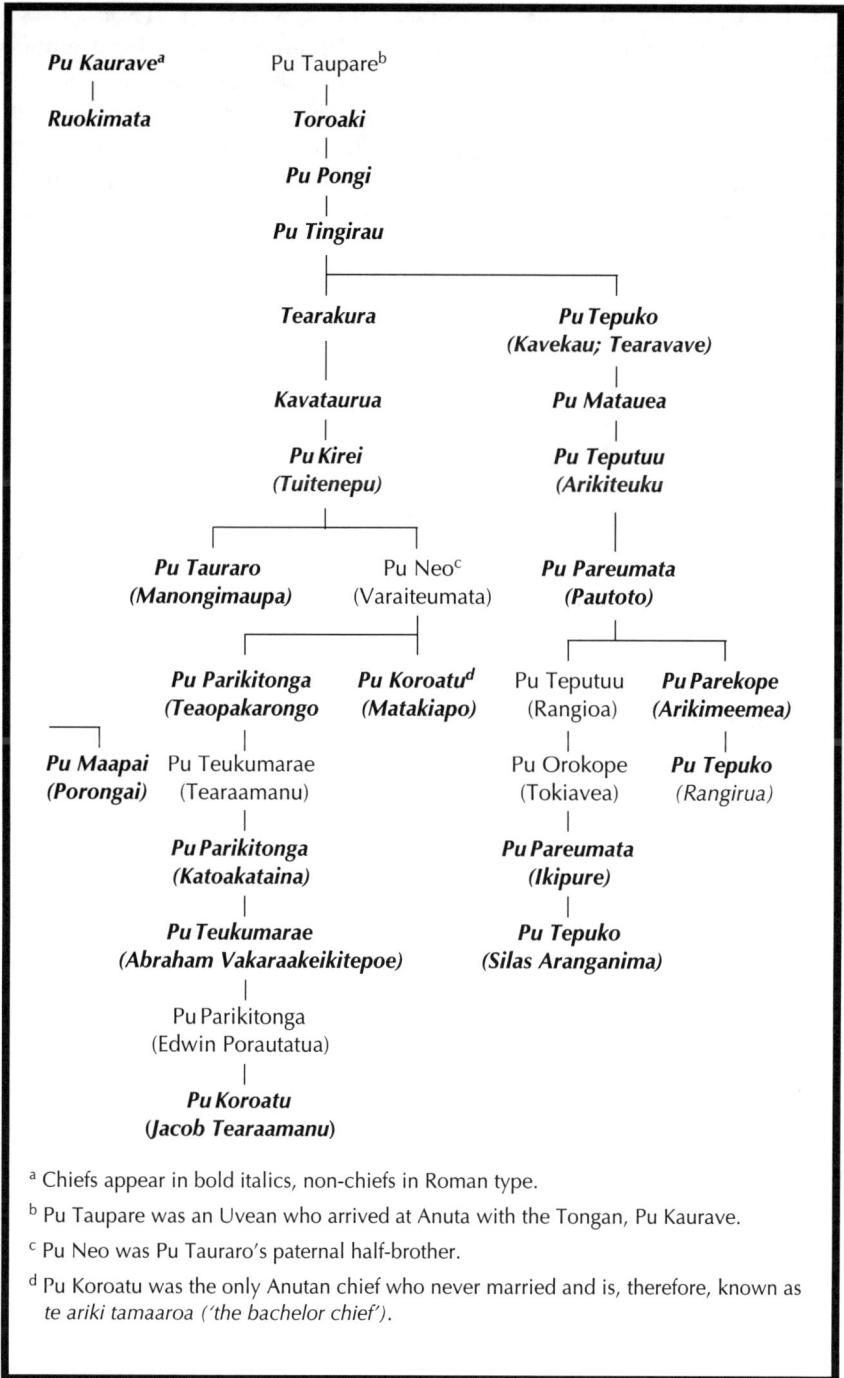

[a] Chiefs appear in bold italics, non-chiefs in Roman type.

[b] Pu Taupare was an Uvean who arrived at Anuta with the Tongan, Pu Kaurave.

[c] Pu Neo was Pu Tauraro's paternal half-brother.

[d] Pu Koroatu was the only Anutan chief who never married and is, therefore, known as *te ariki tamaaroa* ('the bachelor chief').

Figure 6.4 Genealogy of the Anutan Chiefs.

called the *pakaariki* is set aside for each of the two chiefs. If some especially desirable fish is caught, it may be given to one or both chiefs. The chief may either keep such presents for himself and his household or give them to someone toward whom he is favorably inclined. These all are situations constantly arising in the course of everyday events, and during the 1970s the rules were universally and scrupulously followed. By 2000, the *pakaariki* offerings were no longer made as a matter of routine practice. On special occasions such as religious holidays, however, Anutans still show respect for their chiefs by making special presentations.

Anutans pay special respect to one or both chiefs on a variety of ceremonial occasions, and no general feast may start until both chiefs are present. Those immediately around the chief at a meal should not begin to eat before he does, or at least not until he has given the word. I recall one feast in which a hungry populace waited for forty-five minutes with the food spread out in front of them for the Ariki Tepuko to appear so that they could begin their meal. When a chief leaves the island, he is carried down the beach and set in the canoe; and he is not permitted to go without an entourage to assure that he will be adequately cared for. If he is just going fishing for the day, he may walk down the beach but is expected to sit in the canoe while other members of the crew push it through the surf and risk injuring their feet on the fringing reef. The Ariki Tepuko created something of a stir when he left Anuta in June 1972 to visit his sons in Honiara. He and his wife went out to the ship without first publicizing their plans, and his people assumed that the couple had gone to bid farewell to some relatives they knew were leaving. Thus, the chief departed without the proper ceremony and with no entourage to serve as bodyguards and look out for his needs. Many Anutans were upset for a long time over this affair.

Any visitor of note is expected to undergo a greeting ceremony that involves crawling to the two chiefs and attempting to press his nose to each chief's knee as a sign of deference. The chief typically places a hand under the visitor's chin and pulls the guest's head up to the same level as his own, so that they press nose to nose. In this way, the visitor is symbolically elevated for the moment to the chiefs' own honorific status. An Anutan seeing a chief for the first time after a protracted absence goes through the same procedure, and even Tikopians show supreme respect to the Anutan chiefs. Few sights have impressed me more than seeing a young, educated Tikopian, who spoke good English and was working at the Solomon Islands National Museum, drop to his knees and press his nose to the shins of the two Anutan chiefs when they walked into the museum during their visit to Honiara in February 1973.

The Kainanga i Pangatau and Kainanga i Rotomua do not have chiefs, but they do have formal leaders. The Kainanga i Pangatau is said to have three *pare*, one descended from Nau Ariki, the elder of Tearakura's two sisters, one from Nau Pangatau, the younger sister, and one from Pu Matangi, a man who immigrated from Tikopia several generations later. Each of the three houses has its own 'head' (*pokouru*). In 1972, the house descended from Nau Ariki was led by Pu Nukutamaaroa; that descended from Nau Pangatau by Pu Penuakimoana; and that from Pu Matangi by Pu Tuaapi. As might be expected, the line of highest rank is associated with Nau Ariki. More surprisingly, the immigrant line descended from Pu Matangi is second in rank; and Nau Pangatau's descendants are at the bottom.

Photo 6.1 Tikopians' respect for the Anutan chiefs is reciprocal. In this photograph Tikopia's second chief, Te Ariki Tafua, is carried to a feast being held in his honor during a visit to Anuta in 1972.

Each of Pangatau's three leaders is responsible primarily for his own house, although they are referred to collectively as 'the three heads' (*nga pokouru e toru*) of the Kainanga i Pangatau. But while they are officially recognized leaders, they are not chiefs. They have no *ariki* title, are not deferred to in the manner of chiefs, are not given *pakaariki* portions during disbursements of food, and do not sit with the chiefs on ceremonial occasions. While they are responsible for ensuring their subordinates' proper behavior, they do not make policy decisions as do the chiefs. Unlike a chief, 'heads' of the lesser *kainanga* may step down when they reach an age at which the responsibilities of their position become an undue burden. And they derive their position from the *pono* (see chapter 7), which ultimately means appointment by the senior chief. Of the three 'heads' of the Kainanga i Pangatau, only Pu Nukutamaaroa is the most genealogically senior male of his 'house.' Furthermore, it is not necessary for the clan to have three 'heads.' In fact, there was just one until Pu Koroatu, the present senior chief, decided to appoint Pu Tuaapi and Pu Penuakimoana to help Pu Nukutamaaroa maintain order in their descent group.

Leadership in the Kainanga i Rotomua, theoretically, works on the same principles as it does in Pangatau. However, during most of the time that I spent on Anuta, only one adult male from that *kainanga* was present on the island, which made the problem of determining a leader a simple task. In practice the Kainanga i Rotomua, because of its small size, usually participated along with the Kainanga i Pangatau in collective activities.

On Tikopia the word *maru* is used to designate the chiefs' close agnatic male kin, and the *maru* are primarily responsible for seeing that the *ariki*'s policy decisions are implemented. On Anuta, by contrast, all males of responsible age in the two chiefly *kainanga* are referred to as *maru* or *tangata tu*. Men of the lesser clans are known as *pakaaropa*. The Anutan *maru* are expected to perform in the same capacity as their Tikopian counterparts, advising the chiefs, executing their decisions, and maintaining order on the island; but since one is a *maru* by virtue of clan affiliation, it has the appearance of a social stratum rather than an office. The Anutan *maru* have responsibilities which they fulfill to greater or lesser degrees, but one who fails to shoulder his responsibilities does not lose his *maru* status as a result. The only way to lose that status is to withdraw from the chiefly clan, as have Pu Rongovaru and the men of his domestic unit.

Women and children have no formal authority regardless of their clan affiliation or genealogical position. However, a woman may exercise a degree of influence informally through her brothers or her husband. The formal respect a woman is paid depends upon her kinship status. Children are given little ritual respect except when in a restraint relationship (e.g., *tau maa*), and even then, respect and honor are markedly less pronounced than in cases involving an adult.

Role of the *Kainanga*

Presently, the *kainanga* serve primarily to provide Anutans with a definition of their place in the island's social universe. In addition, they sponsor feasts and ceremonies and, on occasion, they participate as units in a ritual exchange. In former times, they may also have acted as collective units of religious practice.

The *kainanga* does not control land in the same direct and immediate manner as the *patongia*. No land belongs to any clan apart from that owned by its constituent households, but the gardens under the control of any elementary unit also may be said to be 'of' or to 'obey' (*pakarongo*) that unit's clan. Anutans gave me conflicting stories about the chiefs' ability to confiscate another person's gardens. Pu Teraupanga told me that if a chief were angry he might take just such action, leaving the offender with no source of food and no alternative but death by starvation. In the abstract, most Anutans might agree that this is a chiefly right, but I could learn of no occasion on which such an occurrence had taken place. And others closer to the seat of chiefly power expressed skepticism as to whether a measure of that sort could be implemented.

The clans' relationship to houses and other forms of property resembles their relationship to garden land. Canoes are not directly owned by *kainanga*, although there are a few, like *Maratautamana*, whose primary owner (*tapitonga*) is one of the chiefs. In such cases, that chief's clan is likely to feel a special sense of attachment to the canoe. Such sentimental attachment, however, does not confer special economic rights or privileges.

Under normal circumstances, each household makes its own decisions as to what crops will be planted on its lands, who is to do the planting and cultivating, when the work is to be done, and so on. Sometimes, however, an island-wide feast or ceremonial exchange requires the clans to act as collective units—or, more commonly, the two chiefly clans act together as one unit and the two commoner clans as another. When a clan acts as a corporate entity, the chief or leader may instruct particular members to go fishing, harvest foods from their gardens, or prepare an oven (*pai umu*) at a particular time; and such instructions override the predilections of any individual or household. This will become clearer as we examine the relationships among clans, especially between the *maru* and the *pakaaropa*, in chapter 7.

The *kainanga* presently serve little if any religious function, but in the traditional religious system, they may well have played a more important role. Any deceased person became a spirit who could be invoked for assistance by his or her descendants. The clans' founding ancestors were among the greatest deities in the Anutan pantheon, and in the traditional system this must have been a powerful tie binding each clan together as a corporate unit with common interests and a common means of promoting those interests. The founder, as a powerful but fundamentally benevolent deity or guardian spirit, is thus the 'basis' or 'source' (termed *tapito*) of the clan's well-being. The chief or leader also is described as the *tapito* since the clan worshipped its gods through him. The chief, on his *kainanga's* behalf, implored the gods to maintain their benevolent disposition and called them into action when assistance was required. Since the fundamental property-owning unit is the *patongia*, one's welfare depends above all on the *patongia's* prosperity. If the clan was successful in maintaining the good will of the major deities, as evidenced by the island's prosperity, individuals would benefit primarily through their membership in one of the domestic units. In this light, the character of the clans as groups of households makes a great deal of sense.

Summary

The Anutan population is divided into four major groupings called *kainanga*. Despite some reservations, I have glossed this term as 'clan.' An Anutan clan generally includes anyone affiliated with a domestic unit whose leader can trace a patrilineal connection to a founding ancestor in the time of Tearakura and the Chiefly Brethren. This characterization must be qualified, however, by the observation that an immigrant with no biological relationship to any Anutan, but who has been integrated into the kinship system through a display of *aropa*, is by virtue of that kinship status a fully acceptable substitute for a patrilineal (in the conventional sense of the term) ancestor. It is possible for a domestic unit to alter its clan affiliation without any genealogical justification, but this is a long and arduous process involving a radical disintegration of *aropa*. The only well remembered case of this occurring involved a threat of exile and subsequent refusal by the threatened unit to engage in economic cooperation with the clan to which it was connected by ties of patrilineal descent, followed by establishment of new bonds through the pooling of resources on appropriate occasions with the domestic units of a different clan.

Rank and leadership within the clan also work on the same principles as in the domestic unit. The leader ideally is the most senior man in the founding ancestor's patriline, although incompetence or failure to exhibit the *aropa* expected of a leader (by generosity in the distribution of material goods) is acceptable grounds for passing over the most genealogically appropriate man in favor of a junior relative. As is true of the domestic unit, when this occurs, leadership should revert to the senior line in the following generation. After a certain time lapse, however, the transition may be anything but smooth. The heads of the non-chiefly clans are selected on the basis of the same criteria as chiefs and *patongia* leaders, but the relative importance of the criteria is reversed. The leaders of the *pakaaropa* are appointed by the *pono* under the direction of the chiefs, whose primary objective is to have an effective leader. But wherever possible that leader should be in the appropriate genealogical position since, other things being equal, the greater one's genealogical seniority the easier it is to be a strong leader. As in the domestic unit, women and children have little formal authority. However, a woman may exert informal influence, and children exercise authority over their still younger kin.

Finally, the *kainanga* do not operate as self-contained units. Rather, their importance lies primarily in defining the structural relationships among sets of domestic units and the individuals who constitute them, as well as structuring the traditional religious system and contemporary pan-island economic activities. Especially important in this respect is the relationship between the chiefly and non-chiefly clans—a point that will emerge more clearly in the coming chapter as we discuss the overall community.

Chapter 7

Kanopenua:
The Overall Community

Anutans enjoy a set of nested identities. Each Anutan is a member of a *patongia*, a *kano a paito*, and a *kainanga*. In addition, Anutans identify themselves very strongly as members of a special and unique community consisting of the island's entire population. This is known as *te kanopenua* ('the contents of the island'), or simply Nga Anuta ('The People of Anuta'). Anutans see themselves as different from Europeans, from Asians, and from other Solomon Islanders. They share a sense of kinship with Tikopia and with the islands of the Polynesian heartland, but even in comparison with their Polynesian brethren, they have a keen sense of themselves as a special people. They are held together by their shared connection to their island—which they perceive as a particularly attractive and nurturing environment—and their special customs (*nga tukutukunga*). Most prominent among those customs are their collective Polynesian heritage, their system of chieftainship, and their adherence to what they view as a distinctively meritorious version of Anglican Christianity. Tying all of this together is commitment to the principles of *aropa*.

Defining the Community

Anutans often operate and think of their community as constituting a unit whose structure parallels that of the household and clan, but on the most inclusive level. In one sense, they view the *kanopenua* as a residential unit, consisting of all persons living on the island. In addition, however, the community includes Anutans living overseas. Conversely, people who visit the island for a short period without being incorporated into the kinship system are not considered members of the *kanopenua*. To put the matter differently, anyone who is part of Anuta's kinship system is automatically incorporated into a *patongia*, a *kainanga*, and the *kanopenua*; anyone who is not part of the kinship system cannot belong to any of the island's social units.

Every Anutan is a member of a *kainanga*, each of which is descended (using the loose sense of "descent" discussed in chapter 6) from a set of siblings. Therefore, if we go back one more generation, we can say that the entire population is descended from Pu Tingirau, father of the Chiefly Brethren. Pu Tingirau himself is a descendant of Pu Taupare, the original Uvean immigrant. Thus, the *kanopenua* may be described as a patrilineal descent group, tracing its ancestry back approximately fifteen generations to Pu Taupare. Yet, as with the other social units, it is possible to become a member of the *kanopenua* without the benefit of genealogical ties by acting as a member of the community should: by living on the island; by functioning as a member of a *patongia*, a *kainanga*, and part of the kinship system; and by following the island's basic customs.[1] In short, like other units constituting Anutan society, inclusion in the *kanopenua* is based upon criteria of genealogy and conduct that is taken to embody *aropa*. Ideally, both are present and mutually reinforcing, but when one is absent the other alone may suffice.

Political Structure

The Ariki i Mua stands at the apex of Anuta's political structure. He is called Tui Anuta, 'Lord of Anuta.' the community's high chief. He generally consults with his *maru* and the second chief before issuing instructions to the community, but he need not. When he speaks, his word is law—although, as we will see in chapter 8, the law is sometimes broken.

Tui Anuta has ultimate say on all island-wide policy matters except for those relating to the church; and there his influence is second only to that of the catechist, who, in 1972–73, was his younger brother. He organizes "public works" projects and has ultimate legislative, executive, and judicial authority. In August 1972, a group of children was caught stealing watermelons. After church that evening, and without consulting anyone, the chief called the community together to announce that henceforth—until further notice to the contrary—no child was to venture out of doors unless accompanied by an adult. I expected this dictum to be half-heartedly followed for a few days and then for the children to slip back into their old patterns. To my surprise, the proclamation remained in force and was strictly obeyed through the time I left Anuta in January of the following year. When conflicts develop, it is the chief's job to resolve them. He may assign particular persons to work at specific tasks like gardening, fishing, or preparing food at a particular time, and such a command takes precedence over all other plans.

The Ariki i Muri has the same powers and responsibilities as the Ariki i Mua, varying primarily in degree. However, there are some respects in which this quantitative variation is sufficient to produce qualitative difference. The whole community owes allegiance to the second chief. He is respected as an *ariki*, and he has authority to issue commands, particularly when the Ariki i Mua is not present. However, he is primarily responsible for his own clan. Anyone wishing to leave the island must first obtain permission from his chief and, except for members of the Kainanga i Tepuko, this means permission from the Ariki i Mua.

The Ariki Tepuko may instruct members of his *kainanga* to prepare an oven or engage in special work projects. He also may issue instructions to members of the other *kainanga*, and he is usually obeyed; but such commands bear less intrinsic weight than those of the high chief. When members of the Kainanga i Rotomua or the Kainanga i Pangatau are asked which chief they listen to, they either exhibit confusion or say that they listen to both. A few people even told me that if the two chiefs issued contradictory instructions they would "listen to the one who is right."[2] Yet, the level of the second chief's political authority is such that at times in the island's history when no Tui Anuta was in office, the leading men of the Kainanga i Mua rather than the Ariki Tepuko are said to have had primary responsibility for overseeing the island.

Between the chiefs and the underlying population—which includes men of the lower *kainanga* as well as all the island's women and children—are the *maru*. They serve as advisors to the chiefs, and about once a week—generally on Sunday evenings—the chiefs and their *maru* gather for a meeting known as *te araara o nga maru mo nga ariki* ('the discussion of the *maru* and the chiefs'). Anutans who speak English sometimes gloss the *maru* as 'the island council' or 'council of elders.' Specific problems and major imminent events, as well as the general state of the community, are thoroughly discussed at council meetings, and everyone present is given a full opportunity to make his voice heard. Votes, however, are not taken. After listening to all sides of an issue the final decision is up to the chiefs.

Photo 7.1 Senior chief, Pu Koroatu, leads a service at the St. James church in 1972.

The morning after such a meeting, islanders convene a *pono* or 'general assembly' of the *kanopenua*. There the previous night's decisions are relayed to the people by the *maru* or, on occasion, by the chiefs themselves. It then is up to the *maru* and the leaders of the chiefless *kainanga* to ensure that the *pono*'s dicta are carried out. The *pono* is not a decision-making body but simply a community meeting at which decisions of the *maru* and the chiefs are relayed to the populace at large. Nevertheless, such decisions usually do not become binding until after they have been formally proclaimed at an island *pono*.

The words *maru* and *tangata tu* refer to the same group of men, and there is no clear line separating the contexts in which it is proper to use one or the other. Literally, *tangata tu* means 'standing man.' indicating that one is in a particularly prominent position. The *maru* are the island's leading men and thus they are designated as the chiefs' *taangata tu*.[3]

Pu Tokerau once explained to me that as the chief's brother his proper designation was not *maru* but *tama nga ariki* ('child of the chiefs'). This conforms with Tikopian usage, and it is true that on occasion Pu Toke stood somewhat aloof from the political process, allowing Pu Paone, Pu Maravai, and some of the others to take the leading roles. He had the right to step in at any time he wished, however, and frequently he exercised that right. In practice, he and the chief's other brothers as well as the sons of the second chief were referred to as *maru*, and they acted the part. These facts suggest that *tama nga ariki* is not a separate category to be distinguished from *maru*, but a subspecies.

In the council meeting (*te araara o nga maru mo nga ariki*) and the *pono*, community leaders discuss matters at all levels of seriousness. Such meetings have produced instructions for people to relieve themselves below the high water mark on the beach so that the waste will be carried away by the tide. I have heard instructions not to use green coconuts and to make sure that papayas were properly ripe before being picked in order to help conserve resources in a time of scarcity. Directions have been given to dump garbage in the sea rather than leave it to rot on the paths or in the villages. It was at *pono* that people were reminded not to let their children go unsupervised, and later it was announced at a *pono* that several youngsters were to be exempted from this regulation as a reward for having dutifully obeyed the assembly's instructions.

Decisions on who is to lead the Kainanga i Pangatau and the Kainanga i Rotomua are in the hands of the two chiefs, but according to the common formulation, the leaders of these *kainanga* are appointed by the *pono*. Normally, a domestic unit's leader is the eldest son of the previous head. When exceptions are made, the decision to break with usual tradition must be ratified by the *pono*. A policy decision may be initiated by anyone, but the chiefs (especially the first chief) have the final say. They speak, however, through the mechanism of the *pono*, and it is not until the *pono* has spoken that decisions become official.

A *pono* is called by one, or possibly both chiefs, and generally— although not necessarily—in consultation with the *maru*. A chief may speak for himself at the assembly to enhance the dramatic effect of what is said, but this is rare. A *pono* may be called at any time. Most often, however, it takes place on Monday mornings immediately after church. The usual time for council meetings is Sunday night, and Monday is the earliest time thereafter when it is practical to call the community together. Before construction of the second church in 1972, *pono* were held in the coconut-leaf shade house just outside the old church at St. John. There the leading *maru*, Pu Maravai and Pu Paone, would relate the previous night's decisions. Sometimes certain decisions were presented by one and the rest by the other; at other times they both would speak on the same topic to reinforce each other's words. Then other *maru* might add their opinions. Anyone was free to raise questions, but only after the two leaders had finished.

After completion of the new church at St. James, except for especially important occasions, the island was divided in two. One of the two leading *maru* addressed the group at St. John while the other instructed the group at St. James. Aside from this, the procedure remained unchanged.

It should be noted that while Pu Maravai was of the second most senior line (after the chief's) in the Kainanga i Mua, Pu Paone was genealogically only the sixth-ranking man in the next line down. His position in the *pono* was due to his recognized status as the "wisest man on the island," to the exemplary life that he was understood to lead, and to the esteem in which his words were held. His ability to comprehend and solve problems and to put the supreme virtues of generosity and hospitality into practice in his own life compensated for any genealogical deficiency and made him the most respected of the *maru*, on a par with his unquestionably senior colleague, as co-leader of the all-important *pono*.

The 'heads' (*pokouru*) of the lower *kainanga* are responsible primarily for maintaining order among their own groups' members, the *pakaaropa*. They have little formal authority over the populace at large, any influence beyond their *kainanga* being based on their personal qualities and powers of persuasion. They occasionally speak at the *pono*, but they do so on the approval of the *maru* and the chiefs.

As in the *patongia* and *kainanga*, women have no formal power at the community level. There are no female *maru* and, aside from Nau Ariki, of whose role little is known, there has been no female chief. In fact, most Anutans insist that Nau Ariki was not a chief, and that her name was given in recognition of her position as the eldest of Tearakura's 'chiefly siblings.' Still, she is recognized as a crucially important and influential personage, a woman with tremendous *manuu* (see below), and a force to be reckoned with in Anuta's pre-Christian spiritual world. In recent times, women have had no voice in council meetings or the *pono*, except perhaps indirectly through their husbands. At a meeting called one night in 1972 to discuss whether the island should accept relief supplies from the government at the possible expense of compromising its sovereignty, all the men, *pakaaropa* as well as *maru*, were encouraged to come and express their opinions. Few women attended, and those who did show up were given no opportunity to speak.[4]

Religion and the Church

In the traditional religious system, a deceased person became an *atua* ('god' or 'spirit'). One's *atua* included one's ancestors, and a person's spiritual power depended upon that of his or her *atua*. Tearakura was the premier deity (*te atua rai*), superior even to those gods who were never human. He was the ultimate source of Anuta's welfare, but as founding ancestor of the Kainanga i Mua, he had a special relationship with the leading clan through its chief. Since he was especially susceptible to their propitiations, the entire island depended on the Kainanga i Mua—and particularly its chief—for its prosperity and health.

Pu Tepuko succeeded Tearakura to the chieftainship, and in the following generation the chiefly office was divided. Thus, the *tapito* of the Kainanga i Tepuko was not only a man who assisted Tearakura during his lifetime, serving as one of his closest and most trusted lieutenants, but he was genealogically inferior only to Tearakura himself and was elevated to the status of *ariki* after his brother's death. When Pu Tepuko died, he became an *atua* also. However, it seems that he was associated primarily with his clan and was invoked by its members in order to promote their welfare; he was not responsible for the community at large, as was Tearakura. His descendants, nevertheless, assisted their senior colleagues when the latter performed kava to Tearakura on behalf of the overall community.[5]

It appears that each clan, in addition to community gods, had its own special deities whom it invoked. The relative positions and roles of these deities corresponded more or less with those of their respective clans. Identification of a *kainanga* with a particular deity must have helped to reinforce the people's identification with their clan, for which the deity was responsible and from whom collective action was necessary in order to maintain the spirit's favor.

In addition to the *kainanga*'s founders, households were able to invoke more recent ancestors. However, it appears that domestic units did not perform kava individually. In general, the lowest-ranking households were those with the least influential deities in their repertoire.

In contrast with the traditional religion, the church is independent of the genealogically oriented units into which Anuta is divided. Even at the start of the twenty-first century, every Anutan with whom I have discussed the matter, including several church leaders, is convinced that the ancient gods existed and continue to do so in some manner. Everyone can relate a tale or two about encounters with the spirits that still haunt the bush at night.[6] The traditional system of religious ritual, however, has been totally abandoned and replaced by Christianity.

At the head of the Anutan church is the catechist, known as *te pakaako*. *Ako* is the Anutan word 'to learn.' and *paka* indicates causation. Thus, *pakaako* is the verb, 'to teach.' and the generic term for 'teacher.' It is applied to the catechist and his assistants since their job is to educate the community in the ways of the Anglican church.

The church is a central institution on Anuta, second to none. Anutans look to it for protection from natural disaster and insurance for their continued well-being. Positions of rank and power as well as most rules for correct behavior are justified by reference to Anglican church doctrine. More than any other single factor, church regulates the Anutans' work schedule, their ceremonial calendar, and the rhythm of daily life. It gets light around 5 A.M., and people get up between 5 and 5:30. The morning service starts at 5:45 or 6:00 A.M., and the evening prayer is around 5:00 P.M. Services last a half hour or more, and all productive activities have to fit between the two services. Fishing canoes typically return between 3:00 and 4:00 P.M., and people working in their gardens or preparing oven food attempt to finish by around 4:00 so they can wash before church.

It would be an exaggeration to say that everyone goes to church every morning and every evening, but almost everyone goes almost all the time. Although people continue to hold the view that the traditional gods and spirits existed and probably still do, the church protects them from having to worry about such potentially dangerous beings. In addition, it has taken over some of the roles of the chiefs.

The church's preeminence makes the catechist one of the island's most important men, and he is honored accordingly. He is not shown the formal deference of a chief. One does not step aside to let a catechist pass by unless already obliged to do so on other grounds. The same may be said for standing in the catechist's presence, turning one's back on him, and other signs of deference normally exhibited toward a person of superior rank. In his dealings with the chief, the catechist is ritually subordinate. At general food distributions, however, in addition to the *pakaariki* offerings for the chiefs, special baskets may be apportioned to the catechist, his assistants, and the local schoolteacher. This type of offering is referred to as *te pakamisionari*. It differs from the *pakaariki* in that it is smaller, and if a *pakaako* is absent, his gift simply is omitted. If a chief is away, the *pakaariki* is retained and presented to someone acting in his stead. Both the *pakaariki* and *pakamisionari* presentations were standard practice in 1972–73. By 2000, they were only offered on special occasions.

Pu Nukumairunga, who served as schoolteacher in 1972–73, was not intrinsically entitled to a *pakamisionari* offering despite his designation as *pakaako* because his teaching role was not directly related to the church. However, he was an immigrant from Tikopia, disabled (his legs were paralyzed and atrophied from polio contracted during the 1950s), and recognized as making a valuable contribution to the island (in addition to teaching young children, he operated the radio, dispensed what medicines were available, and on occasion rendered his services as interpreter for visiting dignitaries). Therefore, Pu Tokerau and the chief decided that it would be appropriate for the community to offer him a gesture of its sympathy and appreciation by including him in the *pakamisionari* disbursements.

The catechist instructs the people, as do the chiefs and the *maru*. Although his proper sphere is church-related matters, virtually everything has its sacred side. As a result, there is no obvious dividing line between the sacred and the secular. The catechist offers instruction in correct moral behavior, and he organizes ceremonies and feasts that are related to the church. He may organize fishing expeditions or tell people to prepare an oven in order to have available the necessary resources for an upcoming celebration. He, along with the Companions (see below), is responsible for ensuring the proper upkeep of the church buildings and any equipment therein. In terms of spiritual power, the catechist is seen to be in the same general class as the two chiefs, and when he speaks, the awe with which people listen to him compares favorably with that afforded an *ariki*.

Assisting the catechists is a church auxiliary known as the Companions of the Brotherhood of Melanesia. The Melanesian Brotherhood is an order of friars founded by a man from Guadalcanal during the reign of John Steward as fifth Bishop of Melanesia. Members of the Brotherhood are expected to take vows of poverty and chastity for short periods, which may later be extended at the member's request. There is no compulsion to maintain membership beyond the minimum two years, and there is no stigma attached to leaving after that period. The Brothers' goal is to assist the official clergy of the Anglican church in their task of bringing new Solomon Islanders to the faith and strengthening the faith of those already converted (Fox n.d.).[7] According to the Melanesian Mission (n.d.) the Companions are:

1. . . . baptized members of the Church, men, women and young people who are joined to the Brothers in their work for the kingdom of God.

2. They help the brothers

   by praying for them and their work

   by giving money and useful things to the Brotherhood

   by taking care of Brothers when they come to visit them or travel through their districts.

3. As the Brothers work for the kingdom of God in places to which they are sent out, so the Companions work for the kingdom of God in the places where they live.

   They help the people who live around them,

   to know and worship God,

   to be strong in the faith,

   to keep the commandments of God and to serve him truly in their daily lives,

   to work for the good of all, serving one another in love and true fellowship,

   to be faithful members of God's holy Church.

   They do all this by their good example and in other ways
   (Melanesian Mission n.d.:1).

On Anuta there are no Brothers, but the Companions (Te Kompanion) serve as lay assistants to the catechist. Members attend to the details necessary for keeping the church in good repair and its activities in smooth operation. They perform various social services, help the infirm and others who have difficulty in caring for themselves, and participate in making decisions regarding church policy. In 1972–73, services in the new church at St. James were run by the Companions while the four *pakaako* all concentrated their efforts in the old church at St. John.

The Companions are respected and appreciated for the services they perform, and they are believed to possess spiritual power as a result of their association with the church. Because of that association others listen to them with deference and respect, but people are rarely afforded outward signs of ritual subordination on the basis of Companion membership.

As with the position of *pakaako*, Kompanion is not a traditional title, and there are no genealogical requirements for membership. One must be willing to devote extra time for prayer (about fifteen minutes a day after the regular services have disbanded), several hours a week for meetings to discuss church policy, and the time, effort, and responsibility for performing the religious and social services for which the Companions were organized. Despite the separation of genealogical rank from church leadership, however, the chiefs and *maru* continue to feel a sense of responsibility for smooth operation of the religious system. It is partly for that reason that the first chief's younger brother was head catechist in the early 1970s, and the *ariki*'s son was one of the assistants. In 2000, the chief's son, Pu Parikitonga (Harry Matakiapo), was serving as one of two head catechists. And it is for the same reason that both chiefs and the leading *maru* have assumed responsibility as Companions.

Religious Activities

Activities requiring collective action of the community at large may be divided into two broad categories: those directly related to the church and those that are not. The first group includes ceremonial feasts and activities directed toward church maintenance.

Major work in construction and maintenance of the church building is performed by the entire male population, under the direction of the catechist and/or chiefs. It was on the senior chief's instructions that Anutans constructed the St. James church; both the chiefs and the catechist contributed their labor in addition to directing operations, and every able-bodied man assisted. Similarly, the coconut-leaf shade house (*pare rau niu*) near the St. James church was constructed by the Anutan men at the catechist's instruction. When the shade house by the old St. John church was blown down in a gale one night, it was reconstructed according to the same procedure. Women sometimes help by carrying thatch and performing other minor chores, but all the carpentry and heavy work is done by men.

Smaller-scale maintenance projects, such as rethatching a church roof or decorating the building for a major festival like Easter or Christmas, are usually performed by the Companions. A few tasks, such as washing the benches once or twice a year, are assigned to the children and unmarried men and women. Should a church bench be badly damaged or defiled by menstrual blood, it is thrown out and another is built to take its place. The new bench, then, is built by one of the skilled carpenters—usually one who belongs to the Companions.

Also in the general category of church maintenance is the practice of collection. The church does not hold regular collections, but on important holy days a cup is passed around and everyone is asked to contribute. In the early 1970s, a normal contribution was about ten cents; in 2000, it was on the order of a dollar or two in Solomon Islands currency—somewhere between 20 and 50 cents U.S. The money is put into a church fund and used to purchase equipment. In 1972–73, the catechist was saving to buy an iron roof for the St. John church, and in the 1990s, the St. James church was rebuilt with milled lumber. Occasionally the catechist may instruct the women to make mats or order the men to plait sennit cord. These items are then sold to Tikopians or other visitors and the proceeds donated to the church fund.

On the ritual side is *te pakaari kai*, 'the presentation of first fruits.' In the days of the traditional religion, the first taro of any harvest was presented to the chief. In the 1970s it usually was presented to the church. The catechist might then keep it for himself and his domestic unit, give it to someone else, or have it used as part of the general food supply at a religious feast. In this way, it closely resembled the *pakaariki* offerings described earlier. In fact, if someone wished to present a first-fruit offering to the chief rather than the church, this still was an acceptable alternative. By 2000, the system had changed further, with the church increasingly taking over the chiefs' traditional role. Now a portion of the first crop to be harvested from a garden after a new planting is taken to the church, where it remains during the evening service. The vegetables then stay there overnight and are eventually sold to raise money for the church.

Fish are treated in a similar fashion. When a canoe goes out for the first time after it has been in storage, the fishermen take some of the catch to the church. Special offerings to the chiefs are now largely restricted to major religious holidays like Christmas and Easter.

All major holy days are celebrated with a feast and dance. In the early 1970s there was at least one such feast every two weeks or so; over the past three decades they have become less frequent. When such an occasion is imminent, the catechist instructs members of each household to go to their gardens and collect some food. Depending on the importance of the occasion and the state of the gardens, he announces the number of ovens to be prepared; and the amount of food the people harvest is thus adjusted. For such island-wide events, the domestic unit to which an oven house 'belongs' makes little difference. The catechist assigns cooking facilities with consideration to such practical concerns as size. The people who staff an oven cross-cut both household and clan. Who works where is flexible, and there are no consistent patterns based on kinship or household and clan membership. To a large degree, the catechist selects the teams, but there is a great deal of individual choice as well.

While the bulk of the community is preparing vegetable foods, one or more canoes go out to fish. Which canoes will go and who will constitute the crew ultimately is up to the catechist, but as in working the ovens, a measure of individual choice comes into play. When Anutans are preparing an exceptionally large feast, the fishing takes place for several days before as well as while the crops are being harvested. Then, on the day that the ovens are prepared, the canoes are temporarily retired, and the crew assists the remainder of the island in 'making oven' (*pai umu*). At times when the surf is too rough to take out the canoes, the catechist may organize a communal fish drive on the reef, and ovens are prepared either that afternoon or the following day.

Following the morning prayer on the day of the celebration, representatives of the *kanopenua* go to the ovens and carry back the food to the shade house by one of the two churches. In 1972–73, most of the celebrations were held outside the old church in Vatiana (see chapter 2), although a few feasts, including the St. James Day celebration, were held near the new church. With some exceptions, to be discussed below, the two congregations did not cook or eat separately. Rather, the community operated together as a single unit.

Quantities of food are such that it usually takes two or three hours to carry it all from the ovens to the site of the feast and distribute it into the usual number of baskets. Each *patongia* then sets up its coconut-leaf *tapakau* mat at its customary spot under the coconut-leaf roof and carries its allotted basket to the mat. The community leaders responsible for the distribution carry the *pakaariki* and *pakamisionari* baskets to the mats of the appropriate *patongia*. In addition, they may set out a separate basket and mat for the crews of the canoes that provided the fish.

Each *patongia* eats together as a unit. Households forming one *ngutuumu* (see chapter 5) share a mat and pool their baskets; and the fishermen usually eat together as a group. After the meal, islanders spend the afternoon dancing in the shade house. Sometimes around mid-afternoon the young men grasp their *tika* darts—long javelin-like implements with reed shafts and hardwood heads—and wander inland to the dart pitch (*te marae tika*) where they spend an hour or two in competition before washing and preparing for the evening service (cf. Firth 1930b). When the evening prayer is finished, the population recongregates at the site of the feast for dinner, and the evening is passed in dancing.

Most celebrations last for just a single day, but some of the more important ones go on for several. Around Christmas and Easter the festivities continue unabated for two to three weeks, during which periods no substantial work is permitted to take place. Gardening and planting are forbidden, as are canoe building, house construction, and all other major projects. The only productive work allowed is that directly involving food preparation, which becomes necessary about every third day.

The yield of a collective oven generally lasts the community about three days, during which time the feasting and dancing goes on

Photo 7.2   A late afternoon dart match in 1972.

without interruption. When the food supply runs down, Anutans take a day off to fish, harvest crops, and prepare what they have gathered in the ovens. The food is disbursed after church the following morning, and the community then has another two to three days of feasting and dancing before the process must be repeated. The cycle, as well as the number of cycles involved in the celebration, is regulated by the catechist, who may impose minor variations at any time.

In addition to the regularly observed holy days, the marriage ceremony and funeral are followed by church-sponsored feasts. These rituals are conducted according to the same patterns as church holidays. Other rites of passage, while not truly secular, are not under the church's authority. Their format was discussed in chapter 5.

Temporal Activities

The success of any economic endeavor depends on the good will of the ancestral deities or, at the present time, the Christian God. Therefore, all activity has its religious side, and there is no clear division between sacred and secular events. It is possible, however, to distinguish between behavior directly involving the church and activities in which the church takes part only indirectly as a means of ensuring success. Although not truly secular, the latter events might be viewed as temporal in that they are performed to satisfy needs other than maintaining the religious system.

During normal times, the *kanopenua* cooperates to perform assorted public works projects, to prepare temporal feasts, and to share or pool certain resources. As indicated in chapter 4, many crops are accessible to the entire community and cannot be reserved for any particular household. Whenever a large canoe, or a fleet of small ones, is taken for a fishing expedition, the fishermen distribute the catch to the *kanopenua*. Public works projects not directly pertaining to the church are organized by the chiefs, especially the Ariki i Mua. Either at the *pono* or in church, and either directly or through their *maru*, the chiefs announce to the population that they should meet at a certain place and time to rebuild an aqueduct, pull coconut seedlings from the ground in order to keep the nuts from sprouting, remove chickens from the hilltop where they might damage young taro plants, or participate in other projects of concern to the community at large.

Many projects include a cross-section of the population without involving every able-bodied individual. A good example of this is turmeric preparation. At any one time, the community is likely to have one or two experts who know the process. When the plants are ready, the experts choose a half dozen or a dozen persons to assist. The procedure still is surrounded by stringent taboos and lasts for several days, so that participation involves sacrifice of considerable personal comfort. Thus, except for the leaders, the team does not remain the same from one occasion to the next. To a large degree the team members are volunteers.

Sago preparation no longer is surrounded with taboos, but it sometimes is performed by a group of people that cross-cuts household boundaries and lines of kinship. Once during my initial study, all the unmarried people joined together to perform this task.

Just as the chief has power to organize public works projects for communal benefit, he may take extraordinary measures to protect the *kanopenua* in times of hardship. For example, as a result of the cyclone that struck Anuta just prior to my first arrival, food was in short supply throughout my period of residence. In response, the *pono*, under the senior chief's leadership, forbade the picking of green coconuts to drink so that they might mature and ensure an adequate supply of brown nuts for cooking. Taboos were placed on a few other crops, most notably papaya, to give the fruit a chance to ripen before being eaten by a hungry populace. In order to conserve food and regulate the utilization of scarce resources, the *pono* announced that during the recovery period each domestic unit would not cook for itself—rather, the community would 'make oven' as a single unit. At two- or three-day intervals, groups of people appointed by the *pono* would harvest foodstuffs from their gardens in predetermined quantities and deposit them at two or three cook houses, which were also designated by the *pono*. That evening after prayer, the baked food would be distributed to the community. Individual households were not forbidden to prepare food on their own, but they generally had all they needed from the regulated community ovens. Since the island's gardens and ovens were being pooled, the *pono* decided that the *kanopenua* should take collective responsibility for a certain amount of cultivation as well, and it declared that for two days each week everyone should participate in a collective work project, cultivating plots of manioc.

In addition to the holy days and rites of passage, Anutans sometimes perform a special type of feast that is intended to honor a deserving person and is not tied to any regular occasion. I took part in two such feasts, called *pungaumu*. The first was initiated by the heads of the Kainanga i Pangatau. It was performed by the two *pakaaropa* clans to honor the two chiefs and show appreciation for their vigilance in protecting the community during its time of hardship. For several days, the *pakaaropa* prepared huge quantities of food, which they took from their own gardens. On the allotted day, the *kanopenua*

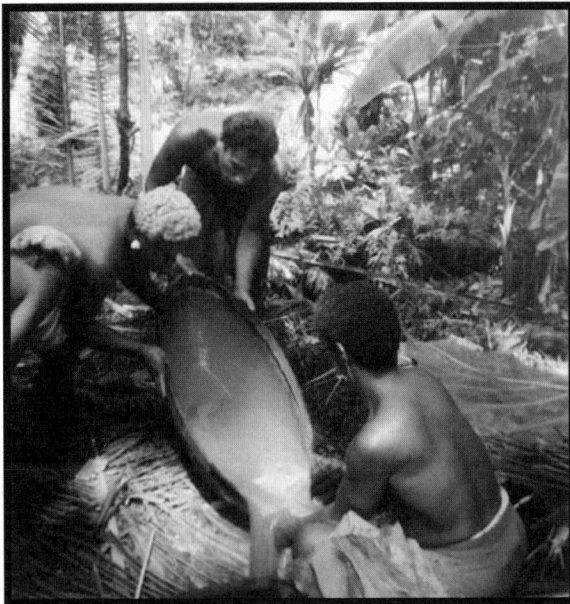

Photo 7.3 Turmeric preparation is still surrounded by elaborate ritual.

gathered outside the house of the senior chief. The latter, along with several invited guests, was painted with turmeric and partook of special portions of the most highly esteemed foods inside his house. The following day, the chiefly clans provided a feast outside the house of Pu Penuakimoana, one of the initiators of the *pungaumu*, as an expression of appreciation to the *pakaaropa* for the honor they had been paid.

The second *pungaumu* was sponsored by the Ariki i Mua in honor of the Ariki Tafua, the second-ranking Tikopian chief, when he came to visit Anuta for several months. This time the island was divided not according to clan membership. Individuals and households attached themselves to one side or the other depending on whether they were most closely related to the Tikopian (through *tauranga* bonds; through the Ariki Tafua's sister, who had married an Anutan man; or through other Tikopians who had settled on Anuta) or to the Anutan chief. Presents of pandanus mats and bark cloth were prepared and exchanged between the two sides. The bark cloth presented by the Tikopian side was made from trees standing in the gardens of Tikopians' *tauranga* or spouses, and that presented by the Anutans' side came from the gardens of the other *patongia*. On this occasion, two weeks elapsed between the initial feast and the counterfeast sponsored by the Tikopian and his kin.

Spiritual Power and Temporal Authority

Anutan social structure is dominated by an interplay between genealogical relationship and code for conduct, both of which are intimately tied to the concept of *aropa*. These considerations, in combination, define the outlines of the kinship system, the social units into which the population is divided, the political and honorific relationships among these social units and the individuals who constitute their membership, the traditional religious system, and even, to a degree, the modern church. No less important, the interplay between these complementary and yet potentially opposing principles governs the merging of these subsystems into an integrated whole.

Manuu or *mana*—Anutans use both terms to similar effect, but the former is more common—designates a kind of power or efficacy, and it is believed generally to be possessed in proportion to one's social rank. It is inherited from one's father—one Anutan even suggested that this is the basis for using *mana* as a term of address for 'father'—and it flows down through the patriline. The higher one's rank, the more *manuu* one has to pass on to the next generation. Anutans believe that it goes to an elder son before a younger, so that by the time it gets to the youngest, there may be relatively little left for him. In other words, its commonest immediate source is genealogical seniority based on primogeniture and patrilineal descent.

Women have less *manuu* than men. Children have little or none regardless of their genealogical position and gender. It increases gradually as they get older and grow into adulthood. A title like *ariki* or *pakaako* brings a great deal of *manuu* to the one who bears it. Despite the varied immediate sources, however, its ultimate origin is the same. In the ancient religion it derived from the traditional deities (or, according to some contemporary Anutans, from Satan); in more recent times it comes from the Christian God, who often is referred to in church services as *te tapito o te manuu katoa*—'the source of all power.'

Manuu is manifested in such qualities as wisdom, physical strength, occupational expertise, and skill in solving problems. Ideally, genealogically senior men are also competent, effective individuals, in which case the genealogical and behavioral determinants of rank are mutually reinforcing. Sometimes, however, people demonstrate through their unusual ability or notable ineptitude that they possess *manuu* in a greater or lesser degree than is expected on the basis of ascriptive genealogical criteria. This is taken as an indication of special favor or disfavor by the gods (or God), and thus there exists a degree of openness in the Anutan systems of political authority and honorific rank.

Anuta's ritual and political hierarchy is enforced by possession of *manuu*. In earlier times, islanders say that if a chief were annoyed at someone he could curse him with illness, misfortune, and even sterility or death; and despite establishment of the church, most Anutans are convinced that chiefs retain such power to this day. Over the past three decades I have recorded many cases of emotional and physical illness, natural disaster, and other misfortunes which Anutans attributed to the victim's alleged disrespect or disobedience toward a chief. Pu Rongomai (see chapter 6) fell ill because he opposed his elder brother, who was also heir apparent to the chieftainship. And while I was on Anuta in the early 1970s, there were at least two physical illnesses, one proving fatal, that were said to have stemmed from the victims' failure to care properly for their aged parents.[8]

Cases such as these illustrate the risk involved in failure to respect persons of superior rank. But the legitimate right to exercise political authority derives from ancient tradition (*te tukutukunga mai mua*) and service as protector of one's subordinates' well-being. This was illustrated most dramatically in the measures taken by the senior chief to deal with the food shortage created by the cyclone of February 1972. No one at the time could know just how severe the scarcity might be, or whether, for that matter, it might develop into a full-fledged famine. It was the chief's feeling that if no corrective measures were taken, some of the poorer members of his community might be in danger of starvation. Therefore, he determined to distribute the wealth so that—as he put it—if any of his followers should starve, all would die together. He did not feel it right for one person to enjoy a surplus while someone else went hungry, so he decided that during the period of scarcity food resources would be pooled and distributed equitably to everyone.

If this were the whole story it would demonstrate the chief's assumption of responsibility for the collective welfare, but there is more. The food that was harvested, cooked, and distributed to the *kanopenua* did not come from *all* the gardens but from those of the Kainanga i Mua; and it was the members of the leading clan who carried out the food preparation and distribution. The Kainanga i Tepuko assisted the Kainanga i Mua with contributions from its gardens, and members of the second clan helped staff the ovens. The *pakaaropa*, by contrast, were able to keep their food as a reserve supply or use it for ceremonial occasions. This arrangement was related neither to numerical superiority nor material wealth. The Kainanga i Pangatau is as large as the Kainanga i Mua and somewhat richer in number of gardens, while the Kainanga i Tepuko in both respects is but a distant third. Rather, it reflects the position of the leading clan, headed by its chief, as protector of the island. The Kainanga i Tepuko followed the example set by its founder in his role as first lieutenant to Tearakura during the latter's lifetime and as chief of the island after his brother's death by assisting Tearakura's descendants in their task of caring for the island.

The relationship between the chiefly and non-chiefly clans is best expressed in the very terms by which the men of the two types of clan are called. *Maru* refers to shade from the sun or shelter from the rain. A husband may be depicted as his wife's *maru*, and I have heard a funeral lament for a dead chief in which the singer describes the *ariki* as "my *maru*." When this is combined with the role of the men in the chiefly clans, who are called by the same term, it may be viewed as a unitary concept translatable as 'guardian' or 'protector.'

The men of the lesser *kainanga*, and the clans themselves, are referred to as *pakaaropa*. *Paka* is the causative prefix, and *aropa*, which I have discussed at length particularly in chapter 3, means something like 'sympathy' or 'pity.' One may roughly translate *pakaaropa*, then, as 'sympathy-producing' or 'pitiable.' The *pakaaropa* are spiritually weak. Because of their genealogical position, they do not have enough *manuu* to take care of themselves and, in traditional times, they did not bear enough influence with the important gods to ensure the continued welfare of the island on which they lived. Thus, they produce feelings of *aropa* in those with greater *manuu*. The *maru* express their *aropa* by providing protection in both the supernatural sphere by performing kava rites to propitiate the gods (or at the present time, by making sure that the church operates smoothly) and in the temporal sphere by ensuring that the *pakaaropa* have the material resources to lead a reasonably comfortable existence. In return for the *maru*'s solicitous behavior, the *pakaaropa* owe the *maru* and their chiefs allegiance, obedience, ritual deference, and occasional offerings of material goods as symbols of their *aropa* (translated in this case, perhaps, as 'appreciation'), which then must be reciprocated.

These dynamics permeate Anutan social structure. Men own the canoes and have primary interest in the gardens.[9] Their economic preeminence is connected with their superior *manuu* and fashions their role as protectors and providers for the welfare of their wives and sisters. It is in this context that male ritual and political dominance must be understood.

Parents care for and protect their children. Because of this assistance and protection, which is provided during a person's most vulnerable period, Anutans say that the respect due to a father is second to none. Significantly, as one grows older and the dependence relationship reverses, respect relations also shift in favor of the child.

Older persons normally are more experienced and, therefore, assumed to be more knowledgeable and competent than their juniors, who depend on them for tutelage and assistance. A strong man, great warrior, or man of outstanding wisdom is expected to use his prowess to protect the island from foreign invasion and to maintain order among the population. And the church as "the source of all power" assumes ultimate responsibility for the community's well-being.

Summary

Structurally, the *kanopenua* resembles the *patongia* and the *kainanga*, but it incorporates the whole community. Most community members share common descent from Pu Taupare, an Uvean immigrant who lived about 15 generations in the past, but this is not necessary for membership in the *kanopenua*. Each resident and each nonresident Anutan who takes part in the kinship system and belongs to a domestic unit is, thereby, a member of a *kainanga* and the *kanopenua* as well. In the absence of a genealogical tie, one may gain *kanopenua* membership by acting as a good Anutan, obeying the *pono* and the chiefs, following the customs of the land, and exhibiting the *aropa* for which every Anutan is responsible.

The *kanopenua's* authority structure resembles that of the lower-level units. At its head is Tui Anuta, the most genealogically senior man on the island. Below the first chief the seniority principle still holds, but when it comes to a choice between a junior member of a senior group or a senior member of a junior group, there is no clear, unequivocal way in which preeminence can be determined. This ambivalence is reflected most vividly in the ambiguous position of the second chief, who is respected and honored as an *ariki* but whose political authority at times may be subordinate to the leading *maru*. At lower levels seniority becomes still less clear but also less important, as such other criteria as kin-class membership are invoked when political authority and ritual deference come into question.

Even where genealogical seniority is clear, it may be overridden by explicit agreement and corresponding social action. A genealogically legitimate successor may nonetheless be denied the chieftainship if he shows deficient *aropa* or lacks the necessary competence and spiritual force. *Manuu* is critical to chiefly succession as it makes possible the *aropa*—that is, the compassion and generosity—that Anutans require of their *ariki*.

A second authority structure centers around the church. Here, the importance of genealogical seniority is minimized. Still, persons of high rank in the temporal sphere feel responsibility for the island's welfare and, thus, for the church's proper operation. For this reason, in 1972–73 the first chief led services at the second church, his brother served as head catechist, and his son served as one of the catechist's three assistants. This pattern has been continued through the start of the new century, with the chief's son now serving as one of Anuta's two head catechists.

Functionally, the *kanopenua* most frequently comes into action as a composite of smaller groups or segments, as when the *pakaaropa* hold a feast in honor of the chiefly clans, or in certain rites of passage where, between ego's maternal and paternal kin, the entire population is included. At other times, the community may act as a single corporate unit under the leadership of the *pono* or the church, as in preparing for religious festivals, carrying out public works projects, distributing fish, or utilizing certain crops. But most importantly perhaps, the *kanopenua* defines itself in contrast to the outside world.

Symbolizing the Anutan community and distinguishing it from the wider world are the island itself, its language, its customs, and its chiefs. Anutans share a profound sense of place. They are proud of

Anutans Identify With:		As Opposed To:
Anuta	vs.	Tikopia
Anuta + Tikopia	vs.	Tonga + Samoa + etc.
Anuta + Tikopia + Tonga + Samoa + etc. = Kiri Toto ('Red Skin')	vs.	Penua Uri ('Melanesians')
Kiri Toto + Penua Uri ('Melanesians') = Penua Uri ('Colored People')	vs.	Paparangi ('Europeans')

Variant A

Penua Uri + Paparangi = Atangata Katoa

Anuta	vs.	Tikopia
Anuta + Tikopia	vs.	Malaita + Makira + etc. = Solomon
Anuta + Tikopia + Malaita + Makira + etc. = Solomon/ Penua Uri	vs.	Paparangi

Variant B

Solomon + Paparangi = Atangata Katoa

Figure 7.1   Anutans' Extended Social Classification.

their customs and jealous of their sovereignty. After the cyclone of February 1972, the protectorate government sent a shipment of relief supplies which the Anutans refused for fear that strings might be attached which would result in compromising their political autonomy. They steadfastly refused to join the local governing council for the Eastern Outer Islands until December 1992 when local authorities agreed to let them be represented by their chiefs, and they have been adamant in their refusal to pay taxes to the national and provincial governments. Yet, Anuta is being pulled inexorably into the larger world community.

The people have come to depend on many services from overseas. They are curious to know about the world beyond the horizon. Many young men are eager for travel and adventure. Anutans depend on the government for transportation and radio contact, such as it is, with other islands. They have come to enjoy European goods of many types and appreciate the opportunity to earn the cash with which to buy them. The proper role of medicine has become a controversial issue, but most Anutans are grateful for whatever medical care the government provides. Thus, despite their independent will and pride in maintaining their autonomy, Anutans find themselves drawn ever more into the orbit of Temotu Province, the Solomon Islands, and the world at large. Even this world, however, is not an undifferentiated unit. Anutans clearly recognize the geographical, physical, linguistic, and cultural affinity between themselves and Tikopia, and they identify with Tikopians in opposition to the remainder of humanity. This is expressed in the special *tauranga* relationship and patterns of intermarriage. When overseas in the central Solomons, Tikopians and Anutans often live together in a single community, occasionally sleeping, eating, and even performing rituals together. On a more distant plane Anutans identify themselves with the Polynesians of Tonga, Samoa, 'Uvea, New Zealand and the various outliers in the Solomon Islands, describing them as *kiri toto* ('red skin') in opposition to the *penua uri* ('black islands' [i.e., Melanesians]) on the one hand and *paparangi* ('Europeans') on the other. Yet in opposition to the Europeans, they identify themselves as *penua uri* along with all the other colored people of the world.[10] Finally, *atangata katoa* includes the whole of humanity—of which the Anutans view themselves as one essential segment and in which they see themselves as playing an integral part.

Chapter 8

Three Decades of Change and an Uncertain Future

A visit to Anuta in the early 1970s made me feel as if I were stepping back two centuries—to an era when traditional Polynesian culture thrived and European contact was a mere speck on the distant horizon. Even thirty years ago, of course, this was an illusion. All cultures experience constant change, and Polynesian communities have always differed from one another in important respects. By the time of my first visit, Anuta had been Christian for over half a century, and the ancient worship rites had been abandoned. Introduced crops such as manioc had become staples, tobacco was perceived as a necessity, and people had come to depend on metal tools, monofilament fishing line, kerosene, batteries, waterproof flashlights, and a host of other imported items of predominantly Western manufacture. Anutans had traveled throughout the Solomons, and a few had visited other countries working aboard ships or on Fijian and Australian sugar plantations. Still, economic life centered on subsistence production. Canoes and houses were built exclusively from locally produced wood, leaves, and sennit cord. Only one man spoke reasonably good English, and but a handful had command of Pijin. Social organization and daily life revolved around the extended family domestic unit, and social relations were structured according to kin ties. The hereditary chieftainship, bolstered by notions of *manuu* and *aropa*, was alive and well, and the chiefs' authority was virtually unchallenged.

191

All that time, the island's welfare was threatened by a food shortage because of a devastating storm and subsequent drought. Yet, Anutans weathered the challenge quite effectively, depending on their own resources and resourcefulness. Thirty years later, Anutans face a new set of challenges grounded on their integration into the wider political sphere of the Solomon Islands and the world market economy. The result has been uneasiness and periodic conflict as Anutans look toward an uncertain future and debate their most appropriate response. In retrospect they view the early 1970s as a golden age when all was right—when people got along well, respected the island's customs and its chiefs, and shared a sense of confidence and purpose. In this chapter, I will try to summarize the Anutan experience of the past three decades, consider where it has led, and offer a few observations about what the future may hold.

External Pressures and Internal Change

Superficially, as of my most recent visit to Anuta in October 2000, remarkably little appeared to have changed. Islanders organized their lives in terms of the old social units. Those units continued to be defined by the same interplay of *aropa* and genealogical connection. The chiefs continued to exercise political control, and the ranking system remained essentially intact. The economy continued to be dominated by subsistence production. And Anutans continued to perform the old life-crisis rites very much as in the 1970s. On closer inspection, however, stress and change were unmistakable.

Anuta, owing to its isolation, small size, and paucity of commercially exploitable resources, has been less affected by external pressures than most communities in the so-called developing world. Nonetheless, two centuries of European contact have yielded access to expanded travel, new ideas, worldly experience, and a variety of European goods. As early as the 1800s, a few Anutans journeyed as deck hands to such far-flung places as New Zealand, Australia, and America's Pacific Coast. The Anglican Church has operated on the island for almost a century. Metal axes, knives, and fishhooks were introduced relatively early, while other imported commodities are now in high demand.

In order to acquire cash to purchase manufactured goods, and as a safety valve for an expanding population, Anutans in increasing numbers have moved off their home island. At first, such emigration was limited to a few individuals joining groups of Tikopian plantation workers—mostly at the Levers copra plantations in the Russell Islands of the central Solomons (Firth 1969; Larson 1966, 1977). Starting around 1960, however, the number of Anutans traveling abroad increased dramatically. By the time of my first visit to Anuta, every adult male had been overseas at some time during his life. In some cases, this amounted only to brief stays on Tikopia; in others it involved a permanent move to the central Solomons. Most émigrés have worked as low-paid manual laborers. A few, however, have attended secondary school and even held prestigious jobs.

Commercialization of Interpersonal Relations

The market economy has made itself felt both on Anuta and among Anutans residing overseas. I initially became aware of the resulting tensions as far back as the mid-1970s. The first issue of contention was sale of taro, betel, tobacco, and bananas by a few households to others that were short of food. Such behavior clearly contradicted the Anutan principles of *aropa* and kinship. Pu Koroatu, the senior chief, viewed himself as guardian of local tradition and quickly forbade the practice. From the sellers' perspective, however, exchanging food for money was part of a new orientation involving commitment to upward mobility in European terms. It provided an opportunity to accrue cash on Anuta and was thus part of a strategy for obtaining Western commodities. Moreover, the first two domestic units to start selling food had children in school overseas whom they felt obliged to support financially. Therefore, those 'houses' did not share the positive value that the chief placed on collective enterprise, discipline, and community harmony. They resisted orders to desist from selling food and, in fact, the practice spread. To make matters worse, several *maru*, on whom the chief depended for enforcement of his orders, joined the opposition.

As tensions waxed and waned over the next several years, the chief's authority—both religious and secular—was challenged. He tried to exercise moral leadership by leading services and preaching sermons in the St. James church. About 1979 or 1980, however, a number of *maru* began putting pressure on the chief to step down as catechist.

At first the chief refused to abandon his post, believing it his duty to protect both custom and the church. When the *maru* remained adamant that one person could not simultaneously be catechist and chief, he announced that he would give up his position as *ariki* rather than relinquish his religious role. The other catechists asked him for permission to discuss the issue at a *pono*. But he told them he could not tender permission as he was no longer chief; instead, they should go to the Ariki Tepuko. Pu Tepuko replied, however, that he was chief by virtue of his relationship with Tui Anuta. "I sit at the bottom of the *tapakau* ('floor mat'); he sits at the top. So ask him. If he is not a chief, neither am I." Thus, an impasse had been reached.

Pu Koroatu eventually acceded to the *maru*'s demand and stepped down not only from his post as catechist, but also as leader of the Companions. Still, tension continued to build. The *ariki* left the village and constructed a small house atop the hill, where he dwelt by himself for a month. During that period, he carried a small adze whenever he went out to walk about the island. Word spread that he planned to massacre his subjects some night while they slept. In truth, he armed himself in fear for his own life. The chief's dramatic action forced people to look at just how serious the situation had become, and in an effort to cool tempers, he finally returned to his village residence.

Around that time, Pu Teukumarae, the chief's younger brother, came to Anuta for a visit. Pu Teukumarae, known to non-Anutans as Frank Kataina, was prominent for many years in the national police force. During that time, he served in such important posts as Superintendent of the Police Training School and chief government prosecutor for criminal cases. Although the youngest of his sibling set, he is the most worldly. He has lived in Australia and New Zealand and speaks three languages eloquently: Anutan, English, and Solomon Islands Pijin. He is a man of poise, self-confidence, and admirable leadership qualities. His responsibilities gave him little chance to return home, but he was kept abreast of developments by Anutans who passed through Honiara; and every three years he was provided with a three-month leave so that he might visit his kin on Anuta. The moment Pu Teuku walked ashore, he told me, he could feel the tension. In church, he felt as if he were attending a "club" rather than a service. After church, another brother, Pu Teaokena, told him in detail what had been going on.

Pu Teuku called the *maru* together to discuss the island's problems. Particularly on the question of selling food, he backed the chief's position. An argument ensued, and the chiefs had to disband the meeting before it turned violent. A *pono* was called, and the catechists addressed the crowd. Pu Tereata (now known as Pu Penuaika) gave a moving speech, which Nau Teukumarae (Frank's wife) related to me. Pu Tereata said, pointing to the Patu o Mangoo ('Shark Rock.' a boulder about a mile off shore):

> See that rock out there. It's out by itself in the ocean. We have no way to get there. I want you all to take buckets of sand from the beach and build a bridge.

> When I was young, I remember the island as being green and beautiful. Now that I'm an adult, it makes me very sad to see everything brown and yellow. It hasn't rained for two years. The crops are dying.

> Why is this? It is because certain people have abandoned the chief. The chief is like that rock out there. If you want this island to become green again, you must build a bridge and renew your relationship, giving the chief appropriate respect and obedience.

At this time, Nau Teuku had a disturbing dream. It was during the Easter celebration, and she dreamed that she was with her husband on Anuta (as indeed she was). People were getting ready for a feast in the coconut-leaf shade house near the St. John church and went up to the hill to get banana leaves. Each one carried a pile of leaves, but there was one left over. She thought that she would carry the extra pile herself and bent down to pick it up. When she lifted the leaves, she found that they were covering a hole. She looked into the hole and saw a giant snake and a centipede. She turned to her husband and said, "I thought you told me that there aren't any snakes or poisonous insects on Anuta." He replied, "That's right. There aren't."[1]

She said, "You're a liar! Come and look in this hole." After arguing for a while, Pu Teuku went to look in the hole. She said, "Look! Isn't that a snake?"

The two animals started climbing out. Pu Teuku dropped his bush knife and ran away. Nau Teuku picked up the knife and killed the two animals. She placed them back down in the hole and replaced the cover. At that point, her husband rolled over in his sleep, hit her, and she awoke. The next morning, they asked Nau Koroatu, the chief's wife, to tell her husband the story and request an interpretation. He refused. The chief's son implored him, but he still refused. So Pu Teuku told his wife to ask the chief herself. The *ariki* told her that he would not give a full interpretation, but he said that as soon as the Easter celebration was over, there would be a time of great sadness.

On Easter Sunday, a woman named Nau Pouro gave birth to a son. The following week the celebration ended. As people began walking back to Rotoapi village from the dance ground, they heard wailing from the woman's house. The moment that the dancing stopped, Nau Pouro's son died. Within a week, an eighteen-year-old youth, Alfred Tauvaka, fell to his death from the cliff at the island's north coast while climbing down to hunt for shellfish. Nau Tanukope, a 60-year-old woman, died. There was great sickness on the island. Everyone but Pu Teuku was incapacitated with influenza and conjunctivitis. Pu Koroatu's leg was paralyzed, so he could not walk to treat the sick; the infirm had to be carried to the chief, who got up from his sick bed to treat them in the traditional manner—by laying on of hands. Pu Teuku tried his best to care for the afflicted, but he could not prepare enough food single-handed. At the same time, crops were failing. There was no taro, papaya, or banana. People survived by eating breadfruit, manioc, and fermented *ma*.

These events were uniformly interpreted as resulting from the social conflicts on the island, and people decided that their entire community would be in jeopardy if the situation were to continue. Both sides, therefore, worked to cool tempers and reestablish overt peace. But this was accomplished by people talking less about the sources of tension—not by resolving them. Families that had been selling food desisted, or at least kept their actions hidden, but they still maintained that their conduct had been appropriate under the circumstances. And the chief refrained from vocal opposition to what he perceived as incorrect behavior, but he registered his protest by refusing to attend church services on Sundays.

Relations with Governmental Bodies

At the same time that factional strife began to tear at the Anutan community, conflicts were taking shape between Anutans and the Solomon Islands government. Regardless of their internal divisions, Anutans have been united in their distrust of the national and provincial governments that claim dominion over them. They are acutely conscious of their status as part of a small Polynesian minority in an overwhelmingly Melanesian country. They perceive the government as being under the control of people who are very different from themselves and who, therefore, have no interest in their welfare.[2] Furthermore, despite some criticism of the chief, the chieftainship itself is a key symbol of Anutan cultural identity, distinctiveness, and self-respect. Anutans agree that traditional custom and local sovereignty are important and should be preserved; and for that reason many Anutans have advocated independence from the Solomon Islands. They have consistently refused to pay taxes and, until recently, boycotted all provincial and national elections. Anutans recognize that they receive important services from the government—most notably—transportation, education, and medical care. In the minds of many, however, the costs of political association with the Solomons outweigh the benefits of those services.

When asked why they refuse participation in governmental bodies, the first issue Anutans cite is taxation. They say, very simply, that they have no source of income and, therefore, cannot pay taxes. At times, the government reportedly has offered to reduce Anuta's tax rate in light of the island's limited resources, but even that conciliatory gesture has met a negative response. The senior chief expressed to me concern that if Anutans were to pay less tax than people of other islands, it would become a source of inter-island animosity and conflict. Some Anutans also feared that the offer was a Machiavellian ploy. Once they committed themselves to the government, they believed, the authorities would raise tax rates and imprison anyone unable to pay. Anutans hold the government responsible, at least in part, for the scarcity of shipping and their island's low priority on shipping schedules. They say that the government has refused assistance in the aftermath of several storms that decimated crops. And, in general, they feel that if they did pay tax, the benefits would go to other islands.

Anutans in 1983 unanimously agreed that whether to join the larger polity was a decision for the chiefs, but on this issue they also strongly supported the chiefs' position. The unsolicited expressions of suspicion and animosity toward governmental bodies were striking. Among Anutans living in the central Solomons, the same underlying feelings were expressed as on Anuta, but these were sometimes tempered by a recognition of governmental power and that in the long run the chiefs would have to come to terms with external authorities.

Anutans in Honiara

At least since the 1950s, Anutans have been traveling to the central Solomons for a variety of reasons. Until recently, most short-term (and some long-term) laborers have worked in the Russell Islands. Other prospective wage earners have gravitated to Honiara.

As the Solomons' capital, Honiara is the country's center of commerce and shipping. It is a convenient stopover point for travelers to and from the Russells. A number of Anutans have attended school on Guadalcanal Island. Others have worked as carpenters or gardeners for the Honiara Town Council, as bus and taxi drivers, as officers in the national police force, or as local security guards. In addition, people sometimes visit Honiara to see kin who have settled there or to enjoy a change of scenery. For those residing in the Honiara area on a long-term basis, material rewards and opportunities for social advancement in Western terms have, at times, been substantial. But the rewards come at a heavy price.

The price lies largely in contradictions between what Anutans view as ancient custom and realities of urban life. Anutans, regardless of where they live, consider themselves to be members of one overarching community. Even those who have spent most of their lives in town and may never return home except for brief visits do not perceive themselves to be part of a community that is in any significant way different from or independent of Anuta and its chiefs. Without exception, Anutans value their home island and its customs (*nga tuku-tukunga*). For Anutans in the central Solomons, what sets them apart from other people with whom they come into daily contact is: their attachment to their island; recognition of the island's chiefs as foci of collective loyalty and centers of authority, even with respect to matters arising outside of Anuta; and participation in a system of relations based on *aropa*. Yet, they are hundreds of miles distant from Anuta. They are subject to a government and system of laws that is wholly independent of the Anutan chiefs. And wage labor, along with production for private profit, directly contradicts the *aropa* ethic. Much of Anutan life in Honiara revolves around the drive to reconcile these contradictory impulses—to strike a balance between custom and the practicalities of living in an urban center, being immersed in the money economy, and being subject to national and local governments whose power is recognized even if their legitimacy is questioned.

Commitment to Anuta and its way of life is visible in many of the Honiara enclave's living arrangements. As of June 1988, I counted sixty Anutans living on Guadalcanal. These included people born on Anuta; their spouses, whether of Anutan birth or not; and all their children. Of the sixty, 36 slept in a cluster of three houses in White River, a Honiara suburb to the west of town. Several others lodged with Tikopians in White River and were regular visitors in the three Anutan houses.

The three houses formed the core of the Anutan community on Guadalcanal. They were all within a few dozen yards of one another, and their residents were in constant contact. Approximately eleven people regularly slept in the smallest house, a simple concrete structure with four bedrooms separated by a central foyer, and graced with electric lighting but no plumbing. A somewhat larger wooden house, with raised floor, indoor plumbing, and a full kitchen, held about a dozen bodies. The largest of the houses—a not-quite-completed structure on stilts, perhaps ten feet off the ground, with two large bedrooms, living room, kitchen, and veranda—held about fourteen persons including myself. People in the largest and the smallest houses operated as a single household, cooking and eating their evening meals together in the foyer of the concrete structure. People in the third house usually ate separately. However, parties and dances drew participants from all three houses plus assorted friends and relatives from the surrounding area.

Within each house, the usual pattern was for a married couple and their children to share a room. Unmarried boys and men slept in a common area like a veranda, cook house, or living room. However, this was flexible. For example, Pu Penuamuri often preferred to sleep outside in a shed next to the middle house to get away from his baby's crying. When the shed was full, he often slept in the living room of the large house. His wife and child shared a bedroom with another woman and her baby.

Each morning someone from each house would heat water for coffee, while someone with a few cents to his credit walked three blocks to the local store to bring back a few loaves of bread. As people awoke, they would help themselves to bread and butter, fix some instant coffee, and drift off to work. Those not holding paying jobs or watching children might go to the nearby garden land which had been allocated to the Anutan community by the Honiara Town Council, and spend a few hours cultivating manioc or yams. Wage workers

Photo 8.1 Pu Avatere (John Tope) performing a dance at a community party inside his house in White River, near Honiara, in 1993.

on their way home at the end of the work day were likely to stop at the market for fresh fish, vegetables, and betel, or at a store for biscuits and tinned fish. This was then pooled with the garden produce, cooked communally, and eaten by the household as a collectivity. On weekends and special occasions, members of all three households plus other Anutans in the area worked together to prepare a variety of traditional foods. These were then shared at communal feasts and dances. Anutans in Honiara have thus done their best to recreate their traditional socioeconomic system under conditions of wage employment and commodity production.

The attempt to retain ancient custom, as well as the difficulties in doing so, also can be seen in marriage patterns. Through the generations, the vast majority of Anutans have married other Anutans. In part, this may be attributed to the insular character of the Anutan community and lack of contact with outsiders. But in large part it is also the result of a conscious decision to maintain Anutan customs and the feeling that, should people marry outside their community, customs would quickly become diluted.

By 1973, there had been a number of marriages between Tikopians and Anutans. Such marriages were deemed acceptable because of the similarity between the two communities. If one goes back six generations or more, oral traditions identify immigrants from several Polynesian islands who married Anutans. However, as of 1973, there was only one Anutan who had ever married a non-Polynesian.

As more Anutans spent increasingly long periods away from home, the old marital patterns became harder to maintain. Long-term emigrants were predominantly male, and by the time they returned home, most women of their age group had already married. Thus, the men were faced with a choice between wedding non-Anutans or remaining single. In the Russell Islands, Anutan men were married to either Anutan or Tikopian women; in Honiara, not one Anutan man in 1983 had an Anutan wife. A few had opted not to marry. Two were married to Tikopians. Two were married to Melanesians—one from Santa Isabel and one from Malaita. And one was married to the daughter of a Tuvaluan couple who had immigrated to the Solomons. Since 1988, the constellation of personnel has included several couples in which both spouses were Anutan. Still, the tendency is more and more to marry non-Anutans.

The dilemma facing Anutan men in Honiara is exemplified by the marriage of Frank Kataina (Pu Teukumarae). In 1983, Frank was a high-ranking official in the national police force, and his wife was the Solomons' first policewoman. Her parents had immigrated to the Solomons from Nanumea in the Ellice Islands (now Tuvalu). She had been raised in Kira Kira, one of the country's main administrative centers, and in Solomon Islands terms she was a city girl. She also was literate, sophisticated, intelligent, and outgoing. Apparently an ideal match.

However, as a "city girl," she had assimilated Western feminist values of independence and self-realization. Although attached to her husband, she continued to associate with many of her old friends, going by herself to concerts, dances, and parties, and sometimes wearing slacks or even shorts—daring attire for a Solomon Islands woman even in Honiara in the 1980s. Had Frank been an ordinary man, people might have registered their disapproval and then left the matter. As he was a leading officer and brother of Anuta's senior chief, however, his wife's behavior was perceived as an attack on the integrity of traditional custom, and pressure mounted upon him to leave her. By June 1984, the two had separated. Four years later, it was clear the break was permanent.

Frank's marriage and its unhappy outcome illustrate the value that Anutans place on keeping their community distinct by maintaining rigid island endogamy. While divorce among Anutans is virtually non-existent, marriages to non-Anutans (with the exception of Tikopians, who are almost regarded as honorary Anutans) most often have dissolved under the influence of social pressure. In this way, even inter-island marriage has served to underscore Anutan distinctiveness and to maintain cultural boundaries rather than break them down.

To operate within the framework of a money economy and remain faithful to the principles of *aropa* poses no fewer problems for Anutans in Honiara than does marriage. Housing and food are expensive—comparable to Western Europe, Australia, or the United States. For government employees, housing is partially subsidized. The government provides a certain amount of garden land. And many people build canoes so they can fish on their days off. Still, the amount of time available and the productivity of garden land and ocean are far below what Anutans enjoy back home. Substantial sums of money, therefore, are essential to survival. Yet many pressures on the wage earner in Honiara make it difficult to save and accumulate financial resources.

All Anutans, regardless of how long they have been overseas, are expected to contribute to their *patongia*'s well-being. Anutans have come, over the years, to depend on a variety of commodities of European manufacture, and their acquisition requires money. In addition, Anutans need funds for boat fare if they are to travel overseas, and to pay tuition for children seeking secondary education. Since opportunities for monetary income on Anuta are almost non-existent, a substantial proportion of the cash that Anutans earn in the central Solomons finds its way back to Anuta. Requests from home by people with little concept of the cost of living in town often are exorbitant. Yet to deny assistance to one's closest kin violates *aropa* and contravenes Anutan moral sensibilities.

Anutans constantly pass through Honiara, visiting for periods of anywhere from a few days to many months—or even years. Typically, these visitors are unemployed with little cash. Furthermore, a housing shortage makes it difficult to find accommodations on short notice even for people who do have money. Thus, visitors inevitably stay in the houses of their employed fellow islanders.

For the people who own or rent a dwelling, it is a burden to accommodate as many as a dozen long-term visitors. The houses become crowded and uncomfortable. Often, the best rooms or sleeping places must be turned over to guests of high rank in the traditional system. These guests use water, electricity, and gas, and they must be fed. They are unfamiliar with city foods, do not shop, and have little concept of the relative expense of various provisions; thus, they often indulge in the most expensive items, which then have to be replaced or done without. In short, visitors rarely contribute financially to the household and often are a major drain. Yet to put them out—or even to suggest that they eat more of the less expensive items—would be a breach of etiquette and is avoided.

It is easy to appreciate the dilemma faced by an Anutan wage earner in Honiara after even a short period of participant observation. For several months in 1983–84, my family and I stayed in the house of Frank Kataina. Of the fifteen or so people with whom I shared the house, only Frank was regularly employed. The two of us, then, were supporting the entire household. The following experiences, recorded a few days before I left, are typical:

> We got a large jar of shampoo for about $4.50. Rachel [a pseudonym] used it to wash clothes, and within one afternoon, the jar was empty.

> Last Thursday, I bought a large tin of Milo [a powdered chocolate drink] so that there would be some for our children to take with their antimalaria medication on Sunday. Sunday morning, my wife went to fix the Milo and it was gone. That afternoon, I got another tin from the Rove store; the next morning, it was finished.

> Frank purchased a case of Taiyo tuna, and the first day, several tins were devoured with rice and potato. Toward the end of the noon meal, a new tin was opened, a few bites taken out, and, as the meal was over, the almost-full tin was fed to the cat. This is the only case of pure waste that I saw; but just three of our current visitors seem quite capable, by themselves, of going through five cans at one evening meal. They also open tins for breakfast and lunch. Among people more accustomed to city life, two tins suffice for a large household for a day.

> A kilo of sugar lasts around three days.

The household has been going through about two rolls of toilet paper a day.

Peanut butter, at $2.80 a 375-gram jar, now lasts about a day.

Two to three loaves of bread last a day. If there is just one loaf, it also lasts; but the more you get, the faster people eat. It does not last any longer.

I bought a block of stick tobacco for the household. I mentioned it to Pu Matapenua [a pseudonym], and within a day, it disappeared.

Water is left running in the sinks.

We boil water to sterilize it for the children, as Honiara tap water is considered to be unsafe. The water is then used for coffee or Milo before we can save it in a jar. Meanwhile, other people fill jars from the tap and put them into the refrigerator, making it impossible to know which water has been boiled and which has not.

A large parcel of matches lasts two to three days.

When someone makes a large pitcher of coffee or Milo for the household, immediately, either Pu Matapenua or Tuku [pseudonym] grabs the pitcher to use it as a personal cup. They may go through a quart apiece at a sitting.

Since the guests tend not to have money, they have no way to pay their own fare back home. Therefore, you have to pay again to get rid of them. Furthermore, they probably don't have the knowledge or initiative to book their own passage. Consequently, you must make arrangements for them or they will stay indefinitely. Frank missed the latest booking deadline and will therefore have all of his visitors for at least another month.

The alternative is a combination of pressure and bribery. Thus, Pu Matapenua was staying for some time with a Tikopian in Rove. For a while, his host accepted the burden with equanimity; but finally, he announced that his wife was soon to give birth and he would need the space for her relatives. He tried to soften the blow by offering to pay Pu Matapenua's fare to the Russells while he awaits transport back to Anuta. Pu Matapenua declined, opting instead, to move back in with Frank.

The remaining defense mechanism is to buy only the bare necessities. Thus, when gas (for the kitchen stove) ran out, Frank declined to order a refill. If I had not contributed, all cooking from that time on would have been over wood fires—as indeed it was for a week.

As all that happens among Anutans in the central Solomons occurs with reference to events back home, the leadership crisis involving the Anutan chief made itself felt in Honiara as well. Factional lines developed following those on Anuta. While some issues of contention on Anuta are attenuated in Honiara, other problems—particularly those involving distance and geographical dispersal—have come to the fore.

In 1983, the structure of authority, in principle, was clear. The senior chief was represented by his brother, Frank. Frank had one or two close confidants with whom he consulted on matters of major importance, but when he spoke, it was with the chief's authority. Tikopia was similarly represented by Fred Soaki (Pa Nukuriaki), the Commissioner of Police, who also was, in the traditional political system, a member of a leading 'house' (*paito*) in Tikopia's leading clan. On matters concerning the two islands jointly, the two leaders would consult, and Soaki then spoke for the combined community. By 1988, the Anutans withdrew from their joint arrangement, complaining that Tikopians had monopolized community resources.

The major difficulty with the authority structure is the population's physical dispersal and the fact that the leaders simply cannot be everywhere at once. Coupled with this problem, the leaders have no enforcement powers; they must depend on moral authority and their subordinates' cooperation to implement decisions. Thus, for the most part, their pronouncements may be ignored with impunity. The one exception occurs where a breach of custom also violates national law. For example, when a community member used funds belonging to a relative for his own bridewealth payment, Frank presented him with the choice of repaying the relative or having the matter turned over to the courts. The accused decided on the former option.

Anutans, then, are faced with a set of pressing dilemmas. Among their chief moral values is *aropa*, which requires kindness, compassion, commitment to mutual assistance in matters related to material well-being, and a communal outlook upon social life. This is associated with chiefly authority as a core symbol of cultural identity and differentiation of Anuta from other communities. In the old system, the chief was expected to ensure the community's prosperity. In doing so, he manifested *aropa* for his people while providing them with the material resources and moral bearing to reciprocate with their own expressions of *aropa* toward him and other men of rank. Every Anutan with whom I have discussed the matter over a period of thirty years has expressed commitment to these symbols, values, and understandings. Yet many Anutans feel pressure to maximize their material welfare by adopting a large measure of self-interested individualism and intra-community competition. Interest in money and competition for its acquisition conflicts with chiefly authority. It encourages individuals and families not to share. Anutans visiting relatively well-off kin residing overseas see a share in their relatives' prosperity as their fundamental right, while the hosts view the demands of less-than-understanding kinfolk as an economic burden even as they feel compelled to display *aropa* in their outward behavior. These conflicts and dilemmas are well illustrated in the case of an Anutan housing project that I had the opportunity to observe during a visit to Honiara in 1983–84.

Housing: Proposed Solutions and New Problems

Over the past three decades, Honiara has experienced a population explosion, and housing is at a premium. A few Anutans have access to their own houses, but most are not so fortunate. A majority of Anutans in Honiara stay with fellow islanders, sleeping on mats strewn about the floor. For example, Frank Kataina's house in 1983 was rather large by Solomon Islands standards—with three good sized bedrooms, a living room, a kitchen, a veranda, and an indoor bath. During my visit, the house's population ranged from twelve to almost twenty persons.

Under these conditions, Anutans in the Honiara area set more and better housing as a priority. Their first attempt to address the problem was to have Anutans in the area contribute toward the purchase of a plot of land near the Tikopian settlement in White River and build a small dwelling. The house was under construction during my visit to Honiara in early 1972 and was completed later that same year.

The building was intended to serve as a collective dwelling for any Anutans in the Honiara area who might need a place to stay. But, according to the story I was told, a man who had been working as a taxi driver convinced the rest of the community that the structure should be titled in the name of one individual for legal purposes. As a sophisticated long-term resident of Honiara, he suggested he should be that individual; and the rest of the community agreed. He then took advantage of his new position and sold the house to the Honiara Town Council. He pocketed the proceeds, resigned from his job, purchased a small fleet of vehicles, and started his own taxi company. At the same time, he purchased for himself an outboard motorboat and a smaller house on the far side of town. Within a few years, the boat sank, the motor was destroyed, the taxis developed mechanical problems, he went out of business, sold his house, and abruptly left the Solomons to work for several years for Nauru Shipping.

After that disaster, Pu Avatere, a man known to non-Anutans as John Tope, took the initiative. Pu Avatere is unusual among Anutans. Inspired by a dream that he took to be divine inspiration, he left home as a boy to attend school on Tikopia, and later on Guadalcanal. He attended Kohimarama Theological College during the early 1970s and trained to become an Anglican priest. However, his assertive ways offended several leaders of the church, and on completion of his training he was not ordained. The decision was eventually reversed, but by that time John had soured on the church, and he refused to join the priesthood. Instead, he took a number of secular positions—first as secretary to the Melanesian Mission and later with the Pijin-language training program for U.S. Peace Corps volunteers. The program at the time was headed by John Roughan, a former Catholic priest from the United States with long experience in the Solomons; he has since become a Solomon Islands citizen. After two years with the Peace Corps, Tope and Roughan left to create the Solomon Islands Development Trust (SIDT), a non-governmental organization that promotes self-reliance and appropriate development in rural villages. Tope became SIDT's first field officer, Roughan its technical adviser.

During the two years that Tope worked for SIDT, he initiated a number of development projects for the Anutan community. His first major project was to build a rest house for Anutans in White River. In an effort to accumulate the capital needed to support his project, John approached governmental agencies, banks, and private individuals to ask for grants and loans. Not surprisingly, lending agencies demanded a plan to guarantee repayment of their loans, and even would-be grantors asked to be assured that the house would have some source of income for continued maintenance once it had been constructed. Thus, by almost imperceptible stages, the plan changed. No longer was the building to be a rest house to provide free lodging for Anutans passing through the nation's capital. Instead, the idea was now to rent the house to non-Anutans. After the loans were repaid, profits would be used to maintain a piped water system, improve the school and clinic, and promote similar development projects on Anuta.

The point at which Tope became aware that the project had changed focus is unclear. It is clear that the process by which the change had come about and the rationale for the change were communicated poorly if at all to the community. By the time the change was common knowledge, many Anutans had already come to distrust Tope's motivations, and the change of plans confirmed their suspicions. John had a tendency to work by himself or with a small circle of confidants. Somehow, he had purchased land at Graciosa Bay, near Lata, the capital of Temotu Province, and on Utupua, a large but sparsely populated island in the Santa Cruz group. No one knew how he obtained the money, the nature of the financial agreements which made those purchases possible, or what he intended to do with that land. It was widely suspected, however, that he had acquired the land to promote his personal self-interest, caring little for the overall community's well-being. The change in plans regarding the White River rest house seemed to fit the larger pattern.

One of John's severest critics was Eric Toarakairunga (Pu Tau-mako), a man who had lived for many years in Honiara. He worked there first as a driver for Peter's Taxi Service; later he drove a bus, eventually working his way up to head driver for the Rainbow Bus Company. According to Eric's story, while he was a taxi driver, he became a trusted friend of Peter, the company's proprietor. Peter also owned a sizable tract of land in White River, and when he left the Solomons upon retirement, he gave the land to his good friend. In 1983, Eric and his Tikopian wife were living in a small leaf cook house erected on that land. Out of a sense of social consciousness, he agreed to allow Tope to build the community rest house there, assuming that it would be used for the collective benefit. However, as suspicions rose about the project and its organizer, Eric grew increasingly annoyed and started threatening to give the land away to someone more deserving, thereby effectively quashing the rest house project.

John's understanding, not surprisingly, was rather different. By his account, Peter never gave the land to anyone. Rather, his intention from the start had been to sell it. Eric expressed interest, and Peter was prepared to sell it to him. However, Eric never tendered the money and the deal would have fallen through had John not bought the land with his own earnings. Therefore, he contended that the land was his, and it was only through his own good graces that others might stay there.

Eventually, the loan applications were turned down because of the amount of money requested and the small likelihood of its being repaid. In addition, potential lending institutions may have been soured on the project as they began to hear murmurings of the community's concerns. Still, Tope persisted, eventually receiving a $10,000 grant from the Canadian Diocese of the Episcopal Church, to be administered by the local Church of Melanesia.[3]

With this grant in hand, construction began. Still, the confusion persisted. Most Anutans remained under the impression that the house was being built for them to occupy. As soon as it was livable, John and his wife moved in, intending to oversee construction and move to different quarters when the building was completed. Imme-diately, other Anutans moved into the house, but with no under-standing that their occupation would be temporary. Soon the building felt the effects of heavy occupancy, and it became apparent that, upon completion, it would not be a new house.

While this was going on, Tope also was involved in several other projects. In partnership with a man from Honiara's resettled Gilbertese community (see Knudsen 1977), he purchased a second house—a small concrete structure a few dozen yards from the one under construction. He successfully petitioned the Honiara Town

Council to return to the Anutans the dwelling that had been sold without community authorization. And he convinced the Town Council to allot a plot of undeveloped land to the Anutans for the purpose of subsistence cultivation.

Many of John's fellow islanders happily availed themselves of the resources that he had procured. At the time of my 1988 visit, three dozen people were living in the three White River houses. The garden land was virtually all cultivated—with manioc, sweet potato, yams, a small stand of taro, and a few fruit trees. Still tension festered and, in fact, increased.

John suggested to the Anutan community in White River that they construct one or more leaf houses in the garden area and vacate the new house so that it might be rented out, as per his agreement with the church. It seemed to most occupants, however, that he wished to expel them in order to convert the building into his personal business enterprise. Almost to a person, his suggestion was resisted. Undeterred, John began construction of a small leaf house by himself, but without assistance this was a slow process.

In the midst of all this turmoil, the man who sold the first White River house returned from Nauru. He claimed that he still owned the building and moved in, along with his wife from Santa Isabel, a number of her kin and fellow islanders, their children, and some Bellonese friends. Anutans in the house now formed a minority.

Other Anutans resented this turn of events. Some complained about their erstwhile comrade returning to the controversial site; most objected to being displaced by people from other islands. Moreover, many felt that Town Council still controlled the dwelling and had agreed to make it available to the Anutan community. Since it was not being used for its intended purpose, Anutans feared that the council might attempt to take it back. However, no one wanted to precipitate a direct confrontation, so a stalemate had been reached.

Controversy also surrounded the small concrete house. Although no one doubted that John had contributed toward its purchase, there were many questions as to where he obtained the money. As of 1988, he had not held a paying job for almost four years. Still, he managed to feed his family, he owned land in the Santa Cruz Islands of Temotu Province, and he purchased a dwelling in White River. Suspicions turned to an earlier scheme to buy a ship.

The Anutans decided in the early 1980s that if they could acquire a ship to be used for transport and commercial fishing, they could effectively be independent of the Solomons. Around that time, John organized the Anuta Community Development Project (ACDP), one of whose goals was to obtain a vessel. In the name of

ACDP, he contacted a number of granting agencies and the govern-ments of many foreign countries. In addition, he took up a collec-tion from Anutans both at home and overseas to contribute toward the purchase of a vessel. From the latter sources he accumulated approximately SI$500.

Eventually, he reported, the government of Singapore came for-ward with an offer of a ship. To finalize the deal, however, he felt he had to travel to Singapore. The trip cost SI$6000 for food, lodging, and air fare. Unfortunately, the deal (if it ever existed) fell through.

John insists that he spent his own savings on the trip. Since the ship never materialized, he declared his intention to return all the contributions. However, as far as I can determine, he has never been able to fulfill that intention. Meanwhile, his detractors were convinced that he pocketed the community's money, used it for his trip to Sin-gapore, and spent the remainder on the White River house.

Given the atmosphere of suspicion, it did not take long for some Anutans to conclude that Tope also was diverting funds allotted by the church for house construction to his own nefarious purposes. These suspicions were reported to the church, which rightly was con-cerned. In order to ensure that their funds would be used as first intended, church leaders determined that the local diocese would hold the grant in trust, select the carpenters, and pay the bills itself. No more money would pass through Tope's hands.

At this point, the house was almost finished. The contractor, however, insisted that his bills had not been fully paid and refused to complete the job until he received what he felt was his due. Since the church would not release the funds, John could not pay him. Some members of the Anutan community convinced the govern-ment to prosecute John for misuse of funds. The contractor sued John for his back fees. And John sued the church for release of the funds so that he could complete the house. As of August 1988, John was cleared of criminal wrongdoing. The civil suits have never been resolved.

Although the most active, John was not the only Anutan pursu-ing plans for community improvement. Alternative leadership in this area was provided especially by Frank Kataina. After retirement from the Royal Solomon Islands Police in 1985, Frank's interests turned to promoting a number of development plans. Initially, he focused on three projects: establishment of a community store to be run as a cooperative rather than for private profit; acquiring a ship; and convincing the Peace Corps to post a teacher or two on Anuta. To date he has made little progress on any of these fronts. The com-munity store proposal was as much a political statement as a plan for economic development. As the chief's brother and leading assistant, he felt compelled to guard tradition and the community's collective identity. For precisely these reasons, however, his efforts met with opposition from several families who were trying to establish their own private stores.

Since these projects met with such limited success, Frank's major contribution was to serve as a kind of watchdog and protect the com-

Photo 8.2 Around 1980 the old areca log aqueduct that carried water from the spring down to the coastal flat was replaced by a system of vinyl piping. While this may look insignificant to most Americans, Anutans regard it as a major improvement to their quality of life.

munity from schemes that might be detrimental to its interests. His long experience with government and public service made him effective in the role. The net effect of his efforts, however, was to thwart most of the projects Tope had promoted. Since John so infrequently delivered on his promises, everybody's worst suspicions were confirmed. And without community support, chances of success for his endeavors were minimal.

By the time of my visit in 2000, political alignments in the Anutan community had shifted and grown more complex. Frank had worked extremely hard for many years to establish a commercial seafood business on Anuta but felt his efforts had been sabotaged by lack of community support. At the same time, many community members had grown suspicious of Frank, as they had toward John years earlier. The common experience had brought the two old adversaries together, and they now regarded one another as allies. Frank, irritated at the lack of Anutan support, decided to turn his efforts to a demonstration project on Taumako, a Polynesian island in the Santa Cruz group about 200 miles from Anuta and perhaps eighty miles from Lata, the Temotu provincial capital. If the project worked on Taumako, he hoped to incorporate the Reef Islands and Utupua—at which point Anuta and Tikopia might request to join the inter-island seafood co-op. A major storm cloud hovering over all such plans, however, is a civil war that broke out in the Solomons in 1998 and has brought the national economy to a virtual standstill.

Development Issues at the Start of the New Millennium

The civil war has centered around the national government and the island of Guadalcanal. One consequence of the fighting is that most Anutans have left the central Solomons and returned home. Despite the influx of former émigrés and consequent overpopulation, Anutans in 2000 seemed generally satisfied with life on their island. They reported having plenty to eat, and they enjoyed a good variety of foods. Fertile soil provided quality produce, and the reefs around the island offered an abundance of fish. Anutans, for the most part, said they enjoyed the work of extracting a living from their environment. Men, as in the past, took pleasure from being near, in, and on the ocean; from building and operating excellent ocean-going canoes; from their myriad techniques of fishing; and from their occasional voyages to Patutaka, thirty miles away. Men and women enjoyed the camaraderie of island life and the daily rhythm of church, work, and recreation. People questioned some leadership decisions, but they were generally satisfied with the *system* of leadership. Even when they disagreed with a decision, they were usually willing to accept their leaders' authority in order to avoid conflict.

Anutans still speak of their island as a special place, and they derive a great deal of pleasure from their physical environment. They talk fondly of the white sand beach; the clean, sweet spring that rushes forth from their 200-foot hill; the clear salt water that covers their productive reef flat; the ocean that is alternately wild or friendly, but which offers an extensive network of reefs that provide more fish than people can consume; and the constant sea breeze that keeps the heat from becoming oppressive. When Anutans travel overseas, they speak longingly of their island and these characteristics. Even the insects, which visitors can easily find overwhelming, Anutans take in stride. They regard flies and cockroaches as an aesthetic nuisance rather than a threat to their health and well-being. The swarms of mosquitoes that follow rainy periods generate complaints, but remarkably few. Invariably Anutans contrast their own mosquitoes with those of the central Solomon Islands, observing that Anutan mosquitoes do not carry malaria. They are unpleasant and their bites hurt and itch; but they are "good mosquitoes"—they do not transmit disease. Anutans have little money and virtually no opportunity to make money without leaving the island. But they have little need for money, especially with the virtual shut-down of Honiara.

Satisfaction with island life is not universal, and it varies in degree. Some islanders complain about the hard physical labor of cultivating hilltop gardens and transporting heavy baskets of food to the dwelling areas to be prepared for consumption. Some miss relatives who still reside in Honiara or elsewhere. Many older Anutans compare their island of today unfavorably with the period when I first visited in 1972. They worry about the younger generation's lack of respect and attention to customary etiquette. And there have been heated arguments over religious matters. But the overall sentiment is strongly positive. So, what if anything do the Anutans want? What, in their opinion, can and should be improved?

Some Anutans insist that they are perfectly happy with the way things are and that nothing should be changed. Such extreme endorsement of the status quo, however, is exceptional. Anutans most commonly respond to questions about possible improvements by citing education, transport, medicine, and medical facilities. A piped water system, once high on the list, has been installed and is working well. Two people mentioned construction of a new church as a priority. One cited creation of a relief fund for emergencies that may arise as a result of natural disaster. And most people would like more ready access to money, at least in modest quantities.

Education

In 1972, Pu Tokerau, the island's one English speaker, occasionally taught school. He was not trained as a teacher, was not accredited, and was not paid for his efforts. The school was a one-room leaf structure, similar in construction to the dwelling houses. It was small, dark, and devoid of books and supplies. Thus, opportunities to obtain a formal education on Anuta were extremely limited.

Present conditions represent a qualitative improvement. School is taught by a qualified headmaster from Tikopia and a capable Anutan assistant. The school compound consists of three classroom buildings and a library/administrative office constructed of "permanent" materials—concrete block, cement, metal roofing, and milled lumber. In addition, the head teacher is provided with a small but substantial "permanent" house. Building materials were purchased with a grant from the World Bank and assembled with local labor. The school currently reaches standard six, which is theoretically

Photo 8.3   Anuta's school compound in 2000.

equivalent to sixth grade in the United States. Books and supplies are still limited but adequate to provide a basic education. Each year, one or two Anutan children usually pass the national exam for admission to secondary school, and the ones who attend seem adequately prepared to compete effectively with their fellow students from other parts of the country.

The consensus is that the school is a major advance, and that it has reached an acceptable, if not optimal, level of operation. Still, people would like to see continued improvement in the quality of instruction and the physical facilities. One spoke of his dream to see a secondary school established on Anuta so that the children would not have to leave the island until they are ready to pursue a university education. This, in his view, would reduce the subversive influence of external contacts and help protect traditional Anutan culture from erosion.

Transport

My October 2000 visit to Anuta left me with the impression that shipping is more regular than was the case in the past. No fewer than five ships make the journey to Temotu Province at least occasionally. Anuta's radio, which had been out of commission about half the time in 1972–73, was working well. It could reach Lata and even Honiara. Via the radio it was possible to hale a ship if it was needed and one was in the province. On my visit, I was able to stay for two weeks, arriving on October 5th aboard *Eastern Trader* and returning on October 18th on *Baruku*. By contrast, in 1972–73, ships most often came at one-month intervals, and a hiatus of three months between ships was not unusual. During my 1988 visit to the Solomons, conditions were still worse; I waited three months for a ship and eventually had to leave without reaching Anuta. The previous year, I was told, a nine-month period passed without a single ship arriving at the provincial capital.

From this perspective, current conditions appear extremely favorable. Still, Anutans reported that shipping can be sporadic. Moreover, the ships tend to be slow, dirty, crowded, and uncomfortable. A vessel carrying 100 passengers and fifteen or twenty crew may have only one working toilet, and deck passengers often end up sleeping on top of one another, sometimes in pools of betel juice or saliva (see Feinberg 2001b). In 2000, the Temotu Province government purchased a large and relatively fast ship from South Korea, and it was placed in service in 2001. Still, the extent to which this ship will actually improve the lives of people in the eastern Solomons remains to be seen.[4]

Health and Medical Care

Medicines and medical facilities are controversial because of disagreements within the community about the proper relationship between medicine and the church. The province has offered to construct and stock a clinic, but the chiefs and *maru*, several years ago, declined the offer. Four reasons were cited. First, God ultimately decides who will get sick and which victims of illness will recover. Therefore, the best medicine is faith, prayer, and involvement with the church. As a corollary, I was told that at times when there has been plenty of medicine on the island, there has also been great sickness; at times when there was no medicine and people depended on prayer, the overall state of the community's health has improved. Third, the island has no one qualified to administer medications, and to put them into the hands of someone without proper training could do more harm than good. And finally, Anuta is a small island, all of whose land is used for planting crops. The question was raised, therefore, of where a proposed clinic might be located. Who would be required to sacrifice a valuable garden in the interest of community health?

To each of these arguments, there has been a pointed response. Many Anutans feel that medicine and prayer are complementary. Thus, there is no reason that medicine should be precluded from working with and "helping" the church. In addition, they say, God put everything here for a reason; he made medicines available with the intention that we would use them. Empirically, many people simply dispute the assertion that the island is healthier when there are fewer medicines. They also point to people who have not been helped by prayer and herbal remedies but have been cured with the administration of modern medications. Some medicines are easy to administer, relatively innocuous, and can be a great help to those in need, so why not at least make those available? People note that someone could be trained to administer the more problematic medications. And they are convinced that the land issue can be equitably resolved in a variety of ways.

Church Construction

The St. James church was originally built of local materials in 1972. Since then, it has been completely rebuilt with "permanent" materials. By contrast, the St. John church probably dates to the 1960s, or perhaps even earlier. Its walls are made from a mixture of *kapia* ('lime') and sand, which looks like cement but is less durable. They are black with mildew, inside and out, and they are starting to deteriorate. The floor is largely sand, covered with coconut-leaf floor mats. When one kneels to pray, it is on a layer of grit, which is hard on the knees. The community has been gradually collecting materials such as metal roofing sheets and concrete blocks to be used in construction. But the materials are expensive, and the process is taking a long time.

Disaster Relief

Anuta is generally well off, with productive soil, good water, and extensive fishing grounds. Still, severe storms or prolonged droughts can threaten Anutans' security. Older people report that a cyclone in 1916 reduced them to eating dirt just to fill their stomachs. After the storm in 1972, Anutans were able to cope without assistance, using their own reserve supplies of *ma*. With population increases, however, the community has been forced to accept relief supplies from the government when they were offered after recent cyclones. Anutans appreciate the assistance, but they prefer not to depend on it. Therefore, creation of their own fund, which they might use to purchase food when gardens become unproductive as a result of natural disaster, has definite appeal.[5]

Money

Anutans do not need much money for personal use, but some is essential. Money is required for ship passage if they are to leave the island to attend school, pursue wage work, or visit relatives overseas. It is needed to purchase manufactured goods upon which Anutans rely for their subsistence production and for such non-essential but highly desired commodities as kerosene, flashlights, radios, batteries, coffee, sugar, rice, and biscuits. Money is needed for occasional church contributions, which in turn are used for building maintenance and new construction. And Anutans need cash for their disaster-relief fund. Despite the need for money, however, opportunities to raise it without going overseas to engage in wage labor have been virtually nil. This is a situation that Anutans would like to change.

Anuta's isolation and small size preclude commercial agricultural exploitation. At one time Anutans attempted to produce coconuts for sale in the form of copra, but transport was so irregular that the coconut meat tended to spoil before it could be shipped to Honiara. Commercial production of such crops as oil palm, cocoa, or rice is out of the question. The island has no exploitable mineral deposits, and earlier rumors of oil beneath its offshore seabed (see Feinberg 1986) now appear unfounded. The Anutans' only possibility for raising cash would appear, then, to be exploitation of their considerable marine resources. They have already done this on a small scale, harvesting shark fins and *bêche-de-mer*; and they have been talking for some time about the possibility of developing a commercial fishing operation. Each of these activities holds promise, but each also poses problems.

Shark Fins.   Anutans have been collecting shark fins on a modest scale and selling them in Honiara for a number of years. The activity is sporadic, and the amount of money generated is marginal, but this has been their most reliable source of income short of leaving the island. Shark fins have the advantage that they are dried, so they do not require refrigeration and, if treated with care, can be stored for many months without losing their value. While international conservationist sentiment to end shark finning has been on the increase, the demand remains high, and dried shark fins fetch a good price. Anutans eat the sharks that they catch, so the carcasses do not go to waste. The scale of Anutan activity is unlikely to have much effect on the world-wide shark population, and Anutans do not consider depletion of the local shark population to be entirely negative. Thus, a continuing small-scale shark-finning operation appears to be a viable source of Anutan income at least in the short term, and possibly beyond.

Bêche-de-mer.   Anutans have, for several years, collected a small amount of *bêche-de-mer*. *Bêche-de-mer*, also known as trepang or sea cucumber, is a fairly large tubular marine animal related to the starfish. It is dried and exported to east Asia, where people make it into soup. According to exporting agent David Low, the quality of Anutan *bêche-de-mer* is low. That could be improved to some degree with better preparation, but the supply of appropriately-sized sea cucumbers of the most desirable types is limited. Furthermore, unlike shark-finning, the possibility of decimating the *bêche-de-mer* population to the point of local extinction is a clear and present danger rather than a vague abstraction. Anutans recognize this and have followed the lead of other tropical maritime communities in monitoring the numbers of sea cucumbers and imposing closed seasons on those varieties that show an excessive decline. Good conservation practice, however, means that income from *bêche-de-mer* production will continue to be a trickle.

Commercial Fishing.   Anuta has a large network of reefs despite the small size of the island itself. In 2000, I spent several days mapping the reef with local experts, who identified approximately 300 coral heads on Anuta's reef shelf, which extends over two miles from the island in all directions. I was told that there are actually many more, but that my paper—which was four and a half feet long by three feet wide—was too small to include the entire inventory and still be legible. Two larger coral banks known as Te Aongo and Te Akau Motu appear in the deep sea within approximately five miles from shore. Patutaka, about thirty miles away, has a substantial reef, and Anutan legend reports the existence of a great coral bank perhaps 50 miles to the east of Patutaka known as Te Rau Akau o Pu Tingirau—named for the early chief, Pu Tingirau, who is said to have died there. No Anutan in many generations has traveled to the Rau Akau o Pu Tingirau. However, nautical charts show two large shoals in the general area described, and clearly Anuta is the nearest populated land. Thus, the community enjoys what appears to be an almost endless supply of fish.

My own inspection shows Anuta's reefs to be mostly dead coral and, perhaps, volcanic rock, with only small patches of live coral here and there. This, however, is the same condition that existed in 1972–73. In fact, there is some new coral growth, and I observed none of the bleaching that I have seen in Port Moresby, Buka, the Santa Cruz Islands, and the Western Solomons. Moreover, there appears to have been little if any drop-off in the reefs' productivity. Indeed, the consensus among Anutans is that they have access to far more fish than they can use, and the commercial exploitation of this resource seems to hold tremendous fund-raising potential. But there are also major obstacles.

The most obvious and immediate is that Anuta is a long way from any potential market. An Anutan fishing business would depend on ships that are notoriously unreliable and come infrequently even when they maintain their assigned schedules. To keep the fish from spoiling would require a dependable freezer system. That, in turn, would necessitate a reliable generator and large quantities of fuel to keep it running. If Anutans are to cover those costs and still turn a profit, they will have to extract fish at a very high rate— much higher in all likelihood than they have been to satisfy their subsistence needs. In contrast with subsistence production, which ceases once dietary needs are met, market production carries no intrinsic limit. Therefore, if Anutans are able to obtain adequate freezer capacity and emphasize exploitation of those reefs that are closest to the island, the seemingly endless supplies could be exhausted very rapidly.

One Anutan fisherman suggested a sensible solution to that problem: reserve the nearby reefs for subsistence fishing and limit commercial activity to those more distant—Te Akau Motu, Patutaka, and Te Rau Akau o Pu Tingirau. The problem with this plan lies precisely in its advantage—those reefs are far away. For Anutans to exploit them regularly, especially in questionable weather, they would need motorized transport, which they currently do not have. Travel to the Rau Akau o Pu Tingirau would also demand a boat large enough to carry many tons of fish and to make a 150-mile round trip in reasonable safety and comfort. Such a boat means major capital expenditures, and that in turn means extraction on a massive scale in order to make ends meet.

An alternative suggestion was that the community might refrain from exploiting reef fish altogether and emphasize pelagic species, particularly tuna. Perhaps adequate reserves are available in nearby waters. However, tuna boats typically travel long distances to harvest enough fish to be commercially viable, and it is likely that this will be true of Anuta as well.

Population Control

The most critical problem facing Anuta at this point is population growth. The number of Anutans has more than doubled in the thirty years since I was first there, and with a resident population of 340 the island has an amazing population density of more than 2,000 people per square mile of land. Currently, the island can support its population surprisingly well. Everyone has plenty to eat. People appear healthy, strong, and energetic, with no obvious signs of malnutrition. However, in case of a major storm, drought, or other natural disaster, the present enviable situation could change very quickly. Perhaps the island can survive with its current population, but if the number continues to climb, it soon will reach a point of non-sustainability.

Not only will population control determine the long-term viability of the subsistence economy; overcrowding is already undermining the quality of life. People are conscious of crowding. Houses are closer together, and it is increasingly difficult to find even a few moments of privacy. At the time of this writing, Anutans get along well, enjoy each other's company, and work hard at avoiding conflict. They recognize, however, that as their population expands, conflict is inevitable and will grow increasingly severe. Even now, Anutans complain about a rise in antisocial behavior such as theft and sexual misconduct; and with a larger population, social control becomes ever more problematic. If the conflict on Guadalcanal can be resolved and people once again feel safe moving to the central Solomons, some of the pressure will be released. Anutans resident in Honiara have been working to acquire land for the community in Independence Valley, just inland from White River; their success would provide an important safety valve. However, in the absence of population control, even that will only be a temporary solution.

Anutans recognize the problem and are aware of the need for "family planning." Several have recommended imposition of a two-child limit per couple. No one, however, has been able to suggest how such a limit might be enforced.

Lessons for America

At this point, let me return to the questions that first drew me to anthropology, which I raised in chapter 1: What do the Anutans have to teach us about the human condition? Can Anutan culture provide clues that we might use in addressing our own myriad and seemingly intractable social problems? Does Anuta offer insights that the Western world might draw upon to fashion a more humane society both for ourselves and for our global neighbors?

The answer is neither obvious nor straightforward. Anutans, like human beings elsewhere, have enormous capacity for contradiction and ambiguity. Their island is no earthly paradise. Life can be difficult, with scorching sun, plagues of insects, periodic epidemics, natural disasters, occasional food shortages, persistent lack of medications, and a constant dearth of information about the outside world. Infant mortality and death in childbirth are alarmingly high, and average life expectancy is distressingly low. Interpersonal rivalry and personality conflicts sometimes give way to debilitating jealousy and mutual suspicion. Public policy disputes involving matters such as the relationship of medicine to Christianity, how to deal with droughts and famines, or the proper mix between tradition and development create episodic rifts in the community. Still, on balance, Anuta offers one of the most benign environments for human habitation of any place on earth. An abundance of crops and fish, along with a high-quality water source, has made it possible for this tiny island to support an extraordinarily dense population in reasonable health and overall good spirits. Anutans are in the enviable position of being able to rely almost entirely on their subsistence economy. Unlike many peoples, they can and do depend primarily on themselves—on their own resources, initiative, and labor.

Within this context, Anutans have maintained a classically Polynesian culture, emphasizing principles of hereditary rank, supernaturally derived power, and kinship as defined in terms of genealogical connection and *aropa*. Since *aropa* so admirably complements Christian principles of love and charity, I found Anuta in the early 1970s to live out its religious ideals with amazing consistency. As the island is drawn into the world capitalist economy, a system of social relations based on *aropa* has grown increasingly difficult to sustain. Nonetheless, Anutans have survived their periods of stress, met the test, and, for the most part, remained faithful to the values of their ancestors. At the start of the twenty-first century, Anutans are living together as a tight-knit community held together by traditional values as reinterpreted through local understandings of Anglican theology. Yet they face a plethora of challenges that will expand as time goes on.

In the most general sense, Anuta demonstrates that people can lead rich, rewarding lives in a community whose social and economic philosophy is very different from ours in the West. As an American steeped in the traditions of the Declaration of Independence, the Bill of Rights, Paine's *Common Sense*, and Lincoln's Gettysburg Address, I am personally repelled by the idea of a hereditary monarchy and a status system based on accident of birth. To crawl on hands and knees before another human being and proffer obedience because that person's father was a chief runs counter to the principles of liberty, equality, and merit-based leadership—principles I have been taught to value on a par with life itself. Yet at the time of my first visit to Anuta, my hosts voiced almost no objections to a genealogically-based system of authority and rank. People in positions of power took their responsibilities seriously, did their best to protect those below them in the social hierarchy, and refrained from taking advantage of their position in the quest for economic gain. Meanwhile, those of lower rank seemed to appreciate their leaders' contributions to the common good. With just a few exceptions, everyone expressed commitment to the system and derived enormous satisfaction from participation in it.

My life on Anuta has forced me to rethink such customary labels as democracy and monarchy for types of political systems. In reality these terms, along with others such as anarchy and oligarchy, designate ideal types; few communities adopt any one of them in unadulterated from. An Anutan chief may theoretically be an unquestioned monarch. He makes policy, commands his subjects, and should be implicitly obeyed. In practice, however, the chief can only lead insofar as his subjects are willing to follow. Therefore, he is keenly aware of public opinion and always takes it into consideration. People are most likely to obey the chief when he demands a course of action they would take in any case. If that is the norm, he can from time to time command his subjects to act counter to their wishes. However, if he does so too often, or if he should exercise his prerogatives in areas about which his subjects feel strongly, he evokes resentment. Should he then persist, resentment may turn into outright opposition. This is what happened to Pu Koroatu with respect to sale of food; and had the matter not been resolved, chiefly authority could have been permanently compromised.[6] Petersen (1982, 1999) has argued along similar lines that Micronesian chiefdoms often combine elements of hierarchy and egalitarianism, thereby making those apparently monarchical communities surprisingly democratic.

If these observations are correct, they may bear implications for our foreign policy. When assessing our relationships with other countries, perhaps we ought to look more closely at the quality of life their citizens enjoy and less at the formal trappings of government. Were we to take such an approach, we might pay more attention, for example, to Cuba's impressive accomplishments in medicine and education and be less preoccupied with the fact that its president has not been subject to electoral challenge for over 40 years. This does not require us to give up our democratic values. But if we recognize that health and happiness can be achieved through a variety of paths, our international relations may become better informed, more nuanced and subtle, and perhaps more effective.

Many Americans agree that racial and ethnic prejudice are evils that we should strive to avoid. Yet we often hear that it is human nature and, therefore, inevitable for people to prefer the company of others who are like themselves. Anutans demonstrate that someone who is very different in physical appearance, cultural background, linguistic ability, and religion can be incorporated into one's kinship system and treated as a brother, sister, son, or daughter, should that person show in concrete terms the 'love' that is expected of close kin.

Connected with political decision making is a community's economic organization. As Americans, we learn that private ownership, competition, and the profit motive are the keys to liberty, prosperity, and happiness. But the practical results too often include alienation, social stratification, poverty, and crime. Anuta demonstrates that economic systems based on private competition and personal accumulation are not a necessary product of the human genome; that an economy based on communal values and collective responsibility can work extraordinarily well at least under certain conditions. Anuta in 1972–73, more than any other community I have encountered, embraced the Christian principles of love and brotherhood, of looking out for one's neighbors, and of valuing equitable distribution of resources above personal profit. To say that such a system was successful on Anuta, however, does not entail that it can simply be transplanted anywhere. Among Anutans, it has been facilitated by certain aspects of the island's culture and conditions of life. Relevant features of Anutan culture include the emphasis on kinship as the basis of all social interaction, a sense of noblesse oblige that underlies political authority and honorific rank, and *aropa* as the central value permeating every aspect of island life. Underpinning the Anutan ethos of sharing, collective responsibility, and mutual support is a system of intensive agriculture and an astoundingly productive network of reefs that provides a remarkable abundance of fish.

The latter point cannot be emphasized too strongly. More than a century ago, Karl Marx surmised that a social system featuring generosity and sharing must be based on an economy of abundance. That is why he expected the first state-level experiments with socialism to occur in Western Europe or the United States; and he would have found the failure of attempts to establish communism in Eastern Europe or North Korea entirely predictable.

Anuta is by no means communist in Marx's sense. Still, it illustrates the importance of material abundance for collective ownership, production, distribution, and consumption. Given the island's small land area families at times become involved in land disputes, while private ownership of reefs or areas of ocean has never been considered. Other islands with a smaller ratio of fishing grounds to population have developed systems of "customary marine tenure" in which descent groups or families claim exclusive jurisdiction over certain reefs and other resources (e.g., Hviding 1996). Such a system would be pointless on Anuta. Similarly, a large canoe after a few hours at sea can almost always provide more than sufficient fish for the community, and the catch is distributed to each domestic group according to its need. By contrast, smaller catches of individual fishermen are kept by the domestic units of the fishermen themselves. In short, Anuta demonstrates that a socioeconomic system predicated upon sharing and compassion and shunning personal accumulation of material wealth not only is possible but may work quite well in a small community with a substantial resource base. Whether such a system can be viable on a national or world scale remains to be seen.

Lastly, we have seen that as Anutans are drawn into a postcolonial political system and the world market, their old cultural and social order have been stressed almost to the breaking point. Anutans are committed to their ancient custom and to interpersonal relations grounded in the principle of *aropa*. But they are also committed to development within a modern capitalist framework. Their success in finding the right balance will determine whether they are able to maintain the rich, rewarding way of life that they have fashioned over fifteen generations on their patch of fertile soil surrounded by the warm, clear, nurturing Pacific Ocean.

Endnotes

Chapter 1

[1] Anutans often use abbreviations for names of more than two syllables. For example, Pu Koroatu usually is rendered Pu Vatu, Pu Nukumanaia is Pu Nuku, Pu Teukumarae is Pu Teuku, and Pu Penuakimoana is Pu Moana. In normal conversation, Anutans shorten Pu Tokerau to Pu Toke.

[2] Four years later, a friend told me that the sign had been changed to read, "Danger! Risk of sharks extreme beyond three feet!" By the time of my next visit to Honiara in 1983, the Solomon Islands had become an independent nation, and acquisition of hard currency was a pressing problem. One proposed solution was to promote tourism. The sign at the Mendana Hotel had been dutifully removed, and people were encouraged to swim. The previous warnings had apparently exaggerated the risk of shark attack.

[3] This approach may be seen in such works as Malinowski's *Argonauts of the Western Pacific* 1984[1922], *Sexual Life of Savages* (1929), and *A Scientific Theory of Culture* 1969 [1944] or Firth's *We, the Tikopia* (1963[1936]), *Primitive Polynesian Economy* 1965[1939], and *Essays on Social Organization and Values* (1964a).

[4] "Interpretive" or "symbolic" anthropology is well illustrated in Geertz's *The Interpretation of Cultures* (1973) or Schneider's *American Kinship* (1968) and *A Critique of the Study of Kinship* (1984). For my views on the concept of culture and its relationship to the social system, see Feinberg (1979b, 1981a, and 2001a).

Chapter 2

[1] For these coordinates and the relative positions of various islands, I am indebted to Paul Teferomu of the Solomon Islands' Hydrography Department and British Admi-

ralty Chart No. 780 (1960). Other estimates have varied slightly from the figures presented here (cf. Yen, et al. 1973:1), but not by more than a few miles. According to the GPS system of the Solomon Islands' ship *MV Eastern Trader* the exact coordinates of Anuta's anchorage, as recorded in October 2000, are 11°36.280 S and 169°50.550 E.

2 On charts and maps, Patutaka is usually listed as Mitre Island or Fataka. The latter is a misrepresentation of the Tikopian pronunciation, Fatutaka—a mistake that is easy to make since in rapid speech the unstressed /u/ has a tendency to disappear. The name is a compound of the Anutan words *patu* and *taka*. *Patu* means 'rock' or 'stone.' while *taka* connotes something that stands alone or wanders about, as an unmarried person. The name, then, might be rendered in English as 'Lone Stone' or 'Wandering Stone'—a rather appropriate designation for a single monolith protruding from the ocean floor thirty miles from the nearest bit of land, that is difficult for even accomplished navigators to locate, and lacks virtually all forms of terrestrial life.

3 A study by Rosendahl and Kirch in late 1971 is the only serious archaeological work ever done on Anuta. The conclusions of this two-month investigation are compiled in Yen and Gordon (1973); for commentaries on this work see Davidson (1975) and Feinberg (1976). Somewhat more attention has been paid to linguistics (Firth 1954; Bayard 1966; Pawley 1967; Elbert n.d.; Green 1971; Yen n.d.; Biggs n.d.a, n.d.b, n.d.c, 1980; Feinberg 1977). In addition, my collection of Anutan oral traditions (Feinberg 1998a) includes 46 Anutan language texts.

4 For a detailed account of Anutan oral traditions, see Feinberg (1998a). Firth (1954:121–22), Yen, et al. (1973:6–8), Kirch and Rosendahl (1973), Davidson (1975), and Feinberg (1976, 1989) also discuss aspects of Anutan history.

5 Motikitiki is related to a character appearing in myths distributed through most of Polynesia. He is known in other communities by such names as Maui (Hawai'i), Maui-a-tikitiki (Maori), Mautikitiki (Rennell and Bellona), and Metikitiki (Tikopia).

6 The story I was given on Anuta coincides in most of its essentials with that related to Firth by Tikopia's Ariki Taumako in 1952 (Firth 1954:121). Pu Ariki is more commonly known on Tikopia as Pu Lasi; both names refer to the same man.

7 According to Moses Purianga, one of Anuta's leading authorities on oral traditions, Pu Kaurave was a member of the Tui Tonga line, but his mother was Uvean, and he was born and raised on Uvea. Purianga also indicated that the Uveans and Tongans voyaged in one double-hulled canoe rather than two single-hulled outrigger vessels (see Feinberg 1998a:13).

8 An Anutan adult typically has a marital name which starts with Pu for a man and Nau for a woman. In addition, every Anutan has at least one 'personal name' (*ingoa tangata* or *ingoa pouri*). I sometimes incorporate the 'personal name' in parentheses to distinguish its bearer from others who might have the same marital name.

9 This observation is supported by linguistic evidence. The Anutan language has retained *puaka*, the common Polynesian word for 'pig.' only in the figurative sense of a slovenly person. *Poi*, the indigenous word for 'swine.' is probably a recent borrowing from the Melanesian Solomon Islands, which evidently supplied a few pigs to Anuta during the twentieth century. Currently, *poi* is falling into disuse and being replace by the English loan word *piki*.

10 As Anutans I include all men and unmarried women who were born on the island, the wives and children of all native-born Anutan men, and all foreigners (as of 1973, this included only immigrants from Tikopia) who appeared to have settled permanently on Anuta. In other words, I include all persons belonging to an Anutan 'household' (*patongia*), to be discussed at length in chapter 4.

11 *Pai kava* ('to perform kava') is the Anutans' term for their traditional worship ceremony. Anutans say, however, that the kava plant, *Piper methysticum*, has never been

found on their island. Thus, despite the name, these rites were performed with water rather than kava liquid.

[12] For a detailed discussion of Anutan canoes, how they are constructed, cared for, and used, see Feinberg (1988a).

[13] Anutans' detailed knowledge of their marine environment is discussed in Feinberg, et al. (n.d.).

[14] *Vanevane*, because of its abundance, is an important fish in the Anutan diet. It is about six inches in length with horizontal yellowish stripes and resembles the French grunts one encounters off the Atlantic coast of southern North America. Firth (1985:591) identifies it as "a blue-striped perch (*Lutjanus quinquelineatus* or *L. kasmira*)."

[15] Pu Nukurava (now known as Pu Ngarumea) used a spool of heavy line and a large hook. When the fish struck, he let out great quantities of line and allowed his quarry to tire itself out trying to escape. Holding his end of the line, he was then able to swim ashore. Once he got to the reef, it was relatively easy to stand there and pull in the fish.

[16] Anuta, however, is unusual in the extent of the reefs surrounding the island. It is that network of coral heads that creates Anuta's extraordinarily productive marine environment despite the absence of a barrier reef or lagoon.

[17] *Bêche-de-mer*, also known as trepang or sea cucumber, is a primitive marine animal that looks roughly like a large brown or black cucumber and is related to the starfish. Certain varieties, when cleaned and dried, may be exported to east Asia, where they are an expensive delicacy. Unfortunately for the divers who collect them, most of the profits go to the export companies.

[18] White people in the Solomon Islands are uniformly characterized as "Europeans," regardless of their actual country of origin. Since the populations of Australia, New Zealand, and the United States are composed predominantly of "Europeans," they are European countries in the Solomon Islanders' sense.

[19] In 2000, Anutans working in Honiara were earning the equivalent of US$150 to $200 per month—considerably better than prevailing wages in the 1970s, but still hardly generous.

[20] A catechist is essentially a mission teacher—the lowest ranking clergy position in the Anglican church and Anuta's highest-ranking clergyman, with the exception of a few brief periods when a priest from elsewhere in the Solomons was assigned to the island. The head catechist at the time of my first visit was Pu Tokerau, younger brother of the island's senior chief.

[21] This excludes a number of men who had been living overseas for many years working at jobs that require skill in English and who are unlikely ever to move permanently back to Anuta.

[22] This was true at the old church, Te Pare Rotu St. John, where services in 1972–73 were led by the catechist. Services in the newly-constructed St. James church were conducted in the Mota language from Vanuatu, which served for decades as the Melanesian Mission's lingua franca. Those services were led by Anuta's senior chief. By 2000, services in both churches were primarily in the local vernacular.

[23] In 2002, civil war devastated the Solomon Islands economy to the point that government hospitals and clinics ran out of medicines and many patients had to be sent home. By the middle of the year, the Ministry of Health could no longer afford to pay medical personnel, and by August most of the physicians went on strike to protest the lack of pay.

[24] For a more complete discussion of health, illness, and Anutan beliefs surrounding them, see Feinberg (1979a).

Chapter 3

[1] Even W. H. R. Rivers, the anthropologist who first propounded "the genealogical method" for studying kinship, vacillated. In 1924, he stated that "defining kinship genealogically . . . excludes metaphorical relationship such as that which is concerned when we call a priest 'father.' any old woman 'mother.' or a fellow-clubman 'brother' . . ." (p. 54). But "metaphorical relationship" for him did not include "artificial relationship, such as blood-brotherhood, when this is so generally recognized as to become part of the social system, and rank with other modes of determining relationship as a means of regulating social duties and privileges" (p. 54). Thus, what Marshall (1977) has called "created kin" may, under certain circumstances, be included in one's genealogy. Yet, in expounding his application of the genealogical method, Rivers (1900:75) appears to reject even such relationships by saying:

> In collecting the genealogies, I ... limited myself to as few terms as possible, and found that I could do all that was necessary with the five terms, father, mother, child, husband, and wife. Care had of course to be taken to limit these terms to their English sense. The term which was open to the most serious liability to error was that of father, but I was able to make the natives understand very thoroughly that I wanted the 'proper father.'

Presumably, then, in asking an informant about his "father," Rivers intended the biological father (or at least the man believed to be the biological father, as physiological paternity is rarely if ever demonstrable), and even an adoptive "father" or, by implication, a "blood-brother" is to be excluded from a proper genealogy. On this matter, Schneider (1972:54) has noted with a sense of irony:

> Rivers says that one cannot define kinship in terms of consanguinity, that it is not a matter of procreation and parturition but of 'social convention.' He then opts for genealogy as the definition of 'kinship.' This means that whoever the informant himself, or the natives themselves, regard as kinsmen by placing them on the genealogy are, therefore, to be considered kin. A place on the genealogy may be obtained by such things as paying the midwife or planting the tree, etc. But when we ask what, then, is a genealogy and how does one obtain one, we are told that the genealogist must be sure the native understands that when we ask for his father, we want his genitor, or the man who has been cohabiting with his mother, and none of this social nonsense at all! For that is what the English sense of this term means, and that is what Rivers says he makes sure his interpreters and informants understand.

[2] In particular, *kano a paito* may also refer to the related but not identical concept of 'kindred.' This is discussed in chapter 5.

[3] "Consanguineal" is a common anthropological term that literally means "related by blood." As I will try to show, this expression is somewhat misleading in the Anutan case and, for that reason, I place it in quotes. I use "consanguineal" despite the lack of precision to distinguish these terms from those for persons who are related through marriage. The latter are, quite properly, identified as affinal.

[4] In some respects, this looks almost like what the "cognitive anthropologists" of the 1950s through 70s referred to as a componential analysis. For further commentary on componential analysis and its limitations in describing Anutan kinship, see Feinberg (1981a, 1981b).

[5] For a discussion of "basic member" versus "total class" definitions of kin terms, see Lounsbury (1969a:207). The total class perspective is exemplified by componential

analysis as well as the symbolic approach of David Schneider and his followers, and it is implicit in any orientation which seeks intensional definitions for kin classes.

[6] The contrast between general and specific senses of kin terms in some ways resembles Morgan's classic distinction between what he called classificatory and descriptive kinship systems. Morgan, however, was concerned with contrasting systems, whereas I suggest that terms may be used in both senses within the same system.

[7] For comments to this effect on the relationship between adoption, genealogy, and kinship, see Scheffler (1970:372). For a similar characterization by a scholar who has made a conscious effort to remain open-minded on the subject, see Carroll (1970:10); also cf. Brady (1976a, 1976b) for analogous formulations.

[8] Goodenough's distinction between "natural," "jural," and "psychological kinship" (1970b; see also Brady 1976a) may be useful here. No Anutan suffered under the illusion that I had a "natural" relationship with anyone on the island, and undoubtedly most people felt differently toward me than toward their indigenous Anutan kin. In a jural sense, however, I was unequivocally integrated into the kinship system. The problem with this formulation is that in Anutan culture, as far as I could tell, "natural kin" do not form a discrete category which is distinguished from "psychological" and "jural kin."

[9] For a more complete account of these conversations and their implications for Anutan chieftainship, see Feinberg (1996a).

[10] This point was repeatedly confirmed by explicit statements as well as many incidents on Anuta. It was most dramatically illustrated, however, by an analogous experience I had on an island in the Polynesian archipelago of Tonga some time after I had left the Solomons.

In Tonga, I spent several days on the island of Tungua in the Ha'apai group. One evening my host offered me a cup of orange-leaf tea with dinner. The drink was good but too heavily sugared for my taste, so I asked for a second cup to wash the syrupy flavor from my mouth. No sooner had I gotten the cup to my lips, however, than I was told in an authoritative voice, "Put some sugar in your tea." I replied that I preferred it without sugar, and again raised the cup to my mouth. My host repeated, "Put some sugar in your tea!" I responded that I really preferred it without sugar and asked, "Isn't it all right if I drink it the way I like it?" He answered no and repeated his command. I did not want to oppose my host, but to drink the tea saturated with sugar would have defeated my purpose, so I poured the liquid back from my cup into the kettle. My host got up and ran out of the house. A few minutes later he returned saying, "Now I know you hate me. Go ahead. Suit yourself. Drink the tea without sugar!" In other words, by offering me the best that he had (that is, tea with sugar) my host was extending his 'love.' When I refused the tea with sugar, I was unwittingly rejecting his 'love' and left him with only one possible conclusion: "Now I know you hate me."

[11] There is a parallel between this argument and that put forth by David Schneider (1968, 1969, 1972, 1984) in his analysis of American kinship. Schneider argued that American kinship is defined in terms of two components: shared biogenetic substance or "blood" and adherence to a code for conduct expressing "diffuse and ensuring solidarity." The latter is known in the vernacular as "love," and formalized in "law." Unequivocal kin possess shared substance *and* adhere to the stipulated code for conduct. Persons sharing natural substance may be termed nonkin if they fail to act in such a way as to express diffuse, enduring solidarity; and a person with whom one has no "known" biological connection but who expresses "love" through his or her behavior may be termed a relative by some American informants. I am not convinced that Schneider's interpretation is entirely correct for the United States (for

a discussion of my position on this matter, see Feinberg 1979b, 2001a). However, a similar situation seems incontrovertible for the Anutans and has now been well documented for many other Pacific Islanders (see Linnekin and Poyer 1990).

Chapter 4

1 See chapter 6 for discussion of the *api*.

2 For a listing of Anuta's canoes and the domestic units that shared ownership in each of them as of 1972, see Feinberg (1981a).

3 For a short while, Anutans attempted to treat even small-scale fishing as a communal enterprise. When productivity of such procedures proved too low to make general distributions viable, however, the experiment was abandoned.

4 The Mothers' Union includes all female Companions of the Brotherhood (see chapter 7). Its primary function is to assist mothers with infant children. Membership is restricted to women, but not to mothers.

5 Nau Paone was the sister of these three men, making them her children's *tuatina*.

6 This is idiomatic usage, as distant cousins of the same sex are called *tau paanau* while even a biological brother and sister are not.

7 The "equivalence of siblings," first discussed by Radcliffe-Brown (1952), was illustrated most dramatically to me when Pu Tokerau explained that a certain pair of men were *tau paanau maori* because they had "the same grandfather." Later, in collecting genealogies, I discovered this was not literally the case and put the matter to my friend. In defense of his initial statement Pu Toke responded that, "their grandfathers were a pair of brothers, which is the same thing." Another striking illustration was presented by Pu Nukurava, who habitually referred to Pu Ropanga, brother of his father's father, as his "first *tupuna*" because he was the firstborn son. His own grandfather, Pu Avakope, was his "second *tupuna*" or "other *tupuna*."

8 This finding on Anuta confirms Firth's report (1963[1936]:179–180) of a similar custom on Tikopia. While *tau kave* in the same domestic unit may sleep close to one another, this liberty is not permitted to cross siblings of different units, regardless of their genealogical proximity.

9 These arrangement may be described as 'fosterage.' in contrast with the more formal 'adoption' relationships discussed below. In Carroll's (1970) and Brady's (1976a) terms, however, even the more formal *kauapi* relationship does not quite qualify as 'adoption' since kinship statuses are not altered except for the degree of closeness, and the new tie is not permanent but only lasts until the 'adoptee' marries.

10 *Epuepu* is a pudding produced by scraping baked taro with a limpet shell and mixing it with unheated coconut cream, making a fine mush. *Pakavatia* is prepared by mixing coconut cream with sago flour and heating it over a fire until it jells. Both foods are highly esteemed and considered particularly suitable for infant consumption.

Chapter 5

1 Pu Teukumarae was a child when his father, the senior chief, passed away. Pu Raropuko thus acted as regent for many years. In addition, Pu Raropuko served as a kind of surrogate father for the heir apparent.

2 Sometime during the 1990s, the households of Pu Nukurava (by then known as Pu Ngarumea) and the senior chief had a falling out, and their *ngutuumu* relationship ended.

³ These observations cast doubt on the general applicability of Radcliffe-Brown's explanation for the existence of *fahu*-like relationships in patrilineal societies (Radcliffe-Brown 1952). From the viewpoint of kinship terminology as well as many other aspects of social structure, Anuta is very similar to Tonga, Fiji, and numerous other societies which emphasize descent through the male line. Yet, unlike Tonga, Fiji, or the Thonga of South Africa, the *tuatina* on Anuta outranks his *iraamutu*. The *iraamutu*'s gender is irrelevant to the *tuatina*'s superior rank. And although the *makitanga* is identified with the *tamana*, the formality and emotional distance between a man and his father's sister is ameliorated rather than intensified by the gender differential.

⁴ In 1972, a number of Anutans reported that the proper term for cross cousins of the same sex is *tau paanau pakakovikovi*, from the word *kovi*, meaning 'bad.' *Pariki* is the Tikopian word for 'bad.' and even in the 1970s most Anutans used the Tikopian expression for cross cousins most of the time. By the 1980s, the older Anutan term was all but forgotten, and several friends told me quite firmly that *tau paanau pakakovikovi* was simply incorrect.

⁵ The logic of this norm is to place sisters and close female cousins in the same domestic unit even after marriage. Thus, Anutan culture affirms the principle of the equivalence of siblings for females as it does for males.

⁶ By saying that neither party inherently outranks the other I mean that although there may be a difference in rank, this would be on grounds such as generation, age, or genealogical seniority, which are separate from the *tau pungona* relationship itself.

⁷ I am indebted to Judith Huntsman (personal communication) for suggesting that *pai*, in this context, be translated as 'to make' in the sense that the ritual is 'making' certain people into 'fathers.' 'mother's brothers.' or 'father's sisters.' My initial inclination was to render this as 'the father's [father's sister's; mother's brother's] side' or 'section.' I now find my earlier interpretation unpersuasive, as 'side' in Anutan is *paai* (with a long /a/) rather than *pai*.

⁸ There are a few exceptions to this rule, as exemplified by the senior chief whose *pai maatuaa* was carried to Pu Nukurava's father, Pu Raropuko, while his *pai makitanga* went to Nau Tavarei, the sister of Pu Tepae, from the unit headed in 1972 by Pu Maravai. This exceptional arrangement was short lived—when the chief's son, Harry Matakiapo, was born, his *pai maatuaa* was presented to Pu Nukurava and the *pai makitanga* to Nau Aatapu, the latter's elder sister. In doing so, the proper custom was restored.

⁹ Included among these oppositions are: high vs. low; upward vs. downward; front vs. back; right vs. left; light vs. dark; male vs. female; man of rank vs. commoner; and genealogy vs. code for conduct. This tendency in Anutan—and perhaps more generally in Polynesian—culture is discussed in greater depth in Feinberg (1980b, 1982a, 1988b).

¹⁰ In practice it is only necessary to have one representative from the *patongia* of each *tamana*, *makitanga*, and *tuatina* respectively. For example, if Pu Tokerau attended the feast it would not be necessary for his brothers, Pu Teaokena and the senior chief, to come as well. However, at least one of them should make an appearance at the *paanaunga* of a baby in their children's generation.

¹¹ *Tipunga* is Anuta's normal word for 'carpenter.' A *tipunga* is skilled at fashioning implements, houses, or canoes from wood. It also is the term by which the man who performs the circumcision is called, perhaps indicating that he is fashioning a kind of raw material into a finished product. In addition, *tipunga* is cognate with the common Polynesian word for 'priest' and may serve to emphasize the ritual properties associated with canoe building, surgery, and other activities covered by the term.

12 In another version of this procedure, I was told that the child sleeps in the *tipunga*'s house while he is recovering from the operation.

13 Anutans, like many peoples, consider blood to be ritually potent and sometimes polluting. A woman, for example, is barred from church attendance during her menstrual period, and if menstrual blood should come into contact with a church bench it must be discarded. For a summary of Polynesian views on the ritual signif-icance of menstrual fluid and female reproductive capacity, see Hanson (1982) and Shore (1989:144–148 and passim).

14 Anutans feel that the mother usually has an interest in her son's settling down, while the father tends to sympathize with the young man's wish for travel and adventure. Therefore, they normally assume that the mother will present a more compelling case than the father on the son's behalf. In addition, Anutans permit greater intimacy between a mother and her son than between a man and his father when it comes to speaking of romance or sex. For these reasons, the mother is the preferred emissary.

15 In fact, except for the *vai pa*, in one way or another the entire population is brought into every major ceremony. It is also significant that the rite of incorporation (*te pakaap-enga*) for anyone who comes from overseas, including an Anutan who has been away for a protracted period, is to share a meal in turn with each *patongia* on the island. The parting rite (*maavae*) for anyone about to leave involves a similar procedure.

16 The husband has expressed his chagrin by withdrawing his domestic unit from his natal clan and throwing in his lot with one of the lower-ranking ones.

17 Lévi-Strauss further notes that restricted exchange is associated with bilateral cross-cousin marriage and generalized exchange is associated with matrilateral cross-cousin marriage. In the former system, ego's mother's brother marries ego's father's sister, and ego (whether male or female) marries the child of that couple. In the latter system, every man is expected to marry his mother's brother's daughter, and every woman is expected to marry her father's sister's son. For a more complete discussion of elementary structures and their implications, see Lévi-Strauss (1969[1949]); Homans and Schneider (1955); Needham (1962); Schneider (1965); Fox (1967); or Buchler and Selby (1968). Anuta has neither of these systems of regular cross-cousin marriage, although marriage to a cross-cousin does sometimes occur.

18 In a Crow system, one calls one's father's sister and father's sister's daughter by the same term. In an Omaha system, ego uses the same term for the mother's brother and the mother's brother's son.

Chapter 6

1 The Tongan *'api*, referring to 'the household group' (Decktor Korn 1974, 1978), or to 'familial lands' (Gifford 1971[1929]:176; Kaeppler 1973:23), may suggest an alterna-tive interpretation for Anuta. In Tonga, *'api* is distinct from *afi*, meaning 'fire.' Since the Tongan /f/ shifts to a /p/ in Anutan, and since the Anutan reflex of the Tongan glottal stop is /0/, one cannot say with certainty which is the Tongan cognate, and the etymological derivation remains obscure. From the viewpoint of the word's sig-nificance to contemporary Anutans it makes little difference, as either way one broaches the same complex of interlocking symbols. Fire (*api*) is used to cook food grown on an *api*'s lands, and access to a common food supply, either presently or in the past, gives an *api* its unity and coherence.

2 *Vaa* can refer literally to a fishing line. For example, the magical cord that the trick-ster, Motikitiki, used to pull up the Pacific islands from the ocean floor is sometimes

termed *te vaa o Motikitiki*. The usual word for 'string' or 'line.' however, is *uka*. *Vaa* can also mean an interval of some sort. Thus, a valley is *vaamaunga*, an 'interval between hills'; and a 'period of time' is *vaatia*. When used by itself, *vaa* most often refers to a social category that might be glossed as 'line.' with more or less the same metaphorical sense that we attribute to that term in English.

3 A generic translation for *tapito* might be 'basis.' 'reason.' 'source,' or 'cause.' The base of a tree, the source of a stream, the basis of a problem, and the causes responsible for any state of affairs are the *tapito* of their respective objects. Analogously, this term is applied to the primary owner of a canoe, the leader of a *patongia* or *kainanga*, or the founding ancestor of any *patongia*, *pare*, or *kainanga*. The sense in which all these people may be thought of as the 'source' or 'basis' of contemporary units is explored below.

4 For details about these conflicts and their outcomes, see Feinberg 1998a.

5 An analogous case might be the Maori *waka*, which Firth (1973[1929]:115) describes as "a group of tribes (*iwi*) whose ancestors formed the crew of one of the famous canoes [which are said to have arrived in New Zealand from Eastern Polynesia in] the fourteenth century." The Maori *waka* are much larger and looser associations than the Anutan *kainanga*, and the ancestral connections—contrary to Anutan practice—may be traced through females. Still, they both are groups of groups connected through ties of common descent. For further illustrations and an excellent theoretical discussion of this issue, see Goodenough (1970a:65–67).

6 In fact, there is a Kainanga i Muri. This is a rarely-used alternative name for the Kainanga i Pangatau and is quite separate from the Kainanga i Tepuko over which the Ariki i Muri presides as chief. The Ariki i Muri derives his title from the fact that he is "behind" (i.e., subordinate to) the Ariki i Mua; the Kainanga i Muri is so called for the unrelated reason that unlike the other *kainanga*, its *tapito* is not a man but a pair of women.

Chapter 7

1 Even in traditional anthropological terms, moreover, to describe the *kanopenua* as a patrilineal descent group is an oversimplification because of the two ancestresses of the Kainanga i Pangatau and the inclusion of immigrants from Tikopia and Rotuma as links to the founding ancestors of the Kainanga i Pangatau and Kainanga i Rotomua, respectively.

2 In practice no situation should ever develop to this point since the two chiefs are expected to defer to each other's judgment and speak in unison. In most cases, if the second chief feels very strongly about some matter, the first chief accedes to his wishes. Should the senior chief be adamant, however, the proper course is for the junior chief to yield.

3 Analogously, a leading carpenter is called *tipunga tu*, and Tikopians refer to the Ariki Kafika, their premier chief, as *te ariki tu* of their island (Firth, personal communication). *Taangata* is the plural of *tangata*.

4 More recently a woman from an important line in the Kainanga i Mua converted to the Seventh-Day Adventist church and took it upon herself to challenge the chief on several religious and political matters in a series of community assemblies. She was almost universally condemned for her allegedly presumptuous behavior and has been banished from the island.

5 *Pai kava* ('make kava') is the name of the procedure by which the most important deities were worshipped. Despite this name, the kava plant (*Piper methysticum*) is absent

from Anuta and not used in the ceremony. In addition to deceased chiefs such as Tearakura, Pu Tepuko, and Toroaki, Nau Ariki, Nau Pangatau, and Tauvakatai also became *atua* after their deaths. However, not much is recalled about them in this role, and most Anutans claim that they never performed kava to these spirits.

[6] For further discussion of Anutan beliefs about traditional spirits and the island's pre-Christian religion, see Feinberg (1979a, 1995, 1996b). Firth (1939, 1970) presents an extensive discussion of an analogous system on Tikopia.

[7] During the recent civil war in the Solomon Islands, which began in 1999, the Brothers played a critical role in helping to mediate and defuse the conflict between the warring factions.

[8] See Feinberg (1979a, 1980a, 1996c, 1998b) for more detailed discussion of these points.

[9] In contrast with canoes and ocean fishing, women work in the gardens and are said to share in their ownership. A man's ties to his gardens, however, are not altered by marriage as are a woman's, and it is in this sense that the bonds between him and his lands are closer than those linking the land to his sisters or his wife.

[10] Some anomalous (to them) categories like African Americans present a conceptual problem for Anutans. America is a *paparangi* country, and yet these dark-skinned, Melanesian-looking people call themselves American. Anutans rarely encounter such people, however, and so they have felt little need to resolve the conflict. Anutan classification of the world's peoples is discussed at greater length in Feinberg (1980b).

Chapter 8

[1] Nau Teuku was a non-Anutan Solomon Islander of Tuvaluan ancestry. This was her first visit to Anuta. She related her experience to me in English; "insects" was her word. In fact, Anuta does have centipedes (*morokau*), but no land snakes.

[2] In the 1990s, the country's administrative structure was changed to reflect some of the Anutans' concerns. First, Anuta and Tikopia were removed from Temotu Province and administered directly by the central government in Honiara. Later, the easternmost islands—Taumako, Vanikoro, Utupua, Tikopia, and Anuta—were reconstituted as a separate constituency within Temotu Province, entitled to elect their own member of parliament. Although the rationale behind this reorganization appears sound, the province—like the nation at large—continues to experience serious political unrest.

[3] Some informants have insisted to me that the amount of the grant was considerably higher than $10,000, and perhaps more than twice as much.

[4] As I was completing this chapter, word came that a ship called *Endeavor*, with a large number of passengers from Temotu Province, went down in a storm. The passengers were rescued at the last moment by a government patrol boat, and I do not know if they included any Anutans. It is a reminder, however, of how precarious travel still can be to outer islands in the western Pacific.

[5] In January 2003, while this book was in press, Anuta and Tikopia were hit by a massive cyclone, with winds reaching a speed of 230 miles per hour. Cyclone Zoe, one of the most powerful storms ever recorded, stalled for two days over the two islands. Amazingly, there was no loss of life, but the destruction was almost indescribable. With the assistance of many overseas friends, Anutans established the Anuta Development and Education Programme. Its first objective is to provide cyclone relief throughout the recovery period. Any funds not needed for relief are to be redirected to scholarships for Anutan children studying overseas and other education-related purposes.

[6] This point is further developed in Feinberg (1978, 1981a, 1996a, 2002a, 2002b). See also Firth (1964[1949]) and elsewhere; Feinberg and Watson-Gegeo (1996).

Glossary

To assist the reader in dealing with the large number of Anutan words presented in this book, I offer the following short list of terms with abbreviated English glosses. I must emphasize that these glosses are rough approximations. For a proper understanding of the terms' signification to Anutans, the reader should refer to the more detailed explanations appearing in the text. Note that in Anutan, long vowels are separate phonemes from short vowels, so /aa/ is listed after /a/, and /ng/ is a single phoneme.

api	patrilineal descent group or descent category of any degree of genealogical depth
angaa	a major ceremony performed during childhood or adolescence
araara (o nga maru mo nga ariki)	'discussion' (of the *maru* and the chiefs); a 'council meeting'
ariki	'chief'
aropa	'love.' 'sympathy.' 'compassion.' 'pity.' or 'affection' as demonstrated through giving and/or sharing of material goods
aavanga	'marriage'; 'to be married'

(*iki nga*) *inati*	presents given to specified persons or sets of persons at rites of passage; the individuals receiving such presents
ingoa	'name'
ingoa pakamaatuaa	'marital name'
ingoa pakauku tapu	'Christian name' or 'baptismal name'
ingoa pouri	traditional 'personal name'
iraamutu	'sister's child'
kainanga	'patrilineal clan'
kano a paito	'kindred'; 'kinsperson'
kano a paito i te paai o te papine	'kindred on the woman's side'
kanopenua	'people of the island'; 'the island community'
kau vaka	'a canoe's (or ship's) crew'
kauapi	'adopted child'
kave	'cross sibling'; sibling or cousin of opposite sex
koroa	'durable goods'
ma	starchy vegetable, fermented in an underground pit
maa	'sibling-in-law of same sex'
maatuaa	'parents' or "title" for 'father-in-law'
makitanga	'father's sister'
manuu	'power'; the Anutan variant of *mana*
maori	'true'; 'near'
maru	'man of rank'; 'protector'; man from one of the chiefly clans
matua	'husband'
mokopuna	'grandchild'; 'descendant'
nopine	'wife'
nga maatuaa e kee	'different parents'
nga maatuaa e tai	'the same parents'
ngutuumu	a set of two or more *patongia* in a formal cooperative relationship

pae	'mother'
pai kava	to 'perform kava'; the traditional worship ceremony
pai makitanga	*inati* offering presented to a ceremonial 'father's sister' during rites of passage; the recipient of such gifts
pai maatuaa	*inati* offering presented to a ceremonial 'father' during rites of passage; the recipient of such gifts
pai paanaunga	rite performed to mark the birth of a couple's first son and first daughter
pai tuatina	*inati* offering given to a ceremonial 'mother's brother' during rites of passage; the recipient of such gifts
pai tupuna	*inati* offering presented to a 'father' of the *pai tuatina* during rites of passage; the recipient of such gifts
pakaako	'catechist'; 'teacher'
pakaapaapa	'distant' in terms of kin relationship
pakaaropa	members of the nonchiefly 'clans'
papine (pl. *paapine*)	'female'; 'woman'
pare	'house'; patrilineal descent group at any level of inclusiveness
pariki	'funeral'
patongia	'household.' usually consisting of a patrilateral extended family; the 'elementary domestic unit'
paai o te papine	'woman's side'; maternal relatives or affines related through a man's wife
paangai ika	a rite of passage taking place when a child is ready to eat its first fish, usually at about a year of age
pono	general assembly of the island's population; any kind of council
punepu	payment by the *patongia* of a deceased person to that person's 'mother's brothers' to compensate them for digging the grave and burying the corpse
pungona	'parent-in-law' or 'child-in-law'; affine of adjacent generation

puru nga kere	boy's circumcision rite, taking place around puberty
taina	'parallel sibling'; sibling or cousin of same sex as ego
tama	'child'
tama pakapiki	'adopted child'
tama tangata	'son'
tamaapine	'daughter'
tamana	'father'
tangata (pl. *taangata*)	'man'; 'male'; 'human being'
tangata tau vaka	one who claims a share in ownership of a canoe
tangata tu	'leading man'; a man of one of the chiefly 'clans'
tapito; tapitonga	'leader'; 'source'; 'cause'; 'base'; 'basis'; 'founding ancestor'
tapu	'taboo'; 'sacred'; 'forbidden'
tau	to be 'linked' in some way (e.g., *tau paanau* = 'linked by birth'; *tau toa* = 'linked as friends'; *tau tamana* = 'linked as father and child')
(te nga) tau paanau	'(a set of) parallel siblings'
tauranga	members of formally linked Tikopian and Anutan domestic units
tipunga	'carpenter'; 'surgeon' in circumcision rite
toa	'formal friend' or 'bond-friend'
tuatina	'mother's brother'
tupuna	'grandparent'; 'ancestor'
urumatua	'firstborn son'; 'firstborn daughter'; 'eldest child'
vai pa	rite of passage performed after a boy's first ocean fishing expedition and upon returning from his first voyage to Patu-taka
vaka	'canoe'; 'ship'; 'vehicle'

References

Bayard, Donn
  1966   The cultural relationships of the Polynesian outliers. Honolulu: Department of Anthropology, The University of Hawai'i. (M.A. thesis)

Berreman, Gerald D.
  1962   *Behind Many Masks: Ethnography and Impression Management in a Himalayan Village*. Monograph 4. Ithaca: Society for Applied Anthropology.
  1963   *Hindus of the Himalayas*. Berkeley and Los Angeles: University of California Press.

Biggs, Bruce
  n.d.a Comments on Feinberg, *The Anutan Language: A Re-evaluation*. Unpublished manuscript.
  n.d.b Anutan reflexes of proto-language reconstructions. Unpublished manuscript.
  n.d.c Inheritance and borrowing in Anutan language. Unpublished manuscript.
  1980   The position of East Uvean and Anutan in the Polynesian language family. *Te Reo* 23:115–134.

Blake, N. M., B. R. Hawkins, R. L. Kirk, K. Bhatia, P. Brown, R. M. Garruto, and D. C. Gajduesek
  1983   A population genetic study of the Banks and Torres Islands (Vanuatu) and of the Santa Cruz Islands and Polynesian Outliers (Solomon Islands). *American Journal of Physical Anthropology* 62:343–361.

Brady, Ivan
  1976a   Problems of description and explanation in the study of adoption.
          In *Transactions in Kinship: Adoption and Fosterage in Oceania*, edited
          by Ivan Brady. ASAO Monograph Number 4. Honolulu: University
          of Hawai'i Press. Pp. 3–27.
  1976b   Adaptive engineering: an overview of adoption in Oceania. In
          Transactions in Kinship: Adoption and Fosterage in Oceania, edited by
          Ivan Brady. ASAO Monograph Number 4. Honolulu: University of
          Hawai'i Press. Pp. 271–293.

British Admiralty
  1890   *Pacific Islands* (second edition). London: British Admiralty.
  1893   *Pacific Islands* (Volume 1). London: British Admiralty.
  1960   Chart 780. London: British Admiralty.

Brown, Paul, William E. Collins, D. Carleton Gajdusek, and Louis H. Miller
  1976   An evaluation of malaria antibody patterns in several remote island
          populations of the New Hebrides, Solomons, Western Carolines,
          and New Guinea. *The American Journal of Tropical Medicine and
          Hygiene* 25(6):775–783.

Buchler, Ira R. and Henry A. Selby
  1968   *Kinship and Social Organization: An Introduction to Theory and Method*.
          New York: Macmillan.

Carroll, Vern
  1966   Nukuoro kinship. Chicago: The University of Chicago. (Ph.D. dis-
          sertation)
  1970   Introduction: what does "adoption" mean? In *Adoption in Eastern
          Oceania*, edited by Vern Carroll. ASAO Monograph Number 1.
          Honolulu: University of Hawai'i Press. Pp. 3–17.

Chagnon, Napoleon
  1997   *The Yanomamö*, 5th ed. Belmont, CA: Wadsworth.

Davidson, Janet
  1975   Review of *Anuta: A Polynesian Outlier in the Solomon Islands*, edited by
          D. Yen and Janet Gordon. *Journal of the Polynesian Society* 84(2):252–253.

Decktor Korn, Shulamit R.
  1974   Tongan kin groups: The noble and the common view. *Journal of the
          Polynesian Society* 83(1):5–13.
  1978   Hunting the ramage: kinship and the organization of political author-
          ity in aboriginal Tonga. *Journal of Pacific History* 13(1–2):107–113.

Elbert, Samuel H.
  n.d.   Anutan word-list. Unpublished manuscript.

Evans-Pritchard, E. E.
  1940   *The Nuer: A Description of the Modes of Livelihood and Political Institutions
          of a Nilotic People*. New York and Oxford: Oxford University Press.

Feinberg, Richard
  1976   Archaeology, oral history, and sequence of occupation on Anuta
          Island. *Journal of the Polynesian Society* 85(1):99–101.

1977   *The Anutan Language Reconsidered: Lexicon and Grammar of a Polyne-
        sian Outlier* (Two Volumes). HRAFlex Books. New Haven, Connect-
        icut: Human Relations Area Files Press.

1978   Rank and authority on Anuta Island. In *Adaptation and Symbolism:
        Essays on Social Organization*, edited by Karen Ann Watson-Gegeo
        and S. Lee Seaton. Honolulu: University of Hawai'i Press. Pp. 1–32.

1979a   *Anutan Concepts of Disease: A Polynesian Study.* Institute for Polyne-
        sian Studies Monograph Number 3. Lā'ie: The Institute for Polyne-
        sian Studies.

1979b   Schneider's symbolic culture theory: an appraisal. *Current Anthro-
        pology* 20(3):541–560.

1979c   Kindred and alliance on Anuta Island. *Journal of the Polynesian Soci-
        ety* 88(3):327–348.

1980a   Supernatural sanctions and the social order on a Polynesian outlier:
        Anuta Island, S. I. *Anthropological Forum* 4(3–4):331–351.

1980b   History and structure: a case of Polynesian dualism. *Journal of
        Anthropological Research* 36(3):361–378.

1981a   *Anuta: Social Structure of a Polynesian Island.* Lā'ie and Copenhagen:
        Institute for Polynesian Studies and the National Museum of
        Denmark.

1981b   The meaning of 'sibling' on Anuta. In *Siblingship in Oceania: Studies
        in the Meaning of Kin Relations*, edited by Mac Marshall. ASAO
        Monograph Number 8. Ann Arbor: University of Michigan Press.
        Pp. 105–148.

1982a   Structural dimensions of sociopolitical change on Anuta. *Proceedings
        of Conference on Evolving Political Cultures in the Pacific Islands*, edited
        by Gloria Cronin. Lā'ie: Institute for Polynesian Studies. Pp. 124–
        142. Reprinted from *Pacific Studies* 5(2).

1986   The "Anuta problem": local sovereignty and national integration in
        the Solomon Islands. *Man* 21(3):438–452.

1988a   *Polynesian Seafaring and Navigation: Ocean Travel in Anutan Culture
        and Society.* Kent, OH: Kent State University Press.

1988b   Socio-spatial symbolism and the logic of rank on two Polynesian
        outliers. *Ethnology* 27(3):291–310.

1989   Possible prehistoric contacts between Tonga and Anuta. *Journal of
        the Polynesian Society* 98(3):303–317.

1990   The Solomon Islands' tenth anniversary of independence: problems
        of national symbolism and national integration. *Pacific Studies*
        13(2):19–40.

1995   Christian Polynesians and pagan spirits: Anuta, Solomon Islands.
        Journal of the Polynesian Society 104(3):267–301.

1996a   Sanctity and power on Anuta: Polynesian chieftainship revisited. In
        *Leadership and Change in the Western Pacific: Essays in Honor of Sir
        Raymond Firth*, edited by Richard Feinberg and Karen Ann Watson-
        Gegeo. London School of Economics Monographs on Social Anthro-
        pology, Number 66. London: Athlone. Pp. 56–92.

1996b Spirit encounters on Anuta, Solomon Islands. In *Spirits in Culture, History, and Mind*, edited by Jeanette Marie Mageo and Alan Howard. New York and London: Routledge. Pp. 99–120.

1996c Outer islanders and urban resettlement in the Solomon Islands: the case of Anutans on Guadalcanal. *Journal de la Société des Océanistes* 103(2):207–217.

1998a *Oral Traditions of Anuta: A Polynesian Outlier in the Solomon Islands*. New York and Oxford: Oxford University Press.

1998b Righting wrongs on Anuta. *Pacific Studies* 21(3):29–49.

2001a Introduction: Schneider's cultural analysis of kinship and its implications for anthropological relativism. In *The Cultural Analysis of Kinship: The Legacy of David M. Schneider*, edited by Richard Feinberg and Martin Ottenheimer. Urbana, IL: University of Illinois Press. Pp. 1–32.

2001b Cruising the South Pacific. *Daily Kent Stater*. February 9, 2001. P. A-12.

2002a A Polynesian people's struggle to maintain community in the Solomon Islands. In *Constructing Moral Communities: Pacific Islander Strategies for Settling in New Places*, edited by Judith Modell. *Pacific Studies* (Special Issue) 25(1/2):45–70.

2002b Elements of leadership in Oceania. *Anthropological Forum* 12(1):9–44.

Feinberg, Richard, Ute Dymon, Pu Paiaki, Pu Rangituteki, Pu Nukuriaki, Matthew Rollins, and Brian George
n.d. Cartographic perceptions of a Polynesian community: Anuta, Solomon Islands. Unpublished manuscript.

Feinberg, Richard, and Karen Ann Watson-Gegeo, eds.
1996 *Leadership and Change in the Western Pacific: Essays in Honor of Sir Raymond Firth*. London School of Economics Monographs on Social Anthropology, Number 66. London: Athlone.

Firth, Raymond
1930a Marriage and the classificatory system of relationship. *Journal of the Royal Anthropological Institute* 60:235–268.

1930b A dart match in Tikopia. *Oceania* 1:64–96.

1939 *The Work of the Gods in Tikopia*. London School of Economics Monographs on Social Anthropology, Numbers 1 and 2. London: Athlone.

1954 Anuta and Tikopia: symbiotic elements in social organization. *Journal of Polynesian Society* 63:87–131.

1957 A note on descent groups in Polynesia. *Man* 57(2):4–8.

1963 *We, The Tikopia: Kinship in Primitive Polynesia*. Boston: Beacon Press. (Original: 1936)

1964a *Essays on Social Organization and Values*. London School of Economics Monographs on Social Anthropology, Number 28. London: Athlone Press.

1964b Authority and public opinion in Tikopia. In *Essays on social organization and values*, by Raymond Firth. London School of Economics Monographs on Social Anthropology, Number 28. London: Athlone. Pp. 123–144. (Original: 1949)

1965   *Primitive Polynesian Economy*. London: Routledge and Kegan Paul. (Original: 1939)

1967   Bond friendship. In *Tikopia Ritual and Belief*, by Raymond Firth. Boston: Beacon Press. Pp. 108–115. (Original: 1936)

1969   Extraterritoriality and the Tikopia chiefs. *Man* NS 21(3):438–452.

1970   *Rank and Religion in Tikopia*. Boston: Beacon Press.

1973   *Economics of the New Zealand Maori*. Wellington, New Zealand: A. R. Government Printer. (Original: 1929)

1985   *Taranga Fakainglisi ma Taranga Fakatikopia*: Tikopia-English Dictionary. Auckland, New Zealand: Oxford University Press in cooperation with the University of Auckland.

Fortes, Meyer
1959   Primitive kinship. *Scientific American* 200(44):146–150.

Fox, C. E.
n.d.   *The Melanesian Brotherhood*. London: The Melanesian Mission.

Fox, Robin
1967   *Kinship and Marriage*. Baltimore: Penguin.

Geertz, Clifford
1973   *The Interpretation of Cultures*. New York: Basic Books.

Gifford, Edward Winslow
1971   *Tongan Society*. New York: Krauss Reprint Company. (First published by the Bernice P. Bishop Museum. Bulletin 61. Honolulu, 1929.)

Goldman, Irving
1970   *Ancient Polynesian Society*. Chicago and London: University of Chicago Press.

Goodenough, Ward H.
1955   A problem in Malayo-Polynesian social organization. *American Anthropologist*: 57(l):71–83.

1970a   *Description and Comparison in Cultural Anthropology*. Chicago: Aldine.

1970b   Epilogue: transactions in parenthood. In *Adoption in Eastern Oceania*, edited by Vern Carroll. ASAO Monograph Number 1. Honolulu: University of Hawai'i Press. Pp. 391–410.

2001   Conclusion: muddles in Schneider's models. In *The Cultural Analysis of Kinship: The Legacy of David M. Schneider*, edited by Richard Feinberg and Martin Ottenheimer. Urbana, IL: University of Illinois Press. Pp. 205–218.

Green, Roger C.
1971   Anuta's position in the subgrouping of Polynesian languages. *Journal of the Polynesian Society* 83(4):427–442.

Hanson, F. Allan

1982   Female pollution in Polynesia. *Journal of the Polynesian Society* 91:335–381.

Homans, George C. and David M. Schneider.
1955   *Marriage, Authority, and Final Causes: A Study of Unilateral Cross-Cousin Marriage*. New York: Free Press.

Hviding, Edvard
1996   *Guardians of the Marovo Lagoon: Practice, Place, and Politics in Maritime Melanesia*. Pacific Islands Monograph Series 14. Honolulu: University of Hawai'i Press.

Kaeppler, Adrienne L.
1973   A comparative note on Anutan social organization. In *Anuta: A Polynesian Outlier in the Solomon Islands*, edited by D. E. Yen and Janet Gordon. Pacific Anthropological Records, Number 21. Honolulu: Bernice P. Bishop Museum Press. Pp. 21–24.

Kirch, Patrick V. and Paul H. Rosendahl
1973   Archaeological investigation of Anuta. In *Anuta: A Polynesian Outlier in the Soloman Islands*, edited by D. E. Yen and Janet Gordon. Pacific Anthropological Records, Number 21. Honolulu: Bernice P. Bishop Museum Press. Pp. 25–108.

Knudsen, Kenneth
1977   Sydney Island, Titiana, and Kamaleai: Southern Gilbertese in the Phoenix and Solomon Islands. In *Exiles and Migrants in Oceania*, edited by Michael D. Lieber. ASAO Monograph Number 5. Honolulu: University of Hawai'i Press. Pp. 195–241.

Larson, Eric
1966   *Nukufero: A Tikopian Colony in the Russell Islands*. Eugene, Oregon: Department of Anthropology, University of Oregon.
1977   Tikopia in the Russell Islands. In *Exiles and Migrants in Oceania*, edited by Michael D. Lieber. ASAO Monograph Number 5. Honolulu: University of Hawai'i Press. Pp. 242–268.

Lévi-Strauss, Claude
1967   Do dual organizations exist? In *Structural Anthropology*, by Claude Lévi-Strauss. New York: Basic Books.
1969   *The Elementary Structures of Kinship*. Boston: Beacon Press. (Original French edition: 1949)

Levy, Marion J.
1952   *The Structure of Society*. Princeton: Princeton University Press.

Linnekin, Jocelyn and Lin Poyer, eds.
1990   *Cultural Identity and Ethnicity in the Pacific*. Honolulu: University of Hawai'i Press.

Lounsbury, Floyd G.

1969a The structural analysis of kinship semantics. In *Cognitive Anthropology*, edited by Stephen Tyler. New York: Holt, Rinehart and Winston. Pp. 193–212. (Original: 1964)

1969b A formal account of Crow- and Omaha-type kinship terminologies. In *Cognitive Anthropology*, edited by Stephen Tyler. New York: Holt, Rinehart and Winston. Pp. 212–255. (Original: 1964)

Malinowski, Bronislaw

1929 *The Sexual Life of Savages in North-Western Melanesia*. New York and London: Harcourt Brace Jovanovich.

1969 *A Scientific Theory of Culture and Other Essays*. Oxford: Oxford University Press. (Original: 1944)

1984 *Argonauts of the Western Pacific*. Prospect Heights, IL: Waveland Press. (Original: 1922)

Markham, A. H.

1873 *The Cruises of the Rosario Among the New Hebrides and Santa Cruz Islands. . . .* London: Dawsons. (1970 reprint)

Marshall, Mac

1977 The nature of nurture. *American Ethnologist* 4(4):643–662.

Melanesian Mission

n.d. *Handbook of the Melanesian Brotherhood*. The Melanesian Mission.

Morgan, Lewis Henry

1871 *Systems of Consanguinity and Affinity of the Human Family*. Smithsonian Contributions to Knowledge, Volume 17. Washington, D.C.: Smithsonian Institution.

Nachman, Steven R.

1986 Discomfiting laughter: *Schadenfreude* among Melanesians. *Journal of Anthropological Research* 42(1):53–67.

Nayacakalou, Rusiate R.

1971 The Fijian system of kinship and marriage. In *Polynesia: Readings on a Culture Area*, edited by Alan Howard. Scranton, PA: Chandler. Pp. 133–161. (Original: 1955 and 1957)

Needham, Rodney

1962 *Structure and Sentiment: A Test Case in Social Anthropology*. Chicago and London: University of Chicago Press.

1973 *Left and Right: Essays on Dual Symbolic Classification*, edited by Rodney Needham. Chicago and London: University of Chicago Press.

Pawley, Andrew K.

1967 The relationships of Polynesian outlier languages. *Journal of the Polynesian Society* 76:259–295.

Petersen, Glenn

1982 *One Man Cannot Rule a Thousand: Fission in a Ponapean Chiefdom*. Ann Arbor: University of Michigan Press.

1999 Sociopolitical rank and conical clanship in the Caroline Islands. *Jour-*

nal of the Polynesian Society 108:367–410.

Radcliffe-Brown, A. R.
   1952   *Structure and Function in Primitive Society.* New York: Free Press.

Rivers, W. H. R.
   1900   A genealogical method of collecting social and vital statistics. *Journal of the Royal Anthropological Institute* 30:74–82.
   1924   *Social Organization.* New York: Knopf.

Rodman, William L. and Margaret C. Rodman
   1990   To die on Ambae: on the possibility of doing fieldwork forever. In *The Humbled Anthropologist: Tales from the Pacific*, edited by Philip R. DeVita. Belmont, CA: Wadsworth. Pp. 101–120.

Scheffler, Harold W.
   1970   Kinship and adoption in the northern New Hebrides. In *Adoption in Eastern Oceania*, edited by Vern Carroll. ASAO Monograph Number 1. Honolulu: University of Hawai'i Press. Pp. 369–389.

Schneider, David M.
   1965   Some muddles in the models: or how the system really works. In *The Relevance of Models for Social Anthropology*, edited by Michael Banton. ASA Monograph Number 1. London: Tavistock. Pp. 25–85.
   1968   *American Kinship: A Cultural Account.* Englewood Cliffs, NJ: Prentice-Hall.
   1969   Kinship, nationality and religion in American culture: toward a definition of kinship. In *Forms of Symbolic Action*, edited by Victor Turner. Proceedings of the annual spring meeting of the American Ethnological Society.
   1972   What is kinship all about? In *Kinship Studies in the Morgan Centennial Year*, edited by Priscilla Reining. Washington, D.C.: The Anthropological Society of Washington.
   1984   *A Critique of the Study of Kinship.* Ann Arbor: University of Michigan Press.

Shore, Bradd
   1976   Incest prohibitions and the logic of power in Samoa. In Incest Prohibitions in Micronesia and Polynesia. *Journal of the Polynesian Society* (Special Issue) 85(2):275–296.
   1989   *Mana* and *tapu*. In *Developments in Polynesian Ethnology*, edited by Alan Howard and Robert Borofsky. Honolulu: University of Hawai'i Press. Pp. 137–173.

van Gennep, Arnold
   1960   *The Rites of Passage.* Chicago and London: University of Chicago Press. (Original French edition: 1908)

Yen, D. E.
   1973   Agriculture in Anutan subsistence. In *Anuta: A Polynesian Outlier in*

the Solomon Islands, edited by D. E. Yen and Janet Gordon. Pacific Anthropological Records, Number 21. Honolulu: Bernice P. Bishop Museum Press. Pp. 112–149.

n.d.   Anuta Word-List. Unpublished manuscript.

Yen, D. E. and Janet Gordon, eds.
1973   *Anuta: A Polynesian Outlier in the Solomon Islands*. Pacific Anthropological Records, Number 21. Honolulu: Bernice P. Bishop Museum Press.

Yen, D. E., Patrick V. Kirch, and Paul H. Rosendahl
1973   Anuta—an introduction. In *Anuta: A Polynesian Outlier in the Solomon Islands*. Edited by D. E. Yen and Janet Gordon. Pacific Anthropological Records, Number 21. Honolulu: Bernice P. Bishop Museum Press. Pp. 1–8.